THE ROMANCE
OF FAILURE

THE ROMANCE
OF FAILURE

*First-Person Fictions of
Poe, Hawthorne, and James*

Jonathan Auerbach

New York   Oxford
OXFORD UNIVERSITY PRESS
1989

Oxford University Press

Oxford   New York   Toronto
Delhi   Bombay   Calcutta   Madras   Karachi
Petaling Jaya   Singapore   Hong Kong   Tokyo
Nairobi   Dar es Salaam   Cape Town
Melbourne   Auckland

and associated companies in
Berlin   Ibadan

Library of Congress Cataloging-in-Publication Data
Auerbach, Jonathan, 1954–
The romance of failure : first-person fictions of Poe, Hawthorne,
and James / Jonathan Auerbach.
p.   cm.
Includes index.
ISBN 0–19–505721–X
1. American fiction—19th century—History and criticism.
2. Failure (Psychology) in literature.   3. First person narrative.
4. Poe, Edgar Allan, 1809–1849—Criticism and interpretation.
5. Hawthorne, Nathaniel, 1804–1864—Criticism and interpretation.
6. James, Henry, 1843–1916—Criticism and interpretation.
I. Title.
PS374.F24A94   1989
813'.3'09353—dc19   88–12634 CIP

2 4 6 8 9 7 5 3 1

Printed in the United States of America
on acid-free paper

For Marijean and Daniel

Acknowledgments

Many of the ideas for this book first took shape in a graduate seminar taught by the late Laurence B. Holland; I trust that his presence will be felt throughout these pages. I subsequently benefited greatly from careful readings by Sharon Cameron and Larzer Ziff, who both guided my efforts with an exemplary combination of patience and rigor. I have since received advice and encouragement from friends and colleagues, including Maurice Bennett, Vincent Carretta, William Kerrigan, Richard Vitzthum, and especially Robert S. Levine and Kerry Larson.

I am also grateful to the University of Maryland Graduate Research Board for providing a summer grant at a crucial juncture of the book's composition, and to Wayne State University Press for permission to publish a revised version of an article entitled "Poe's Other Double: The Reader in the Fiction" that originally appeared in the journal *Criticism* (Fall 1982).

College Park, Md.   J.A.
June 1988

Contents

Introduction: "Proper Identity" and the First Person   3

1. Disfiguring the Perfect Plot: Doubling and
   Self-Betrayal in Poe   20

2. Hawthorne's *The Blithedale Romance* and
   the Death of Enchantment   71

3. The Jamesian Critical Romance   118

Afterword   172

Notes   177

Index   197

THE ROMANCE
OF FAILURE

Introduction: "Proper Identity" and the First Person

There is no outside, no inclosing wall,
no circumference to us.

EMERSON

I

In November 1838, two months after the publication of "Ligeia" and less than a year before "The Fall of the House of Usher" and "William Wilson" were to appear in print, Edgar Allan Poe published a two-part satire entitled "How to Write a Blackwood Article."[1] Setting out to ridicule the popular Gothic fiction of his British contemporaries, Poe ends his burlesque with an extravagant display of self-mockery which dramatizes how an author's experience of writing a story can grow confused with the fictional experience of his characters. The satire begins innocently enough. The tale's first-person narrator, Psyche Zenobia, visits the Edinburgh office of Mr. Blackwood, who teaches the aspiring author how to write a pot-boiler similar to those published by his celebrated literary magazine. Advising Psyche to "pay minute attention to the sensations," Blackwood details an "exact method of composition" that ranges from a consideration of subject matter and narrative tone to "the soul of the whole business," what he calls "*the filling up*," the process of appropriating literary fragments from other authors to give your own work an air of erudition.

Inspired by the incongruous mixture of acute analysis and preposterous illustration that constitutes Mr. Blackwood's philosophy

3

of composition, Psyche rushes out into the streets of Edinburgh in search of some adventure which would put her mentor's advice to the test. The ludicrous tale she tells in "A Predicament," the second part of Poe's satire, suggests the price that the writer must pay in order to translate literary theory into literary practice. As she winds her way to the top of a clock tower, Psyche attempts to follow Blackwood's instructions to the letter, paying such close attention to her sensations that her narrative threatens to dissolve into a self-consumed babble filled with garbled fragments of the same literary scraps that Blackwood had quoted to her in the first part of the satire. Trapped by a language at once half-borrowed and too intimately her own, Psyche soon literally becomes trapped by the massive hands of the tower clock, a hair-raising Gothic denouement worthy of a *Blackwood's* article. Continuing to address her sensations even while her neck is being severed by the clock's hands, our undaunted protagonist remarks, with "not a second to be lost," that she has finally "discovered the literal import of that classic phrase" the "*Scythe of Time.*" Like many of his burlesques, Poe's comedy derives its power from the transformation of metaphoric language into grotesquely literal action.

As the end of both Psyche and her story draws near, brought to a close by the inexorable hands of time, Poe's exaggerated travesty suddenly takes a bizarre twist, the haunting punch line to the whole satire. In a "concerted plot," the "cruel pressure of the machine" forces one eyeball, and then the second, to pop from Psyche's head onto the ground below; with "an insolent air of independence and contempt" they stare up at their former owner, who shortly thereafter loses the entire "head which had occasioned me so much embarrassment." Her relief immediately turns to desperate confusion, however, when she tries to sort out her personal pronouns: "My senses were here and there at one and the same moment. With my head I imagined, at one time, that I the head, was the real Signora Psyche Zenobia—at another I felt convinced that myself, the body, was the proper identity." (355–56).

This is a paradigmatic moment: "I the head" contends with "myself, the body" for "proper identity." During the act of story-telling, the first-person narrator splits into two vying selves, subject and object, a rupture that the speech of the "real Signora Psyche Zenobia," now dislocated somewhere between head and body, strains to comprehend. We end up with two Psyches because of the "cruel pressure of the machine" (the tower clock), a metaphor for the increasing temporal pressure of the narrative, which forces Zenobia to keep recording her sensations in the midst of her agony for the sake of the Gothic plot. Her predicament is that she not only must suffer but must also put her experience down on the page according to Blackwood's set of literary strictures. Psyche thus plays two distinct roles in the writing which rival each other: she is both the central victim of time's agency (what she calls "myself, the body") as well as the keeper of the text who records and analyzes her own actions ("I the head"). Trying, in the end, to make the life of her plot conform to the story of her life, Psyche literally divides in two. Despite the patent absurdities of her attempt at closure (how does she "see" her fallen eyes, "hear" her talking head, or continue to speak at all?), Psyche's doubling retains an uncanny power, compelling us to recognize the familiar dilemma of the writer who would be both historian and hero of his text.

Zenobia's staring eyeballs serve as graphic reminders of the necessary duplicity of writing in the first person. Calling into question the very meaning of a "proper identity," the storyteller's "I" simultaneously plays the part of anguished participant and dispassionate observer, the narrated self who acts in the past and the narrating self who retrospectively analyzes that past action in the present. Unlike the famous transparent eyeball into which Emerson transfigured himself two years earlier in *Nature*, Psyche's eyes do not "see all" but rather a diminished part, their blind ex-mistress, who now literally remains beside herself. The eyes register loss, not universal wholeness. Contemptuously mocking Zenobia's narrative authority, the eyes force Psyche to relinquish control of her own story. Once her head begins to talk back, making a speech which she "could hear but indistinctly," the autonomous double threatens to usurp the role of its former owner, who is compelled to stand by and mutely eyewitness her own beheading. As plot displaces person, the objects of the narrator's discourse (Zenobia's eyes and head) take on a life of their own, so that in the end we are left with the storyteller's literary remains but little trace of the teller herself. With the estranged lament "Alas—*nothing!* I have done" Poe's "how to" travesty draws to a close.

The entire satire is a kind of pretext for this final moment, which literally enacts the consequences of self-objectification. If we continue by running Poe's burlesque in reverse, moreover, the

connection between Psyche's decapitation and the rest of the satire
becomes even clearer. Just as Zenobia's contemptuous eyes comment on her farcical attempt at storytelling, so her story mocks the
literary advice of Blackwood, who stands in the same relation to
Psyche in the first part of the satire as she does in relation to her
talking head in the second part. By exhorting his eager pupil to
write a story based on his literary analysis, Blackwood unleashes
his own autonomous double, who is then free to turn against her
master by carrying his suggestions to an absurd extreme. "How to
Write a Blackwood Article" thus consists of a series of complex
transferences of power from Blackwood to Zenobia and from Zenobia to her disembodied head, transactions of authority which can
finally be traced back to Poe himself, the source of all the doubling
in the tale.

In order to understand how Poe is directly implicated in this
alienating process of self-abstraction, we must look more carefully
at Blackwood's advice itself. As critics have long pointed out, the
theories that Blackwood offers in the first part of the satire bear a
suspiciously close resemblance to Poe's own literary principles.
Blackwood's predilection for pretentious foreign quotations, his
emphasis on the nuances of prose style, and his preference for
plots of impending doom that seriously compromise the firstperson
narrator's ability to bring the story to a close all mirror Poe's
literary practice. Poe even lets his counterpart cite some of the
author's favorite snippets of poetry that express Poe's obsession
with the possibility of life after death. Blackwood's insistence on an
"exact method of composition," moreover, anticipates the theory
of writing for a unified effect that Poe would espouse a few years
later in his reviews of Hawthorne and in his famous essay "The
Philosophy of Composition." In short, Blackwood serves as a kind
of double for Poe, a target of satire that ultimately mocks the
author's own literary pretensions just as Psyche's head mocks her
authorial pretensions. Poe, Blackwood, Zenobia, dismembered head:
one speaking subject, one first person, gives way to another as the
writer's authority censors and betrays itself.

Psyche's apparent disappearance into her plot would seem to
provide grist for the mills of many contemporary narrative theorists, particularly those French structuralists working in what has
come to be called narratology. Assuming from the start some fundamental opposition between "story" and "discourse," Todorov,

Greimas, and Genette, among others, have sought to distinguish
the chronological events of a story from the narrative presentation
of these events in order to arrive at a grammar of narrative which
could be applied to any plot regardless of the particular story it
tells, or the particular person who tells it.[2] Such a grammar treats
texts as autonomous, fixed systems of discourse governed by rules—
semiotic codes or functions—that do not depend on specific acts
of speaking or writing. Subject to the dictates of language's logic,
the individual author or narrator—if invoked at all—is given a
subordinate role to play in the production of a text's meaning. In
this view the dissociation of mind from body which takes place
during the process of Zenobia's mechanical plotting points to the
autonomy of her own discourse, the liberation of her words from
their human origins. And it is only a short step from this kind of
structuralist position to a more radical poststructuralist argument
that would read the dismantling of Psyche as Poe's deconstruction
of the very notion of "the author," what Foucault wryly called "the
principle of thrift in the proliferation of meaning."[3]

Yet if plot exerts pressure on the person of the plotter, it does
so in "How to Write a Blackwood Article" only to suggest a more
primary *identification* between author and text. However divided
Zenobia's allegiances become during her act of narration, her grotesque parodying of Poe (by way of Blackwood) underscores the
role that he has been playing in the tale all along. For all their
apparent autonomy, the narrator's staring eyes and talking head
remain firmly linked to an author outside the story who has made
his presence felt within the story from start to finish. Far from
divorcing writer from writing, Psyche's decapitation enables Poe to
endorse a precariously held authorship that many structuralists and
poststructuralists might prefer to depersonalize and dissolve.

Insofar as Psyche's "I" can be seen to resemble Poe's, the story
thus serves to validate an older Anglo-American tradition of narrative analysis that focuses on the rhetoric of fiction. Building on
distinctions between "showing" and "telling" drawn by Henry James
and Percy Lubbock, Wayne Booth makes "point of view" his central
critical concept in order to examine how "the author's judgment
is always present" in his work. He insists that "though the author
can to some extent choose his disguises," "he can never choose to
disappear."[4] It is therefore Booth's project to look for signs of the
author's "voice" by identifying various kinds of fictional narrators:

personal, impersonal, unreliable, self-conscious, and so on. This inclination to schematize rhetorical functions is even more pronounced in a third group of theorists—mainly German—who classify narratives according to fixed sets of precisely defined formal characteristics (person, mode, perspective, and so on). For these theorists (Franz Stanzel and Dorrit Cohn, most notably) an author's "presence" is primarily determined by the various abstract, transhistoric properties of narrative itself.[5] As in the case of the poststructuralists, such an approach also tends to downplay authorship as an activity, an ongoing process.

In its many implications for narrative theory, the absurdly literal quality of Poe's "how to" formula for tale-telling makes it a useful starting point for my study of the major first-person fictions of Poe, Hawthorne, and James. As my discussion of Poe's Blackwood satire should make clear, I am less intent on establishing either a strict grammar or typology of narrative than in seeing how first-person narration in particular foregrounds the *negotiations* that take place between writer and writing.

Poe's first-person tales, Hawthorne's *The Blithedale Romance*, and James's *The Aspern Papers*, "The Figure in the Carpet," and *The Sacred Fount* all share a similar concern with problems of literary representation: how fictions come to be made and the relation between these fictions and the people who make them. Such fundamental questions are given a special immediacy in these works because of the peculiar duplicity of their first-person narrators, who are both the central actors and the retrospective tellers of their tales. For all three writers, I argue, this double burden of telling and acting entails an attractive but dangerous process of self-revelation which threatens to collapse the distinction between creation and creator, between the action taking place within the fiction and the author's management of that action from without. Focusing on the consequences of this potential collapse between "inside" and "outside," I am interested in seeing how the scrupulous need to preserve form at all costs leads to rhetorical acts of self-betrayal. For both fictional "I" and author these acts serve as last-ditch efforts to affirm an increasingly beleaguered sense of self.

As we shall see, first-person storytelling encourages a special kind of intimacy to develop between author and narrator in these works—an intimacy that narratologists miss when they minimize the significance of the speaking/writing subject to discuss texts as alienated objects cut off from the circumstances of their creation. Typologists also lose sight of this intimacy by neglecting the dynamics of plotting in favor of sophisticated and valuable, but ultimately static, methods of categorizing narratives piecemeal according to technical criteria.[6] However dehumanized or dispossessed the individual becomes during the course of narration (as Psyche's story makes all too literal), the first person is continually trying to define a self *in* language but also over and *against* language. Looking carefully at the fictional first persons of Poe, Hawthorne, and James in action, I am therefore trying to reconfirm more generally the crucial importance of the speaking/writing subject, in all of its provisionality and fragility, for the study of narrative.

By both acting and signifying that action, the "I" narrator serves to bring together, sometimes in uneasy alliance, the mimetic and the semiotic. As such, first-person fiction becomes a particularly fruitful territory to explore the various ways that subjectivity and discourse mutually constitute one another at the same time that they also remain at odds with one another. It is easy enough to disparage this problematic relation between identity and language—more particularly, the degree to which authors invest themselves in their work—by seeing this presumed investment as yet another manifestation of the ideology of the subject: the belief in a unified, essential, sovereign self at the heart of all human endeavor. But "to valorize the decentering of the subject," as Fredric Jameson urges while championing continental theory over the Anglo-American critical tradition, is itself a dubious policy when automatically applied to all texts across the board.[7] What Jameson would dismiss as "American myths of the self" cannot so quickly be discarded, it seems to me, if only because nineteenth-century American writers like Poe, Hawthorne, and James are themselves calling the centrality and autonomy of the self into question in their first-person fictions. By its very marginality the narrating "I" of each of these authors does not negate or abandon the subject but rather attests to its stubborn endurance.

Despite the recent efforts of a host of French writers, the subject still remains very much alive.[8] The Anglo-American emphasis on "point of view" may naively seek to naturalize narration by giving it a simple psychological basis[9]—Booth's characterization of narrators as "reliable" or "unreliable," for example—but a rhetorical

approach to fiction at least is willing to consider what is at stake
for authors themselves in their literary production. The first-person
narrators of all three writers are self-estranged, in fact, precisely
to the degree that their authors remain deeply implicated in their
plotting. And to that degree first-person fiction offers these authors
a way to define the nature of their craft.

What interests me about first-person narration, then, is the
psychology of the form, what it says about an author's relation to
his work. Why does Poe, for instance, invariably rely on a first-
person narrator to tell his stories for him? Why does Hawthorne
turn to the first person after writing two romances in the third
person? Why does James suspect that assuming a fictional "I" will
inevitably lead him to "the darkest abyss of romance"? Such questions can be addressed only if we treat narrative as a performance,
not as a structure. By seeing how first-person plotting develops
during a single act of storytelling, as well as throughout a given
writer's entire career, I intend to explore the form beyond its simple
self-reflexive properties in order to emphasize the author's engagement in his work. Using the author's literary career as my organizing principle, in each case I hope to trace the shifting relation
between writer and writing, as well as to suggest a broader pattern
of development that spans the nineteenth century.

The early part of the century Emerson called "the age of the
first person singular," a period dominated by the all-consuming "I"
of Romanticism.[10] Although Emerson's description would certainly
apply to European forms of Romanticism as well as American, "the
first person singular" plays an especially important role in American
letters. Melville's early novels, Thoreau's writings on nature, Whitman's epic poetry, as well as less canonical spiritual autobiographies,
travel journals, and diaries not only testify collectively to the abun-
dance and range of autobiographical writing in nineteenth-century
American literature but also suggest how these writers tend to treat
literary representation chiefly as a subspecies of self-representation.
Punning on the opening page of *Walden*, for instance, Thoreau
claims that it is "always the first person that is speaking," that all
writing is nothing but thinly veiled confession, the expression of a
"first person" Adamic identity which emerges anew with each act
of creation. In the absence of any authoritative tradition or history
of one's own, Thoreau's pun intimates, the American writer must
be his or her own subject, so that no matter how "other" the characters and events of his writing may seem, the author invents,

discovers, makes something of himself in everything he or she composes. The objective text is not so much a reflection of the self as its very embodiment.

The remainder of this introductory chapter will be devoted to examining how the properties of the grammatical first person specifically make possible such a close relation between author and text; while these linguistic properties pertain to first-person discourse in general, they would also seem to have a particular pertinence for a number of first-person fictions written by Americans during the nineteenth century. It is not my aim to treat this body of writing as a native literary tradition separate from its European counterparts, but rather to appreciate how these romances literalize certain kinds of alienation, intimacy, and anxiety—concerns that in turn have certain implications for our understanding of American culture.

Confining myself to a trio of representative authors, I will be seeking throughout this study to suggest some of these cultural resonances by focusing on the problem of identity, that is, what constitutes the "person" in American first-person narration. As we move from Poe's Gothic horrors to the adventures of Hawthorne's minor poet Miles Coverdale, and on to James's late first-person novel *The Sacred Fount*, we will find that the humanness of the narrator becomes more and more open to sheer caricature, until the very notion of a reified "self" becomes so threatened that it can only be defined strictly by the first person's utter failure to achieve coherence, integrity, or authenticity. Progressively thematized, such failure painfully calls into question the writer's very grounds for self-assertion, and in doing so offers one possible way to gauge the larger transformation in nineteenth-century American letters from romance to realism. While the observations I will be making about the more literal, more troubled, more unstable sense of American selfhood may not be entirely unfamiliar, my emphasis on the fictional representation of the "I" enables me to examine more precisely some of the underlying assumptions about identity that govern many discussions of American romance.

II

When I contend that the first persons of these three American writers enact their authors' concerns, I do not simply mean that these speakers are "artist figures" in a vaguely impressionistic sense. First-person narrators can be doubles for their authors more precisely because of certain fundamental grammatical properties of first-person discourse. Pervasive differences in the use of the pronouns "I," "you," and "he" or "she" that cut across individual languages suggest the way in which these personal pronouns each orient the speaker/writer to the world in fundamentally different ways. When these grammatical differences are expanded to apply specifically to ongoing narratives in which the first-person narrator is also the central agent in his or her tale, then distinguishing between first person and third person begins to have some validity, especially as a basis to discuss the friction between plot and identity generated by literary acts of self-representation.[11]

Most important, first-person discourse, unlike third person, can provide no built-in grammatical barrier—a "he" or "she" or "they" —to mediate between author and text. For an author writing fiction in the first person, this absence of a grammatically objective "other" makes the "I" of discourse refer at once to the writer's own subject and the subject who narrates the fiction. As soon as an author begins to evoke an "I" to do his plotting for him, it becomes more difficult for him to maintain an identity apart from the voice he impersonates in the writing.

One crucial consequence of this linguistic conflation of subjects is that first-person discourse will always remain situated. Merging the story's means with its ends, first-person narration continually calls attention to its own developing status as speech or writing. In other words, what critics frequently call a "dramatized narrator" is more accurately a narrator who is expressly dramatizing the act of narration itself. While texts in general must have contexts, first-person discourse highlights this fact, carrying a context along with it by explicitly showing how the activity of tale-telling is grounded in and emerges from a given experiential source. How and why a self-referring story gets told is inevitably linked to what has happened to the teller in it. Contextualizing itself, first-person narration thus presents us with its own occasion. In third-person narration, on the other hand, or fictions like *Tom Jones* in which the narrator does not directly participate in his story, the circumstances leading to the growth of the plot usually remain separate from the plot itself: an implied author (overtly identified by "I" or not) tells about the experience of another "he," "she," or "them" without entering into it. The narrator's art and his characters' lives may resemble each other, but they are kept distinct. Acting in his own story, however, the first person continually makes available the particular set of conditions that give rise to his narration, so that "art" and "life" tend to merge. In this way first-person fiction is motivated as well as situated, since the reasons for narrating, however mysterious or psychologically obscure (one thinks of Coverdale's surprising "confession" at the end of *The Blithedale Romance*) become part of the story itself.

Discussing the first person's tendency to locate itself in a particular experience, Franz Stanzel defines the form as "embodied" because the first-person narrator shares the same ontological status or plane of reference as the other characters in the fiction.[12] The first person is thus bodied forth in the process of narrating. But it is precisely the difficulty of bodying forth and then maintaining a self during first-person plotting which becomes the main problem in a story like Poe's "How to Write a Blackwood Article." A passive auditor in the first part of the satire, Psyche Zenobia begins to make her physical presence felt in the tale once she takes over narrative control from Blackwood in the second part and begins to talk about her personal sensations. Her act of self-narrating progressively instills in her (and us) a sense of her corporeal identity as a character. As soon as the clock hands begin severing her head from her body, however, this sense of her substance is called into question. We suddenly discover what we must have known all along: instead of referring directly to some objective self, either inside or outside the fiction, the first person's "person" remains a provisional, unstable construct of language functioning for the sake of the plot.

The uncanny effect of Psyche's disembodiment, I would stress again, largely derives from the peculiar nature of the grammatical first person. Insisting on the fundamental differences between first and third person, Emile Benveniste notes that the pronoun "I" does not refer to anything real in the way that the word "chair" or "she" might refer to a particular object or class of objects:

> What then is the reality to which *I* or *you* refers? It is solely a "reality of discourse," and this is a very strange thing. *I* cannot be defined except in terms of "locution," not in terms of objects as a nominal sign is. *I* signifies "the person who is uttering the present instance of the discourse containing *I*." This instance is

unique by definition and has validity only in its uniqueness ... the form of *I* has no linguistic existence except in the act of speaking in which it is uttered. There is thus a combined double instance in this process: the instance of *I* as referent and the instance of discourse containing *I* as the referee. The definition can now be stated precisely as: *I* is "the individual who utters the present instance of discourse containing the linguistic instance *I*."

It is by identifying himself as a unique person pronouncing *I* that each speaker sets himself up in turn as the "subject."

It is the instance of discourse in which *I* designates the speaker that the speaker proclaims himself as the "subject."[13]

Observing that the nonpersonal third person, on the contrary, is never "reflective of the instance of discourse," Benveniste argues that "I" is a uniquely mobile sign that is essentially "empty," non-referential with respect to "reality" (either a real individual or a real concept) until a speaker begins filling it up by introducing it into discourse.[14]

Benveniste's insight into the emptiness of first-person discourse helps us to see how the narrating subject must constantly work to constitute itself in language. Without seizing the instance of discourse, the "I" remains an empty pronoun void of identity. Benveniste also argues that an "I" always presupposes a "you," that a speaker must have or imply a listener. This key observation has important consequences for my study of first-person plotting because it suggests how subjectivity and social relations are absolutely interdependent, with language the defining relation between them. To determine a self means simultaneously constituting an other, since the "I" achieves substance only insofar as it is circumscribed. Creating its own grounds of reference, the first person arrives at an identity by trying to situate itself in the world of the fiction, some otherness outside the self.[15] In the absence of any external source of validation, the narrating subject runs the risk of expanding endlessly to encompass anything and everything.

Representing the person in first-person narration is thus more difficult than it sounds, since the signifying "I" must set its own limits from within. For all three writers I will be examining, this act of self-formation turns into a kind of pursuit specifically following the pattern of quest-romance, which Nothrop Frye has usefully described as "the search of the libido or desiring self for a fulfillment that will deliver it from the anxieties of reality but will still contain that reality."[16] Such containment demands that the first person presume some outside presence—a ghostly double, Blithedale's Veiled Lady, or the meaning of a metaphoric "sacred fount"—which must then be confronted and deciphered if the "I" is to realize itself. The central object of the narrator's plotting, this mysterious other helps to fill or shape an otherwise empty or shapeless "I." Having no life outside the narrative, the first person in this way literally becomes invested in his or her tale of pursuit; as the only means to differentiate between self and other, plot becomes integral, not incidental, to personal identity.

First-person narration serves to actualize and dramatize the process of plotting by giving it a basis in experience, but it does so in a curiously anonymous or nonpsychological way. In this respect the Anglo-American emphasis on authorial "persona" seems inadequate when applied to many first-person fictions. As I will show in my discussion of Poe, the notion of persona seeks to normalize problems of identity by treating narrators as self-contained, psychologically complex characters who are often treated ironically by their authors. "We react to all narrators as persons," claims Booth, a premise that leads him to evaluate narrators as more or less reliable.[17] Such mimetic categories, often overtly moralistic, are designed to fix the troublesome relation between author and narrator, whose reliability can then serve to measure and be measured by his state of mind, motives for action, and so on. As we have seen, however, there is no a priori "self" in first-person discourse. First-person narratives can certainly create the illusion that the person of the narrator exists apart from his narrating, but the three American writers I will be discussing continually betray this illusion for what it is. Taken collectively, the first-person fictions of Poe, Hawthorne, and James suggest that reliability is less a matter of the individual narrator's mind or morals than it is a function of the difficulty of plotting a self. These "unreliable" first-person narrators thus do not simply produce their distorted accounts by nature but are themselves disfigured (recall Poe's Psyche) in the process of narrating.·

Yet the fact that the unreliable narrator is invoked so frequently in critical discussions of Poe's tales, *The Blithedale Romance*, and James's first-person riddles should give us pause. However misplaced by being confined to the figure of the narrator (as character), reliability nonetheless is a key concern in these works, which all exploit the tendency of first-person fiction to expose its own epistemological underpinnings. Since the narrator remains inside his story, how he knows what he knows necessarily becomes part of the story too. As I have suggested, learning about others becomes the central means for these first-person narrators to realize themselves. But in the absence of any privileged, absolute perspective on others, such understanding must be actively gained in the process of plotting. It is not simply that the narrator's perspective is limited (since third-person protagonists as well as implied authors also are made to suffer from partial knowledge) but that these limitations baffle the first person's efforts at self-representation and cannot be contained by an authorial voice in the way that third-person narrative contains and shapes—literally informs—the figures within. In literary conventions governing the traditional nineteenth-century third-person "omniscient" novel, the author is permitted to enter into the minds of characters at will without needing to explain how or why. Even if the author cannot fully penetrate the minds of his or her creations, such a convention nonetheless presumes a clear demarcation between the novel's "inside" and "outside." Authorial explanations and doubts can clearly emerge in third-person narration, but such epistemological issues do not, as a rule, impinge on the presentation of character and action in the narrative proper. By dividing up the labor of the novel between a profoundly discriminating narrator and her erring heroine, a highly organized narrative such as George Eliot's *Middlemarch* can address complex epistemological uncertainties without these problems necessarily intruding on the novel's ontology, its very rendering of events.

First-person narration, however, continually raises such questions from the inside by merging problems of identity with equally fundamental problems of knowing. Poe's many framing devices, which emphasize how information is transmitted; Coverdale's voyeuristic invasions of privacy; and the parasitic prying of James's first-person critics: each, in its way, dramatizes the difficulty of gaining knowledge of the world and then arranging these insights into an explanatory plot. By taking these difficulties as their explicit, if sometimes farcical subject, Poe, Hawthorne, and James test the first person's credibility in order to examine their own efforts to extract meaning from experience.[18]

Instead of trying to match the first person's account against some hypothetical, absolute truth outside the text ("what really happened"), we need to see how this trio of writers makes reliability an issue in order to direct attention to the more crucial problem of how the artist is to assume responsibility for his authority. Denied immediate access to the truth (of self and others), the first person's understanding is necessarily imperfect, compared to the perfection of what Poe calls "the plot of God." Enacting how a narrator comes to know what he knows, as well as what he does not know, first-person fiction betrays the limitations of all human plots and thereby underscores the active role the artist is compelled to play in making them. The discrepancy between divine and human productions throws the writer back on himself and makes him question his power to imitate God. To dramatize the first person's epistemological distress in this way, to cast doubt on his reliability as a plotter, enables these three writers to consider the basis for their own authority to produce fictions which are not simply passive mirrors of reality but aggressive responses to it.

Plots are made, not given; how they turn out depends on who makes them. First-person narration in particular exposes the provisional nature of its authority because, as Benveniste points out, the "I" can be filled only by way of appropriation: "Language is so organized that it permits each speaker to *appropriate to himself* an entire language by designating himself as *I*."[19] The power struggles that occur between Poe's narrators and their doubles, between Miles Coverdale and his rival Hollingsworth, and most explicitly, between James's first-person critics and his third-person authors, Aspern and Vereker, thus often take the form of a struggle to speak, as the "I's" narrative authority is challenged by other dominating characters who threaten to take over the role of master plotter.

The self-authorizing nature of "I" narration clarifies what the first persons of Poe, Hawthorne, and James share in common. For all three writers the narrator's acute awareness of his responsibility for plotting quickly tends to affect the course of that plot. Coverdale's (partially deluded) sense of himself as Blithedale's poet laureate, for instance, helps to explain his desire to pry into the lives of his fellow utopians. The sole source of information in the narrative, the first person is compelled to take credit for the story he is trying to tell. With an increasing degree of self-consciousness and control, Poe, Hawthorne, and James treat this compulsion as their theme.

Here we can see another kind of identification between first-person narrator and author, for such compulsion cannot always be contained within the fiction itself, since it may spill over on occasion and occupy each writer's nonfictional critical prose as well. Poe's infamous essay "The Philosophy of Composition," Hawthorne's remarks on romance in his prefaces, and James's introductions to his New York Edition all cast the relation between writer and writing in terms of the artist's impetus to produce in the first place. More specifically, each piece of critical prose offers a highly stylized autobiographical account of the mysterious genesis of literary creation. The writer's burning desire to vindicate his work after the fact quickly turns into a story about how the literature emerged from a given experience in his life. In their longing to recover the lost origin or first cause of their literature, Poe, Hawthorne, and James each testify to the presence of an authorial "I" who resists being entirely blotted out by the process of writing. Their first-person fictional counterparts similarly try to arrive at a plot which would allow them, from within, to understand their stories, even though such understanding threatens to undermine, by design, the selfhood that they mean to affirm.

First-person form as constituting personal identity; first-person form as constricting personal identity: it is the double-edged quality of "I" narration that unites this trio of American authors. Certainly other important nineteenth-century American first-person literary works—Thoreau's *Walden*, Dickinson's confessional lyrics, Whitman's "Song of Myself," Melville's *Moby-Dick*, and Twain's *The Adventures of Huckleberry Finn*—participate in this sort of doubleness, and could therefore also benefit from a closer look at the "I's" interplay between writer and writing. In these works, too, text and self often stand in uneasy, uncertain relation to one another. But insofar as the interaction between creator and creation in these works does not depend so strictly on the first person's act of fictional plotting itself, the author's literary medium consequently does not necessarily exert the same kind of coercive pressure that we find in Poe, Hawthorne, and James.[20] If I limit myself to this trio of authors, it is because their first-person romances dramatize, with a particular degree of intensity and extravagance, the price which must be paid to achieve a narrative form capable of sustaining and containing personal identity. Guided by each author's theoretical interest in his work—Poe's obsession with the perfect plot, Hawthorne's understanding of the "territory" of his romances, and

James's critical prefaces—I will be examining this price in some detail.

In sum, this study is based on a convergence of formal, psychological, and cultural considerations which in turn depend on a series of implied distinctions: between grammatical first person and third person; between American and non-American attitudes toward the self; and between narrative prose fiction and other forms of literary discourse such as autobiography and lyric poetry. None of these distinctions considered separately is necessary and sufficient to make my case, but taken together they help define a certain kind of romance and a certain set of preoccupations. My argument about these three writers is neither meant to establish an inevitable historical progression nor simply to string together three isolated case studies. Rather, I intend to suggest a continuity of theme and form that extends roughly from Poe's "The Man of the Crowd" (1840) to James's *The Sacred Fount* (1901). Failing to arrive at any coherent self-definition, each of these first-person romances manages to betray in that very human failure the will to persist and the persistence of a will.

1

Disfiguring the Perfect Plot:
Doubling and Self-Betrayal
in Poe

I

I begin with a striking but largely unnoticed fact: with the exception of a small handful of tales, all of Poe's seventy-odd stories and sketches are written in the grammatical first person.[1] Cutting across conventional generic boundaries (grotesque, burlesque, satire, science fiction, and detective fiction), "I" appears with such frequency in Poe's fiction as to suggest that he cannot even conceive of a story without first imagining someone, from within, to tell it. For tale-telling to be at all possible, then, discourse must be made to originate in a particular speaker, one whose presence so fills up the fiction that Poe himself is left with virtually no objective grounds outside the narration from which to survey it. Yet the brutal self-parody of a story like "How to Write a Blackwood Article" reminds us that the first person's domination does not compel the author to withdraw from his subject but rather to slip into it, sharing in a single pronoun the grammatical privileges claimed by his fictional counterparts. The result is that Poe can neither stay out of his stories nor assume the first-person slot as entirely his own. The "I" is up for grabs. In the pages that follow, we will be examining this fictional "I" more carefully, investigating the tension it sets up between author and narrator, as well as the reduplicated tension between the plotting first person and those second selves who haunt so many of Poe's tales.

It may be somewhat misleading to speak of the "particularity" of any given Poe storyteller, for these all-consuming "I's" make their presence felt in the fiction largely without benefit of those key elements of selfhood that we normally think of as constituting personal identity: a past, a family, a network of social relations, some discrete physicality—at its most basic, a face and a body. The typical Poe narrator impresses us less as a fully fledged "person," in fact, than as a disembodied voice, sheer nervous energy seeking to order itself by trying to maintain control over the tale being told. Such narrative control can only be purchased, as we shall see, by some further sacrifice of the "I's" selfhood.

Insofar as Poe's narrators retain only the semblance of personality, these insubstantial figures complicate the ways we are accustomed to reading first-person fiction. The first-person form was so instrumental for the development of the English novel because it could so effortlessly help sustain the illusion of personal verisimilitude. Disguising itself as a retrospective account of factual experience, Defoe's *Robinson Crusoe* begins by detailing the date and place of the first person's birth, his parents and brothers, a certain "famous Colonel Lockhart"—all in an effort to establish his credentials as an individual living in history. Such details quickly become a code signifying "reality" or "truth." We are meant to accept the narrator's selfhood as a given, so that we can then attend to the particular facts of his life, even as that life records his utter isolation from social reality. Laurence Sterne's *Tristram Shandy* parodies this conventional equation between the novel's opening and its narrator's origins by pushing the clock back to predate its first person's birth. But it still takes for granted a kind of traditional verisimilitude by continually referring the quirks and digressions of its narrative form to the personal and national eccentricities of its teller and his equally eccentric family. As in the case of Defoe's novel, we are meant to believe that the "I" exists apart from his narrative, his first name and family name determining the title of the novel itself. In both of these seminal English novels, the first person's "person" is assumed to come first, with his story following.

Take, by way of contrast, the opening line of Poe's early story "MS. Found in a Bottle": "Of my country and of my family I have little to say." After briefly alluding to his "hereditary wealth," the narrator goes on to discuss his "contemplative turn of mind" and "habits of rigid thought," concluding his beginning paragraph by flatly asserting that "the incredible tale I have to tell" is "the positive experience of a mind" closed to "the reveries of fancy." "The positive experience of a mind": this is the quintessential source of validation for Poe's first persons, who have virtually no other facts to go on. Having dismissed absent family and country as irrelevant, the narrator immediately calls his own credibility into question by insisting on it so explicitly; once "mind" is left as the sole foundation for positing identity, then we are compelled to believe the first person, believe in him, simply because he tells us so. But in what sense can thought alone define a self? As in so many of his tales ("Berenice" and "Ligeia," to cite only two examples), Poe is led inward to a vicious Cartesian circle, where "mind" and "self" are meant to constitute one another, with seemingly little of the kind of a priori external grounds that help identify and orient the first persons of Defoe and Sterne. The narrator of "MS. Found in a Bottle" doesn't even give himself the advantage of a proper name, let alone a proper identity, before he is sucked into the story's black abyss.[2] Apparently missing any ready-made terms to mediate between thinking and being, Poe thus is compelled to rely strictly on what Henry James would call romance's "beautiful subterfuge of our thought and our desire" in order to forge an identity and a fictional world for himself.

James's well-known phrase from the New York Edition preface to *The American* is part of his attempt to provide a general epistemological definition of "romance" that would not depend on particular literary conventions or subject matter. Insisting that romance simply offers "experience disengaged, disembroiled, disencumbered," James goes on to suggest that such literature entails "a sacrifice of community."[3] Much earlier in his career James elsewhere described such a sacrifice more pointedly by cataloging the "absent things in American life."[4] Insofar as early nineteenth-century America lacked any densely layered set of social relations, James's famous argument goes, its fiction writers were compelled to turn away from society to explore a more inward, isolated symbolic terrain.[5] My intention here is not to substantiate or dispute the historical validity of James's influential claims, but rather to see how the understanding of romance as a kind of absence, when applied specifically to Poe, helps us to appreciate the trouble Poe and his first persons encounter in trying to discover or invent the foundations of knowledge by which they mean to fabricate some credentials for themselves. While earlier American authors such as Charles Brockden Brown and Washington Irving also seem to have some difficulty securing personal verisimilitude in their first-person fictions, Poe makes this difficulty itself a central feature that is dramatized over and over again in his tales.

Romance seems particularly demanding for Poe, inasmuch as we must add to the long list of perceived absences in his work the absence of any coherent sense of literary tradition that might help to anchor and authorize the storyteller's ego. As we shall soon see, the relation of Poe's fiction to established literary convention is tangential and parodic at best. Denying the very concept of literary influence, Poe substitutes a dualistic scheme pitting absolute originality against shameless plagiarism, with little or nothing in between. While plagiarism can be magically converted into originality by a kind of hocus-pocus, such feigned originality remains cut off from any past relations that would give it meaning. In this way Poe is forced to set the terms by which he wants to be read, and by which his first-person narrators seek to read themselves. Not simply in his critical essays and reviews, or in a "how to" story like the Blackwood satire, but in virtually all of his fiction Poe thus burdens himself with the task of trying at once to originate a self and to make up the literary form with which to contain that self. Neither form nor identity can be assumed to exist independent of one another, with the consequence that the author can possess little confidence in self apart from his fiction, nor can his fictional first persons possess themselves apart from the mocking doubles that repeatedly serve to objectify an otherwise irrevocably divided subjectivity.

In his important essay celebrating Poe's founding of American literature, William Carlos Williams gives a similar but more optimistic assessment of Poe's self-disciplining method: "Poe *gains* by abhorring; flying to the ends of the earth for 'original' material— By such a simple, logical twist does Poe succeed in being the more American [than Hawthorne], heeding more the local necessities, the harder structural imperatives—by standing off to SEE instead of forcing himself too close."[6] Poe's piecemeal yet systematic borrowing from foreign texts, his willingness to treat his own writing as if it belonged to another, paradoxically lets him clear the ground to become the first American writer, according to Williams, to "detach a 'method' from the smear of common usage"(221). Discovering in his predecessor a confirmation of his own literary practice, Williams thus repeatedly calls attention to Poe's "immaculate attack"(220). For Williams it is Poe's self-critical stance, his ability to see the "harder structural imperatives" of his writing, that frees him to cleanse his words of their former ghostly associations.

Williams may or may not be overestimating the value of Poe's method and his status in the canon. But he certainly is underestimating the difficulty of Poe's efforts at situating himself in his fiction, efforts which mostly end in failure. Williams is not alone here, for the majority of Anglo-American critics writing on Poe tend to reduce the tales to single-minded allegories that succeed, in one way or another, in firmly establishing the author at the center of his work. The critics can be roughly divided into two main groups which, taken together, recapitulate the duplicity of Poe's own fiction: those who tend to treat the narrator and author as one and those who conveniently divorce Poe from his narrators to call attention to the author's ironic control of the narrative. The first group has held sway ever since the mid nineteenth century, when Baudelaire and Rufus Griswold each began using Poe's stories to transform his life into a weird mixture of literary biography, myth, and gossip.[7] Continuing to equate Poe with his fiction, modern critics working under this paradigm commonly read the tales as transparent confessions directly offering key psychological and philosophical insights into Poe's life and thought. Richard Wilbur, to cite one influential example, interprets the tales as a series of allegorical representations of dream experience taking place within the mind of Poe the visionary poet, who seeks to return to a primal state of transcendental unity.[8]

This established view has been challenged during the past three decades by a number of New Critics who insist that Poe remains detached from his narratives, deliberately manipulating his deluded narrators to produce an ironic effect. Arguing against what they term the "supernatural" bias of earlier readings, these critics interpret the strange goings-on in Poe's stories as signs of the defective moral and intellectual perception of his first-person narrators—well-formed, internally consistent personae whose mad versions of events are slyly discredited by shrewd author and knowing reader.[9] The unreliable narrator of "Ligeia," for instance, conjures up the apparition of an ideal dead lover so that he may justify the murder of his real wife, Rowena.[10]

Each critical camp thus tends to fix unequivocally on either the content of the narration or, more recently, the figure of the narrator, without quite seeing that Poe often seems more interested in exploring the interaction that takes place between storytellers and their creative constructs.[11] If anything, the New Critical emphasis on Poe's ironic distance is more misleading since it tends to stabilize the relation between author and narrator, a relationship which I take to be unstable and fluctuating, intimate yet volatile. Treating these nervous first-person speakers as well-wrought characters in their own right allows the New Critics to restore to Poe the kind of mastery over his fiction that he himself seems unwilling or unable to assume. To account for the behavior of the first person apart from his ongoing act of narration, as the New Critics and their nineteenth-century critical predecessors both tend to do, risks draining the stories of their haunting power by refusing to admit the extent to which Poe has invested himself in his own fiction. This authorial investment, I would argue, is inextricably linked to Poe's failure to maintain absolute control over his "I," as well as the associated failure of his fictional surrogates to understand the tales they tell about themselves.

This last point may need some amplification, since the exasperating obtuseness of Poe's narrators is frequently a crux in the secondary criticism. Why do these first persons so often and so blindly resist acknowledging what remains obvious to the reader? Noting this remarkable obtuseness, Michael Bell speaks for a host of critics when he complains that Poe's narrators "refuse the implications of their own suggestive symbols."[12] Bell points out, for example, that the narrator of "The Fall of the House of Usher" fails to make the obvious allegorical connection between Roderick's head and the mansion even as he belabors the analogy with numerous descriptive details. Such an appalling lack of self-awareness is even more troublesome when we consider how Poe's first persons repeatedly fail to recognize themselves in their doubles ("William Wilson" being the most glaring example) even as they obsessively seek to confront and kill off their alter egos.

This paradoxical pattern of physical confrontation and cognitive avoidance only makes sense by seeing it as a sign of a more fundamental problem: Poe's inability to conceive of human relationship altogether. In a bracing series of insights that mark a decided advance in Poe criticism, Donald Pease has recently argued that the failure of Poe's speakers to reflect, to gain some objective distance themselves, is a symptom of a larger cultural disconnection called modernity: the severance of the present from the past; the tyranny of the instantaneous moment; the dispossession of memory by immediate sensation; and, most important for my argument, a kind of paralyzing subjectivity that makes it impossible to distinguish between self and other, as if all other persons were simply displaced versions of an inescapable "I." Poe, according to Pease, does not unequivocally embrace this modernity, as the poststructuralists would have it, but instead reacts with loathing and dread, seeking to fashion some semblance of a lost aristocratic, ancestral past out of the very shocks of the new.[13]

While Pease primarily focuses on relations taking place within the tales, or on external relations between Poe and his culture, his insights also help to illuminate the interaction between author and narrator. This relation between creator and creation is so disturbing, I have suggested, largely because difference is so difficult to maintain in the grammatical first person. Yet such difference is also crucial. If the fictional "I" knew as much as the authorial "I," there would be no story to tell. Having articulation depend on ignorance, Poe's tales are set in motion and energized by the first person's groping inability to ever know, a blindness that Poe simultaneously relies on, participates in, and tries to remove himself from. To return more specifically to "Usher," as long as the narrator remains within the house, prey to his companion's stupefying paranoia, he can never wholly comprehend his own allegory. Poe thereby allows his narrator to share Usher's terrifying experience but escape his fate. Without preserving the illusion of difference between author and narrator for the duration of the story, without admitting some epistemological gap between the two "I's," the fiction's inside and outside would collapse together into one unspeakable mass. Obtuseness becomes Poe's way of protecting himself from his own fiction.

Rather than condescending to Poe's blind narrators, or even blaming Poe for impersonating them, we need to explore how the first person, held in suspension between Poe and the narrated self, manages to construe the narrative. His narrators are not simply crazy people who just happen to tell stories, as some New Critics seem to assume, but storytellers whose precarious identities largely depend on the alienating act of inventing some coherent literary form to contain and explain themselves (Psyche Zenobia's predicament). Oscillating wildly between farce and tragedy, these acts of narration share some common characteristics, regardless of the particular first person Poe imagines is doing the talking. First, the narrator's scheming tends to be a substitute for self-knowledge, as the rigid requirements of form come to obscure the possibility of insight. Second, this compulsive plotting most often follows the pattern of a regression or decomposition, as the first person moves backward to search for a first cause that would make sense of his current confusion. And, third, it is this search for origins which accounts for the emergence of the double, for in the absence of even the most minimal confidence in the self's temporal continuity (who I am will essentially be the same tomorrow as today), the narrating "I" must project an alter ego as an intimate presence outside but close to the chaos of his own immediate experience.

Possessing the corporeal identity that the first person finds missing in himself, the double permits the "I" to construct some structure of cause and effect, a plot, that could help give the narrator some objective sense of himself. The first person's pursuit of his double serves to mirror the confusing interplay between author and narrator and thereby allows Poe to work out his relation with his fiction. These encounters between first person and other, as we shall see, often end in a mock self-destruction in which the "I" strains to regain its original integrity by first positing a second self, then plotting to destroy that self, and subsequently destroying his own seamless plot in order to be approved as an ingenious contriver by some objective outsider (the police, a confidant, or the reader). The logic of confession and failure, not mastery and control, drives Poe's fiction, as its narrators struggle to gain some identity for themselves.

No story of Poe's dramatizes the double-edged nature of these self-confrontations more starkly than his enigmatic masterpiece "The Man of the Crowd." Published in November 1840, a few months before "The Murders in the Rue Morgue," the narrative deserves to be classified as Poe's first tale of ratiocination, the purest kind of detective fiction. The intrigue centers on the attempts of the first-person narrator to track down and uncover the identity of a wandering stranger who becomes "the type and the genius of deep crime" (515) by the end of his story. As in "The Purloined Letter," the clues remain on the surface of Poe's fiction—the plot—

despite the narrator's best efforts to find some deep structure which would decipher the disturbing stranger. In both detective stories Poe thus makes the method of solving the crime, the interpretive quest, more mysterious than the crime itself.

The problems the narrator encounters in trying to assign meaning to the old man mock our own attempts to penetrate the text, as any survey of the criticism on "The Man of the Crowd" will demonstrate. Richard Wilbur, for instance, claims that in the story "the soul of a poet 'detects' and confronts the evil or brutal principle in itself," while G. R. Thompson has more recently noted that the tale may be read as "the deluded romanticizing of the tipsy narrator, who perversely attributes a romantic significance to an old drunk who wanders from bistro to bistro."[14] Thompson and Wilbur reproduce in miniature the two poles of Poe criticism with a kind of painful clarity which suggests that Poe has deliberately constructed the story simply to confirm each of our own interpretive presuppositions. By writing a tale whose reflecting surface "does not permit itself to be read," to quote the German motto framing the story, Poe provides a gloss on our critical practices as well as on his own literary procedures. As we shall see, the narrator's quest dramatizes how meaning must be simultaneously posited and denied in order to plot experience and coerce potential threats into coherent structures.

The search for conceptual categories to explain the stranger is only half the story, however. Until the old man enters the picture midway through the tale, the narrator finds significance wherever he looks, decoding the transparent social relations of an urban crowd with absolute precision. "The Man of the Crowd" can thus be sharply divided into two parts, two ways of seeing that comment on each other. In the first half of the story the narrator offers a static representation of society which he blithely believes to be a divinely ordained pattern, a stable hierarchy based on an aristocratic set of assumptions. Once the lonely man of the crowd appears on the scene, however, the narrator's conceptual paradigm dissolves into a more democratic, more disturbing perception that finds people bound together solely by their common depravity. To see the wanderer clearly, both narrator and reader must now interpret him, a risky enterprise that draws the first-person speaker out into the streets.

Like Poe's other detectives Dupin and Legrand, the narrator

begins the process of ratiocination in a heightened mental state "of the keenest appetency" following a recent illness. His intellect becomes "electrified" by virtue of his intense isolation; as he sits alone in a London coffeehouse, he enjoys a "delicious novelty of emotion," a self-satisfied, self-absorbed calm that enables him to analyze the crowd passing outside his window with perfect lucidity. The narrator is protected from the masses outside, in fact, in direct proportion to his ability to see them in their abstract "aggregate relations" (507). Occupying the detached, inviolate analytic perspective which we have come to associate with Psyche's dislocated eyes, the narrator confidently contemplates "the scene without" to provide us with a complete social taxonomy patterned after seventeenth- and eighteenth-century Theophrastian character sketches.[15] He identifies a descending scale of human types based on external traits ("figure, dress, air, gait, visage") which correspond precisely to the vocation of each type: "I observed an order of men somewhat different in habits, but still birds of a kindred feather. They may be defined as the gentlemen who live by their wits. They seem to prey upon the public in two battalions—that of the dandies and that of the military men. Of the first grade the leading features are long locks and smiles; of the second frogged coats and frowns."

He can define types with such assurance because, as his metaphors suggest, he perceives the social structure as a given of nature, something actually "out there" rather than of his own imaginative construction. The narrator's systematic binary differentiating thus turns his fellow humans into a set of exaggerated caricatures, the price he must pay to signify order, and see things whole. What he gains in comprehension he loses in depth, however, for his classifying becomes increasingly sketchy as he moves down the social scale to encounter "darker and deeper themes for speculation": peddlers, invalids, beggars, and prostitutes. With the introduction of these threatening figures, marginal creatures similar to those portrayed by Charles Dickens early in his career,[16] the narrator's secure perception of a fixed social hierarchy gradually disintegrates into a sequence of discrete character portraits whose power partially derives from his inability to classify them any longer as uniform, representative types: "I saw ... drunkards innumerable and indescribable—some in shreds and patches, reeling inarticulate, with bruised visage and lack-lustre eyes ... some in whole although filthy garments, with a slightly unsteady swagger ... others clothed in materials which had once been good . . . but whose countenances were fearfully pale, whose eyes hideously wild and red . . . " (510). Confronted with such troubling, fragmentary glimpses of isolated depravity, the narrator must abandon his analytic discourse for a more subjective set of metaphors depicting the sordid masses of the city as a shadowy tableau of Gothic proportions:

> As the night deepened, so deepened to me the interest of the scene; for not only did the general character of the crowd materially alter (its gentler features retiring in the gradual withdrawal of the more orderly portion of the people, and its harsher ones coming out into bolder relief, as the late hour brought forth every species of infamy from its den,) but the rays of the gas-lamps, feeble at first in their struggle with the dying day, had now at length gained ascendancy, and threw over everything a fitful and garish lustre. All was dark yet splendid. . . . (510–11)

The narrator's clear view of a natural social order gives way to a darker image of humans as solitary figures of discordant artifice whose histories must be "read." This lapse from vision to interpretation, moreover, quickly forces the narrator to participate in the "aggregate relations" that he had previously only observed. In order to get a closer view of the now "individual faces" of the crowd outside, the narrator bends his "brow to the glass." At this precise moment the figure of the old man suddenly seizes his attention. Simultaneously window and mirror, an instrument of self-reflection as well as vision, the glass calls forth the mysterious stranger, whose "absolute idiosyncrasy of . . . expression" at once defies and compels the narrator to read the history "written within that bosom." Only by trying to keep the cloaked figure in view, pursuing him through the streets of London, can the narrator hope "to form some analysis of the meaning conveyed" (511).

The unsettling appearance of the stranger generates the plot proper, which at its most rudimentary depends upon action, movement in time, some relief from the static, spatial overview of society that the narrator envisioned earlier. The plot actually emerges from a curious double movement: as the narrator descends the social scale, moving *inward* to begin to reflect on his own depravity, the double abruptly appears, compelling him to venture *outward* into the crowd. Leaving his fixed observation post to haunt the streets in quest of the old man's significance, the narrator seeks to escape impending introspection, to flee the torments of self-analysis. The self metamorphoses into an other, the old man, whose wanderings permit the narrator to mingle with the masses he had formerly simply watched. Discussing Baudelaire's modernity, Paul de Man has noted that the writer's attraction to the crowd signals his desire to run away from his art and experience the anonymity of the immediate present.[17] Yet the search for anonymous experience only increases the individual's sense of self-conscious isolation. In "The Man of the Crowd" the narrating self, the head, tries to plunge into sheer temporality by investing meaning in his narrated self, the body, a figure of pure motion "without apparent object" (515), whose resistance to detection ultimately returns the narrator to his own subjective prison. But by making the double an object of analysis, the same and yet other, the narrator is able to interpret his story and participate in it simultaneously.

Positing some underlying significance and then doggedly pursuing it, the narrator constructs his plot. The "mad energy" he notices in the old man's aimless movements reflects his own passionate compulsion to detect some secret meaning, to turn the wanderer into some profound archetype. His task is both simplified and complicated by the fact that his suspect, immersed in the immediacy of the present, never speaks. Unlike the Wandering Jew or Coleridge's Ancient Mariner, Poe's social outcast prefers to suffer his fate silently; it is as if the Wedding Guest were forced to tell the Mariner's story for him. Here we clearly see Poe's antagonism toward one key strain of high European Romanticism, the literary tradition that fostered him. By shifting attention away from the conventional wanderer figure to focus on the narrator, Poe suggests that quest-romances, histories of the soul, can no longer be simply recited but must be compulsively framed and interpreted by another: the narrator penetrates the surface to try to "read" the "written" depths below. Given the pursued object's resistance to signification, however, the wanderer's circuitous journey may culminate not in self-knowledge and power but instead turn into a dead end, that is, become an empty cipher rather than a transcendental spiral.[18]

   The narrator thus ends up where he began (in front of the coffeehouse), and so do we. Closure, a respite from perpetual interpretation, can only be purchased by a rhetorical ruse: the narrator halts his twenty-four-hour pursuit by concluding that the wanderer "is the type and the genius" of a deep crime whose secrets must remain undivulged. The narrated self does not permit itself to be read, to be detached from the faceless crowd, a fact that the narrator dramatically announces by means of the German quotation which opens and closes his narrative ("*er lasst sich nicht lesen*"). Yet in the very act of treating the old man as if he were some impenetrable book, Poe's first person sheds light on the construction of his own opaque text, a kind of parable which serves to confess obliquely the alienating subjectivity from which he seeks to escape. Although the stranger's refusal to reveal himself heightens suspense and teases both the narrator and the reader into pursuit, the narrative shows that we can never close the gap between self and other opened up by the sudden appearance of the double.
   The old man's manic movements incessantly mock the narrator's attempts—as well as our own—to uncover some past mystery that would explain his attraction to the crowd. Forever dislodged from the structural paradigm which allowed him to analyze dispassionately the "aggregate relations" of the urban masses, the narrator suddenly finds himself in the midst of the city's buzzing confusion. Observing and recording the ceaseless wanderings of the stranger with an insane kind of precision, he can only accumulate information as a substitute for the wholly meaningful gestures he saw the crowd convey earlier from his secure post of observation. He comes to play the part of a journalist who simply reports raw data that can no longer be assimilated by experience, while the plot itself gets filled up with an extravagant amount of irrelevant detail—factual descriptions of appearance, time, and place similar to the countless details that the narrators of "Ligeia" and "Berenice" lavish on their subjects. In each of these stories such clues pretend to possess significance but always manage to fall just short, leaving in their wake a residual atmosphere of mystery. In "The Fall of the House of Usher," as we shall see, this process of constructing an atmosphere verging on portentous meaning becomes what Mr. Blackwood calls "the soul of the business," a process analogous to Psyche Zenobia's efforts to piece together

quotations that create an air of erudition. In the case of "The Man of the Crowd," the tale fills up with glimpses of the labyrinthine windings of London. While pursuing his double, the narrator incidentally charts the haunting desolation and dissonance of the wretched urban setting: "By the dim light of an accidental lamp, tall, antique, worm-eaten, wooden tenements were seen tottering to their fall, in directions so many and capricious that scarce the semblance of a passage was discernible between them. The paving-stones lay at random, displaced from their beds by the rankly-growing grass" (514). Such details accumulate to create a senseless, sickening atmosphere of chaos that mutely complements the silent old man's own grim movements.

By the end of the story the urban backdrop has become part of the mystery itself. In contrast to the narrator's former vision of social order, the "human bustle and activity" of the modern city offers a more menacing, haphazard inscription of human relations. The labyrinths of London, however, and the old man's wanderings through them, are not perfectly random, for the pursuing narrator does manage to perceive some kind of pattern to his double's frantic motion. The stranger is, after all, the man of the crowd; it is his compulsion to lose himself among the masses, to bury his personal identity, which paradoxically marks him as a type of the social misfit. The relation between the old man and the urban crowd upon whom he depends, then, mirrors the interaction between the wanderer and the narrator, who follows his fugitive double through the streets of London in order to flee from himself. Their interplay, in turn, represents the relation between author and narrator, as well as the relation between the story and its readers. By the tale's conclusion we have become, along with Poe, the narrator's "ghostly confessor[s]," interpreting an impenetrable text to distract us from our own loneliness. As the chilling epigraph to the tale suggests, the entire story documents the desperate attempt to escape the self-estrangement of consciousness by pursuing the meaning of an other: "Ce grand malheur, de ne pouvoir être seul" ("This great misery, to be unable to be alone"). The awkward efforts at human contact that take place between the old man and the crowd, between the narrator and his double, and between Poe and his fiction only testify to "the feeling in solitude on account of the very denseness of the company around," as the first person says early in his description of the restless movements of the crowd, whose furtive, mechanical gestures anticipate his own alienating experience of the city.

II

Against the dim silhouette of a dissolute and decaying city, the narrator of "The Man of the Crowd" searches for the "essence of all crime," a confession that might account for the old man's presence as well as the detective's own self-estranged behavior. Only by trying to trace effects back to their causes can the speculating narrator expect to understand his present circumstances. This impulse to touch bottom, to discover some explanatory first cause or primal self, dominated Poe's thinking from his earliest writings to *Eureka* (1848). In his colloquy "The Power of Words" (1845), Poe calls this backward movement "analytic retrogradation," a regression, by means of analysis, to the self-annihilating center of all thought, namely, God. The individual particles of language themselves, the angels of the colloquy contend, might be traced back through "the medium of creation" to their divine source. Although *Eureka* provides the most explicit discussion of a diffused universe tending to return to original unity, the tales also frequently gesture toward some assumed origin that is a point of self-destruction as well. In "MS. Found in a Bottle" and "A Descent into the Maelström," for instance, personal identity is obliterated by voyaging into some fearful vortex or abyss, an expression of Poe's desire to return to the womb, according to psychoanalytically inclined critics.[19] John Irwin, on the other hand, takes a slightly different tack when he interprets Pym's journey as Poe's search for the linguistic origins of self.[20] In the case of all three of these tales, the pattern of the voyage is the same: the narrative progresses forward in time, while the first-person protagonist moves toward some primal reunion with God prior to self-consciousness. In *A Grammar of Motives* Kenneth Burke explains that this kind of double movement depends on the dialectical conversion of a set of ambiguous metaphors. Burke dubs this conversion "the temporizing of essence":

> Because of the pun whereby the logically prior can be expressed
> in terms of the temporally prior, and *v.v.*, the ways of transcend-

ence, in aiming at the discovery of *essential* motives, may often take the historicist form of symbolic *regression*. That is, if one is seeking for the "essence" of motives, one can only express such a search in the terms of imaginative literature as a process of "going back." And conversely, one given to retrospect may conceptualize his concern as a search for "essence."[21]

Most of Poe's plots operate dialectically between temporal and essential modes of thinking. The narration of "The Man of the Crowd," for example, works forward to track the meanderings of the stranger and backward by grasping for some first cause to interpret his devious ways. The narrator and his double thus engage in a mutual haunting. Like the demon in Poe's "Shadow—A Parable" the *idea* of the specter as something "vague, formless, indefinite" enthralls the narrator, while he in turn pursues the wanderer's *presence*. When the narrator verges on physical contact, a face-to-face encounter, the double withdraws into an even more self-contained enigma, just as the individuals of the crowd feel their solitude most acutely when they are massed together. The tale's inversely symmetrical relation between interpretation and presence, the narrator who signifies and the restless indeterminate actor, rehearses the dynamics between spiritual repulsion and material attraction that Poe infers in *Eureka* as the basic principle at the heart of a universe returning to unity: "Suffering them [atoms] infinitely to approximate, while denying them positive contact" (16:211). In other words, this assumed unity—"God," "Infinity," or "First Cause"—serves to constitute the particularity (and isolation) of both atoms and people, as Poe intimates in *Eureka*: "A word, in fine, was demanded, by means of which one human being might put himself in relation at once with another human being and with a certain *tendency* of the human intellect. Out of this demand arose the word 'Infinity,' which is thus the representative but of the thought of a thought" (16:200).

Poe's interesting emphasis on the word "tendency" helps to illuminate his reasoning throughout *Eureka*, as well as his narration in the fiction.[22] Words like "God" and "Infinity" are not "expression[s] of an idea" for Poe, but metaterms that enable us to think about the "direction" of our thoughts methodically. By assuming the absolute value of such words, we self-consciously forge our own identities. The primal unity which so many of Poe's critics treat as

some kind of ultimate transcendental destination—whether it be
the womb or linguistic self-oblivion, functions instead as a posited
intention that spurs the infinitely regressing quests of his narrators,
who displace desire onto first causes in an attempt to erect some
structure—a plot—to explain themselves. To propose an origin is
to propose a self. Yet Poe seems more interested in systematically
exploring the process of composing, or decomposing, than he is in
arriving at any particular goal that thought may tend toward. In
his reviews of Hawthorne, "The Philosophy of Composition," and
Eureka—every time in his critical prose that he insists on writing
for a preconceived unity of effect—Poe couches his analysis of the
mechanics of plotting in terms of intention and tendency, from the
Latin root *tendere*, a stretching towards: "It is only with the *denouement* constantly in view that we can give a plot its indispensable
air of consequence, or causation, by making the incidents, and
especially the tone at all points, tend to the development of the
intention" (14:193). Poe thus projects an intended origin or first
cause, assumed as unattainable, from which all else follows. This
constantly receding horizon thereby generates a suggestive "air of
causation" that remains the source of Poe's effective power, as he
hints in *Eureka*: "I design but to suggest—and to convince through
the suggestion" (16:221).

Because we cannot know God (since we are not gods ourselves),
we must speculate on "the intention of the Deity" (8:281), a guessing
game that compels us to construct our own imperfect plots. The
primary difficulty for any author confronted with "Silence . . . the
eternal voice of God" ("Al Aaraaf") is to make a beginning. Poe
faces the problem squarely in a *Marginalia* note written about the
same time as *Eureka*: "The true genius shudders at incompleteness
. . . He is so filled with his theme that he is dumb, first from not
knowing how to begin, where there seems eternally beginning behind beginning, and secondly from perceiving his true end at so
infinitely a distance" (16:127). Here Poe outlines a predicament
that Henry James would raise more delicately in his preface to
Roderick Hudson: "Really, universally, relations stop nowhere, and
the exquisite problem of the artist is eternally but to draw, by a
geometry of his own, the circle within which they shall happily
appear to do so."[23] Insisting that art circumscribes reality by a geometry of appearance, James elaborates Poe's guiding calculus of
"intention." For both James and Poe, experience can be transmuted

into fiction only by assuming some method to set the boundaries of the artist's form.

Interpreting an intention that appears to be an origin, Poe provides a starting point for his plots. Author and reader pretend that the man of the crowd embodies the essence of crime so that we may follow the narrator through the streets, even though that search for a secret first cause is given up as futile by the end of the story. Barred from any direct access to divine authority, the writer must inaugurate his own act of authorship by a provisional hypothesis which entertains the possibility of an essence. As I shall argue later in this study, the notion of beginning by interpretation also gives us an insight into Poe's own sense of originality as a secular act of *bricolage* rather than as a Coleridgean imitation of God; for it is precisely Poe's realization of his distance from an unknowable God that induces him to assume some transcendent origin in the first place. Although critics usually cite Poe's famous aphorism from *Eureka* that "the Universe is a plot of God" to show the profound significance Poe placed on his authorship, I am more interested in examining the differences Poe sees between God's constructions and his own. The key difference centers on what he calls divine "mutuality of adaptation":

> In human constructions a particular cause has a particular effect; a particular intention brings to pass a particular object; but this is all; we see no reciprocity. The effect does not react upon the cause; the intention does not change relations with the object. In Divine constructions the object is either design or object as we choose to regard it—and we may take at any time a cause for an effect, or the converse—so that we can never absolutely decide which is which. (16:291–92)

Once set in motion by the divine act, "determinate and discontinued," God's constructions sustain a life of their own through a resonating interplay between cause and effect that prevents us from fixing any single function of the universal plot. The perfect symmetry between intention and object in God's narratives thus stands as a model for the flawed authorial transactions between Poe's narrators and their doubles, who appear to cause the narration as much as result from it.

The perfect plot, however, would be no plot at all but rather an undifferentiated unity where cause and effect would be entirely indistinguishable. God's constructions dissolve object and intention into pure design, a seamless whole that the ornate arabesque decor of a story like "Ligeia" serves to reproduce. Yet the more Poe's art aspires to the condition of transcendent oneness, the closer it moves toward death, an absolutely perfect state of selfless abstraction. Just as the self maintains personal identity by resisting unity, so must Poe's plotting resist divine symmetry by exposing the creaky narrative machinery it pretends to conceal. "The pleasure which we derive from any display of human ingenuity," Poe reasons in *Eureka*, "is in the ratio of the *approach* to this species of [divine] reciprocity" (16:292). Because humans, unlike God, are unable to be alone, as "The Man of the Crowd" reminds us, our ingenuity has meaning only when it is displayed in public. In order to be appreciated as cunning artificers, Poe's narrators compulsively maim their own productions. By self-consciously deforming the artless surface of their work, Poe and his first-person agents call attention to their plots as reactions to the world, not descriptions of it. Suddenly we see why so many of Poe's tales are cast in the form of confessional monologues: the need to admit the artifice of plotting becomes the force driving the expression of self.

Nowhere does Poe confess his own sleight of hand more openly than in his essay "The Philosophy of Composition." By trying to articulate systematically the principles implicit in his artistic act (writing "The Raven"), Poe provides a crucial model for the prefaces of Hawthorne as well as James, who used the publication of the New York Edition as an occasion to analyze the motives and shape of his craft from the retrospective "standpoint on the ground gained."[24] Each time James replays "the thrilling ups and downs, the intricate ins and outs, of the compositional problem"[25] in the prefaces, he becomes obsessed with detecting and recovering the elusive "germ" of the novel, the original intent or impulse that sparked the imaginary process. Although Poe, too, offers us his germ of creativity, it is much more rigidly circumscribed than James's: "Let us dismiss, as irrelevant to the poem per se, the circumstance—or say the necessity—which, in the first place, gave rise to the intention of composing a poem that should suit at once the popular and the critical taste" (14:195–96). Displacing psychological motives onto formal issues, as always, Poe commences with "intention" to detail the exact method of composition by which he arrived at the length, effect, and subject matter of his poem. But as Kenneth Burke has noted, Poe draws out his intention by following a logical rather than a narrative sequence, another form of temporizing essence.[26] Claiming to describe the step-by-step genetic process of composition, Poe offers instead a set of generic principles that logically precede the specific act of writing "The Raven." Like his surrogate Psyche Zenobia, Poe pretends to translate theory into practice when, in fact, he analytically derives the theory implicit in the practice. He thereby confounds the experience of composing the poem with his interpretation of that process, a confusion that should remind us of Psyche's own predicament.

The version of plotting Poe presents in "The Philosophy of Composition" approaches divine reciprocity by making cause and effect simultaneously follow a chain of logic and a temporal sequence. Equating the "effect" of a poem, its persuasive end product, with its own essential "cause," Poe converts the process of writing into reading: the author must assume the role of his reader in order to foresee the temporal outcome of his as yet uncreated creation. This circular symmetry which Poe posits in theory reaffirms my inital distinction between narrating self and narrated self. The writer removes himself from the immediacy of the present to design an interpretive structure based on premeditated effect. To use the famous Russian formalist distinction, the narrated self acts in the *fabula*, while the narrating self arranges this basic story into the *sjûzet*, his explanatory discourse.[27] It is precisely the inability to differentiate between *sjûzet* and *fabula*, however, which gives Poe's first-person narrators such fits. Events never simply happen in Poe's world without someone trying to gloss them from a second perspective. Although Poe claims in "The Murders in the Rue Morgue" that the analytic power "disentangles," a tale like "The Black Cat" dramatizes how analysis, which can be appreciated "only in [its] effects," creates more mysteries than it tends to solve when it turns inward upon itself.

Trying to reform his experience into a gallows confession, the narrator of "The Black Cat" falls victim to his own seductive reasoning. Although he assures us that his "immediate purpose is to place before the world plainly, succinctly, and without comment, a series of mere household events"(849), his subsequent testimony betrays that he is not, as he pretends, "above the weakness of seeking to establish a sequence of cause and effect." He thus burdens himself with the task he reserves for his "less excitable" readers: to perceive a "succession of very natural causes and effects" in the "wild, yet most homely narrative which I am about to pen." The mere act of recounting his tale compels him to comment on it, commentary that quickly leads to a farcical self-representation by which the first person seeks to compensate, after the fact, for a botched life. From the introduction of Pluto, the first cat, to his final identification of Pluto's replacement as "the Arch-Fiend," the narrator gets entangled in a web of explanation that turns the mere household events of his life into a miniature allegory of diabolical crime and punishment. Parodying the structure of an early Victorian temperance tale, Poe thus thematizes his first person's loss of control in the hope of maintaining some control of his own.

Only by desperately seizing upon one interpretation after another to account for his unaccountable behavior can the narrator hope to convince us, as well as himself, that he possesses some coherent identity, that his past actions and his present narration express the same person. He first blames his violence on drinking, "Fiend Intemperance," but by the middle of his story he transforms this cause into an effect produced by an even larger capital letter cause: "the spirit of PERVERSENESS" (852). It must be this "indivisible primary faculty," he assumes, that compels his "original soul"to take flight just before he cuts out Pluto's evil eye with his "penknife," a weapon whose compound construction (pen/knife) conflates *sjûzet* and *fabula* to suggest how a literal maiming will turn into a figurative self-maiming once the narrator retrospectively attempts to contain his violence in writing. Like Psyche Zenobia's dislocated eyeballs, the cat's obliterated organ of sight mocks its master's efforts to tell a story straight. The narrative thus follows the regressive patterns of Poe's other fiction, as one first cause gets displaced onto another, until the narrator, no longer quite himself, finally traces his cruel acts to some vague demonic source represented by the black cat itself. When he claims that he hanged the cat *"because* I knew that it had loved me," he seeks to coerce his perverse desire into an explanatory principle that would force the victims of his hatred to share responsibility for his ungovernable violence. Without projecting onto the world such a causal principle, a theory of evil, the narrator could not construct his plot, a necessary species of allegory.

The problem, however, is that during this process of plotting the restless cat refuses to let the master fix its value with certainty. The "deep impression" produced by the ever-present feline lingers on, despite the narrator's best efforts (murder) to put it to rest once and for all. The significance of the symbol constantly eludes its creator: the murdered Pluto is reborn as a "*bas relief*" graven in plaster, which then comes to life as another one-eyed black cat (with the outlines of a gallows on its chest), which finally turns into the Arch-Fiend himself. The story of the black cat, a recurring series of events alternating between the animal and its image, thus always manages to keep one agile step ahead of the narrator's explanation of it. Unlike the narrator of "The Man of the Crowd," this plotter cannot even present a double stable enough to invest in; as a result he tends to lose control of his narrative, jumping from one kind of explanation to the next to produce, on occasion, a wildly literal, and therefore comic, version of events. When he returns to survey the burnt house, for example, he reasons that the mysterious figure etched on the solitary remaining wall has been created by a neighbor who threw the dead cat into his bedroom to warn him of the conflagration.

The gigantic "graven" image of the cat stands for Poe's art, which leaves its own disturbing traces on the ruins of his narrator's rickety plot. By offering a crucial "link" between "disaster and atrocity," the inscription on the wall serves to sustain a dubious structure of cause and effect verging on dissolution. The wall "resist[s] the action of the fire" that threatened to bring the narrative to a premature close, only to be transformed into the blank facade that the narrator later builds to hide the corpse of his wife. This second wall represents the plotter's final attempt to salvage a coherent narrative structure out of the chaos of his experience. With the painstaking precision characteristic of Poe's other first-person narrators, he constructs the wall to distract him from the horror of his crime, which he carefully glosses over with proud deliberation: "Here at least, then, my labor has not been in vain" (857). His life may be a complete failure, a shambles, but the first person can go on as long as his plot remains intact. When the police arrive, he publicly calls attention to his "well constructed house," a secure "place of concealment" analogous to the coffeehouse that served to shield the narrator of "The Man of the Crowd" from outside threats.

Yet in the very act of bragging about his construction, the

narrator betrays the flimsy face of his narrative, his inability to make
the black cat conform to the contours of his allegory. The cat howls
from the depths of the tomb, revealing the secret its master has
sought to cover up all along: the nameless, speechless wife, whose
haunting presence lies at the heart of the tale, as Daniel Hoffman
has suggested.[28] Maintaining her husband's formerly placid dis-
position, the "uncomplaining" victim of his "personal violence" surfaces at key moments in his narrative. She procures Pluto, alludes
to the cat as a witch, and points out to her mate the gallows on the
chest of her beloved substitute, a form which gradually assumes a
"rigorous distinctness of outline," a kind of counterplot. The wife,
not the black cat, remains the uncanny double, the mysterious
measure of the guilty plotter's depravity. In order to protect himself
from this terrible knowledge, he blindly erects a structure of displaced cause and effect, a wall that conceals the offending reminder
of his tottering domestic and narrative authority.

Obsessively bent on constructing a seamless surface to rival the
perfect designs of God, the narrator tries to suppress disturbing
suggestions that repeatedly erupt in Poe's stories to puncture the
mechanical unity of cause and effect. The black cat returns to betray
its master the very moment he consummates his plot, which needs
to be approved by an other, the inquiring audience of detectives.
The police stand in the same relation to the narrated self as the
reader to the narrating self, who compulsively exposes the *modus
operandi* of his narrative apparatus by unraveling as he weaves,
"letting the public take a peep behind the scenes" (14:194), if only
to see the backside of the props. Poe's first-person narrators can't
help but galvanize back to life those entombed corpses that they have
murdered for the sake of the perfect plot; the triumph of their
complete self-enclosure must be objectified by a "less excitable"
outsider, as Poe uneasily acknowledges in an important passage
elaborating the French epigraph that prefaces "The Man of the
Crowd": "What flippant Frenchman was it who said . . . 'la solitude
est une belle chose; mais il faut quelqu'un pour vous dire que la
solitude est une belle chose'? ['solitude is a fine thing, but there
must be someone to tell you that solitude is a fine thing']" ("The
Island of the Fay," 602).

In "The Black Cat" the narrator's overwhelming urge to display
his self-concealment disturbs the illusory reciprocity between cause
and effect that he has labored to forge. Although he can wall off

the victims of his self-consuming hatred from his sight, and deliberately obliterate the cat's own mocking organ of vision, the narrator cannot stop his ears; the accusing sound of the "hideous beast" penetrates through the narrator's barrier to reveal the confession behind the confession. Poe's description of the cat's "informing voice" is extraordinary enough to quote in full:

> I was answered by a voice within the tomb!—by a cry, at first muffled and broken, like the sobbing of a child, and then quickly swelling into one long, loud, and continuous scream, utterly anomalous and inhuman—a howl—a wailing shriek, half of horror and half of triumph, such as might have arisen out of hell conjointly from the throats of the damned in their agony and of the demons that exult in the damnation. (858–59)

The "utterly anomalous" voice retains an unholy power which is not only hidden from the sphere of the visual but also resides apart from the message it conveys. I suspect Poe's fascination with an autonomous verbal power beyond sight and sense owes something to his American predecessor Charles Brockden Brown, who persistently contrasts the sensation of hearing with seeing in his Gothic romance *Wieland*. Because hearing is a more internalized process than sight insofar as it depends less on the outside world for verification, the voice for Brown, as for Poe, holds a potent but dangerous sway over the imagination that threatens to escape the mastery of both speaker and listener. Transforming his voice into a hypostatized, uncontrollable instrument of deception, Carwin's ventriloquism also conspires to convert Wieland's religious fervor into murderous madness. Only by tracing the alien sounds back to their legitimate owner can the mystery be solved and the deluding voice fettered. Carwin's voice, however, is not the only source of ungodly power in the romance. Brown repeatedly calls attention to the arresting "enchantments" and "sensations" produced by the speech of his first-person narrator, Clara Wieland who refers to herself as both "historian . . . and sufferer of these disasters."[29] Her enchanting narration, in turn, points to Brown's own act of ventriloquism, his thrilling impersonation of Clara's voice through the writing of his novel.

Poe takes Brown's self-reflexive reification of voice one step further by appearing to truncate the power of expression entirely from

meaning. Morella's "sad musical tones," Ligeia's "thrilling and enthralling eloquence," William Wilson's "low whisper," and Usher's
"perfectly modulated guttural utterance" all retain in their own
way some absolute power, imperishable and unmediated, beyond
personal identity and the contingencies of interpretation. Aspiring
to the condition of music, the voice's mystical quality depends on
its enchanting effects. Yet this buried utterance, like the fugitive
man of the crowd, only moves when it is the object of a second
kind of utterance, the social voice of the narrating self, whose own
authority to speak remains a precarious but tangible commodity
subject to worldly pressures. As we shall see, the "hollow" groans
produced by Valdemar's corpse, suspended beyond the grave, are
also "thrillingly distinct." For all its utter anomaly, the black cat's
demonic howl is still an "informing voice," communicating what its
owner himself wants to betray all along.

The common complaint that Poe severs the form of expression
(the body) from significance (the head) in order to indulge in a
solipsistic ritual of incantation needs to be drastically revised.[30] The
author is more interested in exploring the relation between private
experience and the public act of narration. As my introductory
discussion of "How to Write a Blackwood Article" has shown, this
interplay often takes the form of a struggle for the authority to
speak. In "The Murders in the Rue Morgue," to touch on another
example, criminal and detective act out this equivocal power play
within as well as between each other. Dupin's social tenor corresponds to the culprit sailor's easily identified gruff voice, while the
detective's high-pitched treble, excited by the process of ratiocination, bears a striking resemblance to the orangutan's own shrill
voice, at once polyglot and beyond language. Ratiocination and
bestiality thus become strange bedfellows: both detective and animal counterpart operate in a dangerous zone beyond cause and
effect which interpretation constantly tries to circumscribe. For the
sake of his companion, the tale's nameless narrator, Dupin retrospectively translates the spontaneous intuition which possessed him
to solve the crime. The sailor similarly traces the random movements of his pet after it has escaped his dominion to run amok.
The voice of the master can no longer control his bestial double,
which can only be narrated into submission by Dupin, working in
part from newspaper accounts, another form of social mediation.
The narrating detective fits the terrifying ape into his retrospective

scheme of cause and effect by first identifying the "startling absence of motive" (557) for the atrocious murders and then converting this absence into the key piece of evidence incriminating the beast. Anarchic violence incarnate, the orangutan becomes domesticated into intelligibility by its very resistance to meaning.

The translation of violent energy into ordered information thus depends upon the negotiations between autonomous utterance and the social voice, an authority continually put on the defensive. While Poe desires to think of himself out of thought, to become beast or ratiocinator, he also wants to live in order to tell the world about it, to divulge "some exciting knowledge—some never-to-be-imparted secret" (145) as he verges on self-obliteration. Just as Poe's detectives need to be themselves detected (the function of the first-person narrator/confidant), so must Poe's criminals, who gain identity as master plotters only when they are caught by baffled police or reader. Stories like "The Man of the Crowd" and "The Black Cat" suggest that the urge to confess is in direct ratio to the absence of any central motive. This absence, in turn, is framed by the plot's unity of design, the self-contained illusion of cause and effect that the detective and criminal construct to gloss a mysterious universe. The theory of PERVERSENESS posited by the narrator of "The Black Cat," for instance, only calls attention to the disturbing disappearance of any key to unlock his impenetrably private domestic life. Even though the wife plays a crucial part in his story, she can never be anything more than a shadowy mystery; human relations must be cut off, ignored, and buried if the plotter is to avoid self-recognition, that is, to avoid seeing himself reflected in the eyes of another. No wonder that so many of Poe's victims—the nameless wife, Madeline Usher, Berenice—only gain substance in death.

Poe explores the complementary relationship between confession and isolation most intensely in "The Tell-Tale Heart," a companion piece to "The Black Cat." Here the narrator's compulsion to contain his alter ego within the confines of a self-concealing plot forecloses the kind of elaborate allegorizing the narrator of "The Black Cat" offers up to account for himself. By identifying, almost arbitrarily, all "object" and "passion" with the old man's Evil Eye, the narrator seeks to transfer his guilty desires bodily onto his victim and then kill this other evil "I" for good. As in "The Man of the Crowd" and "The Black Cat," horror for Poe is relational: only when his master's eye is open, seeing and being seen, does it terrify the first person. Dispensing with rational explanations, the narrating self is free to concentrate on the convincing "manner" of the murder, a source of growing terror precisely because it has no object but itself. To test his sanity he defers the death of his double,[31] filling up his performance with countless procedural details which only serve to prolong the agony of narrator and victim (and reader). These minute precautions (unhinging the lantern, opening the door, and so on) activate the ticking heart, which, like the cruel pressure of Psyche's narrative machine, serves to mark his time as a self-conscious storyteller. When he permanently shuts the Evil Eye, the sole justification for his scheming, the narrator's acute senses contract to the intolerable sounds of the body, the internalized narrated self. He nervously discovers, as does Poe at the end of *Eureka*, that the throbbing heart divine is his own. Trapped in an accelerating feedback system, he can conceal all clues except himself: the heart literally becomes "tell-tale" by compelling the narrator to announce the motiveless crime he has committed for the perfect plot.

When he confidently dismisses all "object" and "passion," the narrator forces himself to construct a plot out of a series of precisely controlled gestures tenuously connected by temporal sequence alone. In lieu of any central motive, each of these highly mannered details becomes equally significant, leveling all sense of a climax to produce what Robert Caserio has called Poe's "exciting sameness."[32] Without a stable first cause to give their actions a purposeful design, Poe's agents cannot rest; once God excuses himself from the world, every moment of experience may hold crucial significance for the plot. Confronted with such a dreary possibility, the acutely sensitive narrator of "The Tell-Tale Heart" finally shares his terrifying burden with an outsider. Speculating on the presence of description in the novel, Martin Price suggests the consequences of completely flooding a narrative with significance: "Yet to live in a state of unrelieved and intense relevance is something like paranoia, a condition of lucid and overdeterminate design. Such a vision imposes its design at every point, obsessively and repetitiously."[33] Poe's insistence that "the Universe is a plot of God" suddenly takes on new meaning. The details Poe's narrators accumulate while pursuing their doubles pose as pieces of a mysterious universal conspiracy taunting us to weigh accurately the value of any human action or perception. Denied transcendent privilege, Poe's first persons are

driven by the kind of disease that fixes the attention of the confessing narrator of "Berenice": "In my case, the primary object was
invariably frivolous, although assuming, through the medium of my
distempered vision, a refracted and unreal importance" (212).

Paranoia, then, becomes the prime mover of the imagination,
the contriver of arabesque plots. The Greek derivation of the word
(*para* = beside; *nous* = mind) suggests the kind of alienating mental
drama paranoia stages. The subject projects his own meaning onto
a mysterious world to recover a transcendent text, or a text that
seems to escape transcendence. Conscious of his own interpretive
designs, the subject splits in two, generating a second self mocking
the attempt to comprehend the whole (recall Psyche's eyes). Self-
censorship, in turn, fuels the impulse to conceal loss and inadequacy
by discharging these feelings outside the self. The double is killed
and buried; the universe becomes the true source of alien malev-
olence. Yet the urge to obliterate self-consciousness only redoubles
subjectivity, until the isolated criminal is obliged to confess to another that his flawed schemes are excited by his own inexpressible
imaginative desires, not God's. Breaking out of their fabricated
tombs, Poe's restless corpses testify to the power of paranoia to
galvanize the world into meaning. However grotesque and distorted these paranoid monsters may be, they seem preferable to
the only alternative available in Poe's world, namely, objectless en-
nui, a living death.

Poe's greatest paean to the power of paranoia is the inside
narrative "The Fall of the House of Usher." Here the "close cir-
cumscription of space" Poe found essential for "the insulated effect"
(14:204) of a poem or short story produces a claustrophobic climate
that encourages our worst suspicions. Unlike "The Black Cat" or
"The Tell-Tale Heart," Poe has already framed a bounded place
of concealment for his narrator, a haunted palace which is also
Usher's head. To paraphrase Legrand's method of decoding in
"The Gold–Bug," the narrator encounters a context without a text
(833), which he then tries to decipher from within. In order to tap
his companion's central nervous system, as it were, he must charge
the Gothic arabesques inside with significance. Playing his own fears
against the structure·of Usher's mind, he conspires with his friend
to provoke insane stupor into imagination. As we shall soon see,
this tacit contract between first-person narrator and double depends on the paranoia-inducing notion of "sentience."

Even before he enters the house of Usher, the narrator begins "goading the imagination" into "artificial excitement" to give the sullen setting a suggestive air of terror. His self-conscious pauses and repetitions serve as reminders, on the threshold of the house, that he can participate in the action which he is about to narrate only by forming a "different arrangement of the particulars of the scene." This "somewhat childish experiment" of reflection, looking into the still tarn and then back at the house, produces "remodelled and inverted images" more unnerving than their originals. By using the tarn to "work upon my imagination," he thus literally and figuratively construes Usher's brooding atmosphere, which rises out of the rapidly accelerating interaction between the narrator's mind and his surroundings.

Like Poe's other narrators, however, the storyteller must expose the artifice of his own oppressive construction. Noting the "wild inconsistency" between the "perfect adaptation" of the whole and the "crumbling condition" of each detail, the narrator points out a possible flaw in the edifice: "Perhaps the eye of a scrutinizing observer might have discovered a barely perceptible fissure, which, extending from the roof of the building in front, made its way down the wall in a zigzag direction, until it became lost in the sullen waters of the tarn" (400). To protect his plot from prematurely unraveling, the narrator assumes the eye of another "scrutinizing observer" *outside* the action who can objectify his account of the house, which begins and ends in the subjective mirror of the tarn.

Once inside the house, all is mystery—a series of crumbling details pretending to participate in some pervasive pattern. The physician's menacing glance, Usher's ambiguous greeting, and Madeline's ghostly step all vaguely gesture toward some profound meaning hidden just beyond the comprehension of the narrator. Alternately speculating on and resisting the sinister implications of these details, the narrator excites the imagination by hinting at some higher agency orchestrating the discrete phenomena of the house. For Usher this mysterious agency manifests itself as "sentience," a version of Poe's "mutuality of adaptation," which makes it impossible to distinguish intention from object. Investing sense in every feature of his house, Usher testifies to the symbolic power of the artist to turn the world into an emblem of his mind. Yet once he unleashes the potential for meaning everywhere, he can no longer command the self-governing system of living terror that feeds off his inbred fancies. A grotesquely exaggerated external animation of his fears, the house assumes control over its paranoid owner. The acutely sensitive contriver is thus left, along with the narrator, to infer some unknown external authority responsible for the sentience, which he reads as an overdetermined sign of the disease gradually disordering his mind.

Usher's notion of sentience, however, is only a symptom of his disease, not its cause. As we might have anticipated, the narrative follows a regressive path tending toward the origins of the strange illness debilitating Roderick and his sister, only to reach a baffling set of dead ends. It is simply an unquestioned given that Madeline—like Poe's other heroines Berenice, Morella, Ligeia, and Eleonora—must inexplicably suffer and then die from a malady diagnosed simply as "settled apathy." Poe thus suggests that life itself is little more than an incurable disease which gains importance only after the fact. We fare no better at uncovering the mysterious agency controlling Usher's degeneration, although critics have spent a lot of time looking at the products of his feverish imagination for clues.[34] These works of art—the painting, the wild dirges, and the allegorical poem "The Haunted Palace"—repeatedly turn inward on themselves to ridicule our efforts to bring the psychic turmoil of their creator to the surface. The poem, for instance, only pretends to open up Usher's mind; the palace is originally said to be haunted by "evil things," a wonderfully vague phrase that refuses to divulge why the artist fell into self-consciousness. We are put in the position of Madeline's physicians, eagerly waiting for the patient to die so that we may dissect the mocking corpse to see what made it tick. (We may, in fact, have already caught a brief glimpse of ourselves when we passed the cunning but perplexed family doctor on the stairs.)

By prematurely burying the secrets of the body and leaving behind nothing but the pure abstractions of the head, the paranoid plotter eventually becomes "a victim to the terrors he had anticipated," as the narrator himself remarks. It is as if Usher were afraid that if we violated his sister's corpse to trace effects back to causes, we would find nothing inside other than "settled apathy," the terrifying absence of meaning or motive that compels Roderick and his companion frantically to generate their own artificial and immediate excitement, to will their horror into some semblance of belief. The ghostly double returns, then, to expose the thrilling, visceral tendency to fear around which the flimsy story is built and on which the tottering structure finally collapses.[35]

The fissure widens and the plot unravels with the reading of Sir Launcelot Canning's "Mad Trist." An "excessive impersonation of a prior degenerate form,"[36] as James Cox has noted, this curious episode parodies the exaggerated Gothic claptrap Poe has relied on throughout the tale. The romance also raises a set of intriguing allegorical correspondences between Ethelred's dragon-slaying and the events simultaneously occurring in Poe's story. But the contents of this absurd fiction are less important than the sheer fact of their narration, the *only* action the narrator inaugurates during his entire stay in the house. Up to this point in the story, Usher's nameless companion has passively followed his friend's designs without offering any resistance. Although his reason occasionally intrudes to dismiss Usher's beliefs as "superstitions," the narrator must let himself become "infected" by his double's madness in order to experience the immediate terror of his own narrative. Paranoia blossoms when the gap between narrating subject and narrated object narrows. The moment he tries to distract Usher by reading the "Mad Trist," however, he suddenly resumes the narrating role he has been playing all along. Insofar as he is able to retell another's story, he no longer directly suffers his companion's plot, a nightmare he is powerless to alter. Our attention thus shifts from Usher's insane power to contrive abstract arabesques to the narrator's own authority to excite the imagination by secondary means. The ready-made Gothic text reminds the narrator that he is performing an elocutionary act apart from the world which that act conjures up. Twice removed from Roderick's madness, the narrator's self-conscious performance begins to break Usher's spell by pretending to initiate rather than imitate the events that follow. His proleptic utterance helps reinvoke the stirring specter of Madeline, whose accusing cry becomes "the exact counterpart of what my fancy had already conjured up for the dragon's unnatural shriek as described by the romancer." With the return of Usher's twin, the artifice of the plot reaches an intolerable, terrifying pitch. We are compelled to witness a final, fatal embrace that takes place inside the house, inside Usher's mind, inside the "Mad Trist," and ultimately inside the narrator's own construction. The whole self-consuming production comes tumbling down, to be swallowed up by the still waters of the mirroring tarn.

Reading a Gothic romance out loud, the narrator avoids being prematurely buried by his own story, falling permanently into Usher's paranoid state. Like Melville's Ishmael, the narrator escapes alone to tell thee by actively rearranging Usher's fears so that he can resume the self-conscious posturing on which he depended earlier to help contrive the mansion's atmosphere. The performing self identifies with his suffering double, yet still retains a social voice. Usher, on the other hand, falls victim to his anticipated dread because he cannot assume any outside perspective: all is repetition without difference, God's paranoid "mutuality of adaptation." At the last moment Usher turns away from his companion to obey the inner summons of his twin, while the mortified storyteller breaks free from his double to escape the disintegrating structure that his fears have helped to sustain throughout his narrative.

On the verge of plunging headlong into a series of inwardly spiraling doublings—from author to narrator to Usher to ghostly twin—Poe suddenly pulls back to reaffirm some perspective outside the house. By having his narrator recite the "Mad Trist," Poe reminds himself that he, too, is telling his tale to someone, a presence figured in the fiction by that "scrutinizing observer" who is initially presumed to be able to detect the flaws in Usher's construction. However dim or ill-defined, this mysterious outsider expresses Poe's sense of a reader, somebody really out there. Despite the frantic efforts of Poe's first persons to sever all human relation by murdering their doubles, there always remains beyond the grasp of the criminal an unknown other who serves to verify the plotter's identity. Even at its most self-absorbed, as in "Usher," Poe's fiction retains sight of an audience, if only to prevent the seamless plots from collapsing in on themselves. In the third and final section of this chapter I hope to show how Poe's recognition of an audience grew much clearer during the last decade of his life (from the publication of "Usher" in 1839 to his death in 1849), when he began to arrive at a mutual understanding with his readers: to accommodate their expectations and educate them in the ways of his fiction.

III

From the very start of his career, the problem of an audience for Poe was intimately bound up with his conception of writing and publishing. Three essays Poe wrote in 1836, while editing the *South-*

ern Literary Messenger, help us to understand precisely what was at
stake for the ambitious young writer as he initially tried to attract
a wide readership. In a popular *jeu d'esprit* known as "Autography"
Poe reproduced and analyzed the signatures of famous contemporary authors to deduce those particular "mental qualities" that
"have a tendency to impress the MS." (16:18).[37] What seems to
interest Poe in this game of connecting celebrated authors to their
works is the possibility that the personality of the writer is as much
an interpreted effect of the writing as its cause; the literary signature becomes a means of personally endorsing a group of otherwise autonomous documents which circulate quite independently
in newspapers and periodicals. A few months later Poe gave the
world the first inklings of his notorious lifelong obsession with
plagiarism when he published a set of "cullings" entitled "Pinaki-
dia," which diligently set out to trace famous lines of poetry back
to their rightful owners. Here, too, Poe is fascinated by the tendency
of the written word to escape the command of its creator, a tendency
the paranoid journalist attempted to counter by supposing that any
form of literary imitation must be an intentional act of thievery.
The same impulse of individuals to reassert control over their way-
ward productions underlies yet another 1836 article, "Mäelzel's
Chess-Player." Exposing a popular hoax then touring America, Poe
devotes thirty closely reasoned pages to prove that within the chess-
playing automaton there must be a concealed dwarf moving the
pieces. Without such a prime mover, Poe realizes, the invention
would be a "pure machine, unconnected with human agency"
(14:6)—a troubling yet curiously appealing prospect Poe held for
his own art, one which continued to haunt him up to his death.

  Taken collectively, these three articles point to Poe's early intuition that writing is a self-sustaining form of discourse which
acquires currency apart from the person or authority of the writer,
who threatens to fade into obscurity as soon as his work enters the
public domain. Once the author expresses himself in public, his
written identity becomes common property, subject to ceaseless
duplication and appropriation. In the absence of strict copyright
laws to prevent the common practice of piracy, the threat of anonymity was especially acute for American magazine writers publishing in the 1830s and 1840s.[38] Craving recognition as an original
American genius yet fearing the consequences of public exposure,
Poe the professional journalist, engaged in the day-to-day business
of winning over readers, faced the precarious conditions of his

craft with characteristic ambivalence. At the same time that publishing tends to dissolve the individual author in the whole of discourse, it also protects him from potentially hostile reaction and frees him to explore and objectify his desires on the page in relative privacy. The problem we must address, then, is how Poe sought to reconcile the contradictory pressures of private and public, that is, how he sought to encode the self in a written form that would allow him to maintain control over his fiction after it was exposed to public scrutiny.

Only after his great Gothic arabesques "Ligeia," "The Fall of the House of Usher," and "William Wilson" failed to attract widespread acclaim when published in 1839–40 did Poe turn his attention directly in his fiction to the problem of an audience. This change in his writing can be documented in a number of related ways. First, as Michael Allen has pointed out, around 1839 Poe began simplifying his ornate prose style in an attempt to appeal to a mass readership.[39] Second, paralleling this simplification of style, Poe's first-person narrators for the most part become less individualized, less introspective, less bent on pursuing their shadowy counterparts. Third, the ethereal figure of the double tends to vanish altogether, replaced by more substantial presences who no longer simply mirror the speaker's obsessions but act independently in the tales. Whereas in the early tales the object of analysis is usually the narrator's own mind (see "Berenice," for example), in many of these later stories Poe's narrators are more concerned with examining the relation between their thoughts, and the thoughts and actions of those around them, than in reflectively tyrannizing over their narratives. Compared with their detective friends, for instance, the first-person speakers who tell the tales of ratiocination (1841–43) are compelled to play secondary roles in their own stories. Finally, we can note that Poe begins to use this more balanced ratio between narrating subject and narrative object as a metaphor dramatizing his relation with his readers. Concentrating on a sequence of four lesser-known tales which Poe published during the last decade of his life, ("The Man That Was Used Up" [1839], "The Premature Burial" [1844], "The Facts in the Case of M. Valdemar" [1845], and "Von Kempelen and His Discovery" [1849]), I shall argue that although Poe never fully masters his fear of the reader, he eventually manages to put it into perspective by writing stories which treat this fear as an explicit theme.

Late in 1839, when Poe's quest for an authentic, inviolate iden-

tity reached its zenith in "Usher" and "William Wilson," his trust
in his readers' capacity to appreciate that identity conversely
reached its nadir in "The Man That Was Used Up," a bitter satire
he published only two months before "William Wilson." One of the
author's favorite stories, the comedy fits the mold of Poe's earlier
burlesques "Loss of Breath" and "How To Write a Blackwood Article" by literalizing a figure of speech into a surreal image of fragmentation and self-loss. The central character, General John A. B.
C. Smith, is a lionized Indian fighter whose "remarkable . . . manner" compels the first-person narrator to solve the mystery behind
the man's striking appearance. Given the general's prominence in
the public eye, the narrator decides to frequent social gatherings,
attend the church and the theater in order to pick up some gossip
that will explain the celebrity's mysterious presence. When this idle
cocktail chatter fails to disclose the hero's secret, the narrator finally
confronts the general himself. Entering Smith's inner sanctum, his
private dressing room, the narrator stumbles across an "odd-
looking bundle" which proceeds, with the aid of a servant, to make
itself up step-by-step into a full-fledged "personal man" (388). Suddenly the mystery is solved: the general is nothing more than the
sum total of a number of prosthetic devices—limbs, arms, eyes, wig,
chest—an artificial contrivance, a "nondescript" mechanical "thing"
first mutilated by Indians and then "used up" by his adoring public.
Even the hero's "thrilling" voice, a person's most authentic possession for Poe, is merely the product of a "singular-looking machine"
inserted in the mouth of Brevet Brigadier General A. B. C. Smith.

What are we to make of this strange, unpleasant, vaguely sinister comedy that Poe so highly regarded? Whether General Smith
is modeled after the Indian fighter General Winfred Scott or Van
Buren's vice-president, Richard M. Johnson, as critics have var-
iously suggested,[40] it is clear that the target of Poe's satire is the
Jacksonian self-made man, a figure, to use the historian Michael
Rogin's terms, "born free of traditional restraints, who determines
his own fate in the market-place,"[41] thereby achieving the kind of
success and self-sufficiency that Poe desired for his own writing.
Viewing this mythic figure with a mixture of contempt and envy,
Poe fiercely turns the self-begotten hero into a grotesque monster
living at the mercy of the democratic mob, which creates such
creatures to feed its own delusions of self-sufficiency. By literalizing
the image of the self-made man, Poe brilliantly gives the lie to the

Jacksonian ideal and shows how the repudiation of traditional authority forces the enterprising Adam to depend on the public at large for his identity. Without the public, General Smith literally remains "no body," a bundle of lifeless fragments, a total nonentity. Poe's self-raised hero thus survives only as a kind of property held in common (hence his nondescript name), a pasteboard composite cosmetically pieced together from the scraps of information and praise that the narrator and his friends casually trade with each other. Sustained by this gossip, the pretender can confidently venture into society, ironically praising "the rapid march of mechanical invention" (381) of which he himself is America's proudest example, a hollow automaton à la Mäelzel's chess-playing machine.

Despite the obvious relish with which Poe cruelly exposes the general's masquerade, we should view the Indian fighter as a victim of Jacksonian democracy who does not control the mob but rather is controlled by it. A disposable commodity consumed by his public, the figure of the self-made man in fact serves to image the writer's own status in society, once we understand that the phrase "to use up" is not a casual choice on Poe's part but a crucial expression with a precise meaning for the nineteenth-century American artist. Applied to politicians, actors, and authors who received bad reviews in the press, "to use up" appears throughout Poe's letters and essays:

> Have you seen Griswold's Book of Poetry? It is a most outrageous humbug, and I sincerely wish you would "use it up."[42]

> Graham has had, for 9 months, a review of mine on Longfellow's "Spanish Student" which I have "used up," and in which I have exposed some of the grossest plagiarisms ever perpetrated.[43]

> M——, having been "used up" in the "——- Review," goes about the town lauding his critic ... with tears in his eyes. (14:174)

Poe applies the term to the person of the writer as well as to his work, so that an individual's reputation, manufactured by public opinion and dispersed among the masses, soon comes to stand for the individual himself. Linking Poe's dread of self-loss with his fear of public performance, the key phrase "to use up" thus implicates the writer in his own satire and exposes Poe's hostility toward the democratic mob, which he was forced to depend on for his livelihood.

In one sense Poe's nemesis is not so much the magazine reading public per se but information itself, the proliferation of facts and gossip about figures like General Smith that society hungers to consume in mass quantities. Journalism fulfills exactly this demand, offering countless useful items which can be effortlessly digested, used up. Remarking that "the whole tendency of the age is Magazine-ward," Poe insisted that "we now demand the light artillery of the intellect; we need the curt, the condensed, the pointed, the readily diffused—in place of the verbose, the detailed, the voluminous, the inaccessible" (16:117–118). Sounding a little like his own A. B. C. Smith, Poe even went so far as to praise the technology of "the readily diffused" by calling attention to a new printing process, "Anastatic Printing," which could reproduce "a vast number of absolute facsimiles" after the fashion of a xerox machine. What especially intrigued Poe about the invention was its tendency "to cheapen information, to diffuse knowledge and amusement, and to bring before the public the very class of works which are most valuable" (16:156). Despite his apparent enthusiasm, Poe's phrase "to cheapen information" neatly captures the ambivalence the journalist felt toward his profession, an ambivalence partly derived from his misgivings about the written word itself. The mechanical reproduction of writing enables the journalist to diffuse information on a far greater scale than an author working in more traditional literary forms; the wider the diffusion, moreover, the larger the audience, and the greater the writer's commercial success. Yet once the published word becomes a commodity to be proliferated endlessly, the journalist loses control over his creations and finds the identity he has invested in the writing dispersed and dislocated among the masses. The writer's sense of integrity, of an integral self, disintegrates, while his language becomes "cheapened" in the marketplace, accessible to all consumers but devalued, cut off from the experience which originally gave it meaning.

Poe himself helped introduce to America a new word—"magazinist"—to describe this recently invented literary creature, the professional journalist, who was rapidly gaining influence in the early nineteenth-century Anglo-American world of letters. Shaped by the middle-class tastes of his mass-circulation reading public, Poe's chameleon magazinist (N. P. Willis in particular) learned to transform himself, with equal facility, into "a paragraphist, an essayist, or rather 'sketcher,' a tale writer, and a poet" (15:11), as the occasion demanded. What formerly belonged to the province of the traditional storyteller was now being converted into the monotonous copy of the self-made magazine writer, a process which Walter Benjamin has examined with exquisite perception. Analyzing the profound consequences of journalism's ascendancy over storytelling as the central channel of cultural communication, Benjamin gives us an insight into the crisis facing Poe:

> Man's inner concerns do not have their issueless character by nature. They do so only when he is increasingly unable to assimilate the data of the world around him by way of experience... The intention of the press [is not] to have the reader assimilate the information it supplies as part of his own experience... [but] to isolate what happens from the realm in which it could affect the experience of the reader. The principles of journalistic information (freshness of the news, brevity, comprehensibility, and above all, lack of connection between the individual news items) contribute... [to] the isolation of information from experience.[44]

Emphasizing precisely the same characteristics of journalism that Poe himself stressed (freshness, brevity, comprehensibility), Benjamin shows how information produces a leveling effect similar to the "exciting sameness" of Poe's plots. Felt experience becomes transmuted into a series of unconnected facts whose value depends solely on their capacity to be promptly used up by the reader's sensations. For both writer and reader, Benjamin suggests, disseminating information is an alienating act that dissolves the shared traditions that once bound people together. The narrator of "The Man of the Crowd," for example, accumulates countless superficial facts while pursuing his double but cannot use this data to explain his mystifying experience. In the decentered world of Poe's tales, as we shall see, esoteric knowledge, intense personal anguish, and trivia exist side by side, all bits of information to be processed and then digested.

Although Poe professed to champion "the rush of the age" (16:118) and the magazine writing which accompanied that rush, stories like "The Man That Was Used Up" and "The Man of the Crowd" lead us to suspect that the journalist knew full well the alienating consequences of the public's reliance on information. As Michael Allen has pointed out, Poe clung to the conventional belief that literature was a species of learning, a way to pass down wisdom.[45] To borrow Benjamin's terms, Poe saw himself as a storyteller

living at a time when the intimate ritual of sharing experience had
been dispossessed by more efficient but remoter forms of communication. Seeking to resume the traditional role of the storyteller,
Poe continually reminds us (in stories such as "The Black Cat,"
"Loss of Breath," "The Murders on the Rue Morgue," and "Morella") of the power of the speaking voice. Buried, imitated, turned
into a mechanical contrivance, the voice still remains the most profound measure of an authentic self, Poe's sign of the storyteller's
vanishing authority to move a close circle of listeners. Once this
intimate circle widens in the nineteenth century to encompass a
faceless mass of unknown interlocutors, the storyteller gives way
to the fearful "magazinist," who masks his identity to protect himself from the mockery of his readers. Poe's task, then, is to recharge
his tales with personal significance, to retain "sight of man the
individual, in man the mass," as he put it,[46] and yet remain aloof
from the consequences of his writing. While Poe's poems try to
restore the artist's sacred powers of incantation by dreamily re-
treating into the self, falling back upon exhausted Romantic conventions (one reason why the poetry is less interesting than his
fiction), Poe's best stories openly embrace modern modes of communication to exploit the tension between journalism and more
traditional forms of literature. Particularly in the late hoaxes, I
suggest, Poe discovers how to convert his audience's dependence
on information into a source of creative energy.

    Take, for instance, "The Premature Burial," a late tale (1844)
which recapitulates one of Poe's favorite Gothic themes. Opening
his story by vaguely musing on "the purposes of legitimate fiction,"
the first-person narrator proceeds to relate a number of "well authenticated instances" that graphically depict premature burial. To
prove his claim that "truth is, indeed, stranger than fiction," he
enthusiastically cites case histories from such esteemed medical au-
thorities as "The 'Chirurgical Journal' of Leipsic." Only after in-
dulging in four of these dramatic stories does the narrator turn to
his own case history, which he insists is "of my own actual knowledge—of my own positive and personal experience." Poe's protagonist is haunted by the idea of premature burial because he suffers
from cataleptic fits which simulate death. To counteract his grim
fantasies, he remodels the family crypt with a set of elaborate contraptions which would let him survive in the tomb upon waking
from a deathlike trance. When he actually finds himself reviving

from such a trance, the contraptions have all vanished, replaced by a common wooden coffin. Like the walled-up black cat that unleashed a "long, loud, and continuous scream" in an earlier Poe tale, the narrator of "The Premature Burial" frantically gives voice to a suspiciously similar demonic utterance:

> A long, wild, and continuous shriek, or yell, of agony, re-
> sponded through the realms of the Subterrene Night.
> "Hillo! hillo, there!" said a gruff voice in reply . . . "What do
> you mean by yowling in that ere kind of style, like a catty-mount?"
> said a fourth. (967–68)

Chastened by this figurative slap in the face, the narrator's lurid Gothic "style" takes a sobering turn once he discovers that he has fallen asleep in the hold of a ship. The ironic contrast between his overwrought mannerisms and the matter-of-fact colloquialisms of the sailors is matched by an even more incongruous juxtaposition near the end of the tale:

> My soul acquired tone—acquired temper. I went aboard. I took
> vigorous exercises. I breathed the free air of Heaven. I thought
> upon other subjects than Death. I discarded my medical books.
> "Buchan" I burned. I read no "Night Thoughts"—no fustian
> about church-yards—no bugaboo tales—*such as this*. (969)

With a sudden shift in perspective that recalls the end of "A Pre-dicament," the narrator abruptly exposes the fictionality of his story by stepping out of his narrative to remind us that his past actions in the tale are isolated from his present act of telling it, the melodramatic claptrap he has invoked to rival other "well authenticated" case histories.

Turning the narrative inside out, the phrase "such as this" underscores the disturbing dislocation in "The Premature Burial" between the narrator's style and his subject. This dislocation, in turn, derives from a more profound rift in the story between the case histories offered in the first half of the tale and the narrator's preposterous efforts in the second half to convey his "positive and personal experience." Before he can commence with his own story, the speaker feels compelled to give us enough information—dates, names, journal citations—to legitimize his narrative. The storyteller's power to convince no longer resides in his personality but depends on the sheer bulk of facts he can muster for his readers. The more energetically he presents this commonly held information, the less control he has over his own language, riddled as it is with Gothic clichés. Wayne Booth is thus more right than he realizes when he complains that the narrator is "divorced from the effects of his own rhetoric,"[47] that Poe provides "no context" for the self-conscious rigmarole prefacing the narrator's own experience of premature burial. The elaborate devices that he rigs up as a precaution against entombment ("accoutrements and conveniences," Robert Adams wittily suggests, "for a camping trip in the grave"[48]) stand for the clumsy narrative apparatus that the speaker initially sets in motion to help authenticate his private horror. Unable to understand or express the intensity of his fear, Poe's estranged tale-teller is reduced to verifying that fear by importing other people's facts. Despite its obvious air of farce, the story remains strangely moving precisely because of its failure to communicate authentic experience.

Before he can even reach his Gothic denouement, the narrator of "The Premature Burial" becomes prematurely buried by information itself. The facts he accumulates to lend credence to his experience act as a kind of mocking double in the narrative, smothering the storyteller's identity and suffocating his language. Over and over again in Poe's tales his first-person narrators must compete against rival accounts—pseudoscientific reports, newspaper gossip, esoteric literary allusion—while they also desperately struggle to relate their own stories. Overwhelming the action within the stories, this self-perpetuating rhetoric disseminated by the press turns experience into "a world of words" ("El Aaraaf"), a universe of wall-to-wall discourse which threatens to choke off the personal speaking voice. The typical Poe hero is thus either born in a library, trapped in the margins of books (Egaeus of "Berenice"), or else becomes "a dealer in antiquities" (145) whose inexpressible horror translates into cryptic messages that emerge intermittently out of a bottle like Morse code distress signals from another planet ("MS. Found in a Bottle").

If experience is always secondary to rhetoric in Poe's world, and if rhetoric itself depends on an infinitely regressing series of borrowings, then originality, the expression of an inviolate, authentic identity that so dominated Poe's thinking, remains a dubious prospect. When we examine images of writing that appear in the tales, for instance, we note that the written message is almost invariably found, stumbled across, and then decoded, but never willfully created. These recurring figures of hieroglyphic inscription in the tales suggest that language for Poe cannot be invented *ex nihilo* but must be interpretively reconstructed. The writer thus compiles and rearranges previous anonymous texts, picks and chooses, to piece together his own text, somewhat in the manner that General A. B. C. Smith composes himself from disparate fragments.

To comprehend fully Poe's belief that "originality . . . demands in its attainment less of invention than negation" (14:203), it might be useful to contrast Poe's view of creativity with Coleridge's concept of the imagination, a notion which had already become a cornerstone of Romantic poetic theory by Poe's day. Although critics commonly claim that Poe's ideas about art closely follow Coleridge's thinking,[49] the differences between the two are quite striking. For Coleridge man's capacity to synthesize the world into a coherent artistic whole directly originated from God's own creative powers, the primary source of all poetic imagination. Even in his earliest critical writings (the famous 1836 "Drake-Halleck" review) Poe takes issue with Coleridge's belief that art is a divinely inspired imitation of God's thought: "Imagination is, possibly in man, a lesser degree of the creative power in God. What the Deity imagines, *is*, but *was not* before. What man imagines, *is*, but *was* also. The mind of man cannot imagine what is *not*" (8:283, n. 2) Lacking God's perfect "mutuality of adaptation," man fails to gain perfect self-containment; because we cannot stand to be alone ("The Man of the Crowd"), we must always imagine ourselves in relation to others and create in relation to other previous creations. Poe marks the unbridgeable rift between man and God even more insistently in a later passage directly attacking Coleridge's major premise:

> "Fancy," says the author of "Aids to Reflection," (who aided Reflection to much better purpose in his "Genevieve")—"Fancy combines—Imagination creates." This was intended and has been received, as a distinction; but it is a distinction without a difference—without even a difference of degree. The Fancy as nearly creates as the imagination, and neither at all. Novel conceptions are merely unusual combinations. The mind of man can imagine

nothing which does not exist:—if it could, it would create not only
ideally, but substantially—as do the thoughts of God. (12:37,
15:13, n. 2)

While Poe does, on occasion, invoke Coleridge's concept of imagination, the effect is like pulling a rabbit out of a hat; he concludes
the protracted exchange of letters known as "The Longfellow War,"
for instance, by abruptly referring to "secondary origination within
his own soul" and "primary origination without" (12:105–6), Coleridgean mumbo jumbo that lets him off the hook, allows him to
close the infamous controversy about plagiarism without really re-
solving any of the troublesome questions that the controversy had
raised.

"To originate, is carefully, patiently, and understandingly to
combine" (14:73). This assessment from one of Poe's earliest reviews ("Peter Snook," October 1836) sums up the writer's lifelong
attitude toward his work, which is built by secular acts of *bricolage*,
the deliberate tinkering of a mechanic/engineer who can never
hope to achieve transcendence. Poe's understanding of the creative
process, in fact, bears a marked resemblance to the process of
plotting enacted by his criminals and detectives. The entire plot of
"The Tell-Tale Heart," for example, is filled with the painstaking
combining of the confessing narrator, who relates step-by-step a
series of procedural details about the crime—sheer information—
as a substitute for any explanation of his motives, which remain
entirely beyond his grasp. Carefully and patiently the first-person
speaker mechanically constructs his plot, only to destroy what he
has made once the police arrive on the scene, outsiders who represent Poe's sense of his readers. Poe thus uses the story to dramatize his relation with an audience, a drama that becomes even more
clear when we compare the events in the tale with a critical comment
Poe published while he was most likely writing "The Tell-Tale
Heart" (1842): "The voice of him who maintains fearlessly what he
believes honestly, is pretty sure to find an echo (if the speaker be
not mad) in the vast heart of the world at large" (15:247). Punc-
turing the ostensible optimism of the passage, that parenthetical
aside about madness remains a cynical reminder for Poe that, like
his confessing narrator, the response which he hears from "the
world at large" may be of his own contriving.

In the last ten years of his life Poe began to realize that his early attempts to fashion his readers in his own image were a mad-man's vain delusion. Understanding that he could neither escape an audience nor completely incorporate that unknown other into the world of his fiction (recall "The Man of the Crowd"), Poe embarked on a third course: to turn his confessional impulses outward, embodying the expectations of the reading public, their hunger for information, as a second self, a censorial double acting from without instead of from within. By addressing the concerns of some other presence assumed to exist outside the writer, Poe protects his mind from its own alienating self-analysis; by veiling the other behind a cloak of silence, Poe protects himself from that outside reality.

We can best document Poe's growing acceptance of his readers as substantial shapers of his fiction by contrasting the writer's early hoaxes with his later ones. Directly challenging the reader to confuse reality with fiction, Poe's hoaxing remains the most crucial index for assessing the author's attitude toward his audience. In the early hoaxes Poe contemptuously tries to widen the distance between elite writer and common reader by duping his unsuspecting audience into mistaking his fantasies for provable truth. The bulk of "The Unparalleled Adventure of One Hans Pfaall" (1835), for example, is given over to a series of detailed calculations simulating scientific fact: the construction of the balloon; its means of ascent; the distance from the earth to the moon; and so on. Earnestly applying these scientific principles to his imaginary flight, Poe implicitly chastises his readers for their ignorance. In a later story that rehearses a similar imaginary voyage by balloon, "The Balloon Hoax" (1844), the contents of the hoax are less important than its form, which imitates the prose style of the newly introduced, fabulously popular "Penny Dailies."[50] The only story of Poe's to be published in a newspaper (an extra edition of the *New York Sun*), "The Balloon Hoax" (originally untitled) is launched with a series of wild headlines: "Astounding News by Express, *via* Norfolk!—The Atlantic crossed in Three Days! Signal Triumph of Mr. Monck Mason's Flying Machine!" It concludes with an equally hyperbolic flourish: "This is unquestionably the most stupendous, the most interesting, and the most important undertaking, ever accomplished or even attempted by man" (1082). Ironically claiming that "the more intelligent believed [the hoax], while the rabble . . . rejected the whole with disdain,"[51]Poe seems less interested in cre-

ating a convincing air of verisimilitude based on scientific fact than
in simulating a certain popular journalistic prose style. As it narrows
the gap between writer and reader, the medium by which information becomes disseminated prevails over the information itself.

Poe exploits the way in which narrative conveys information
most brilliantly in "The Facts in the Case of M. Valdemar" (1845),
another late hoax published a little more than a year after "The
Balloon Hoax" and "The Premature Burial." Portraying the mesmeric suspension of a body on the verge of death, the story follows
Poe's practice of transforming a theme he had previously treated
philosophically (see "The Mesmeric Revelation") into a graphic
mockery whose power derives from its impossible literalness. Before he gets down to the specifics of Valdemar's "extraordinary
case," the first-person narrator "P" emphasizes that he must now
present "the *facts*" objectively in order to correct the "garbled or
exaggerated . . . misrepresentations" of the affair which have already been circulating in public. The very element of the uncanny
or incredible that he wishes to suppress, however, creeps into his
own vocabulary as soon as he alludes to the misinformed public
response that has occasioned his narrative act in the first place: it
would have been a "matter for wonder" and a "miracle," he acknowledges, if such distorted rumors had not been spreading. The
narrator thus heightens our suspense by using popular sensation
to bind inextricably the "extraordinary" to the "facts," a conflation
of the supernatural with the scientific which becomes crucial once
"P" identifies himself as the mesmerist of his dying friend
Valdemar.

Hypothesizing how long "the encroachments of Death might
be arrested" by hypnotism, the narrator pursues his "experiment,"
and his factual account of that experiment, with absolute clinical
precision, verifying for the reader dates, names, and "reliable witnesses." He also offers a detailed diagnosis of his mesmeric subject:
"The left lung had been for eighteen months in a semi-osseous or
cartilaginous state . . . while the lower region was merely a mass of
purulent tubercles." The act of hypnosis itself, on the other hand,
performed as the patient "approach[es] dissolution," evokes the
atmosphere of a religious ceremony, a magic ritual that casts doubt
on the mesmerist's pose as a disinterested physician: "While he
spoke thus, I commenced the passes which I had already found
most effectual in subduing him. He was evidently influenced with

the first lateral stroke of my hand across his forehead... I pro-
ceeded without hesitation—exchanging, however, the lateral passes
for downward ones, and directing my gaze entirely into the right
eye of the sufferer" (1236–37). This excited emergence of the extraordinary from the ordinary, a process in which the mysterious
power of performance overwhelms "the facts," reaches a climax
when "P" compels his mesmerized subject to answer a question
from beyond the grave:

> I now feel that I have reached a point of this narrative at
> which every reader will be startled into positive disbelief. It is my
> business, however, simply to proceed.
>   There was no longer the faintest sign of vitality in M. Val-
> demar... there issued from the distended and motionless jaws a
> voice—such as it would be madness in me to attempt describing
> ... the sound was harsh, and broken and hollow; but the hideous
> whole is indescribable, for the simple reason that no similar
> sounds have ever jarred upon the ear of humanity... the voice
> seemed to reach our ears—at least mine—from a vast distance,
> or from some deep cavern within the earth... it impressed me (I
> fear, indeed, that it will be impossible to make myself compre-
> hended) as gelatinous or glutinous matters impress the sense of
> touch.
>   I have spoken both of "sound" and of "voice." I mean to say
> that the sound was one of distinct... of even wonderfully, thrill-
> ingly distinct—syllabification... He now said: "Yes;-no;-I *have
> been* sleeping-and now-now-*I am dead*." (1240)

Questioning the narrator's "business" to inform us of "the facts,"
Valdemar's voice remains the single most vivid expression in Poe's
fiction of a deathless, visceral utterance, authenticating and unmediated, which is nonetheless "wonderfully, thrillingly distinct."
And only Poe could have found a message to match such a voice:
"I am dead." To play Poe's own game in "The Philosophy of Composition" for a moment by inferring causes from effects, it is as if
the plotter first conceived this uncanny declaration and then
worked backward to construct some literal context which would
make such a statement plausible. Yet if the context of Valdemar's
announcement is credible (especially given the nineteenth-century
reader's understanding of mesmerism), the statement is not nor
can it be. As Roland Barthes has suggested, "I am dead" is an

"énonciation impossible," an impossible uttering, an unheard of phrase that is absolutely beyond our assimilation.[52] Barthes calls Valdemar's statement, suspended as it is between life and death, perfectly "useless" since it short-circuits the structure of language, occupying a blind spot midway between a constantive and a performative. A fact which can refer to nothing, spoken by a voice without a self, the impossible "I am dead" cuts short the tale's accelerating rivalry between scientific and supernatural forms of persuasion, forcing us to realize that such terms are inadequate to explain the experience, which aims to erode utterly our faith in the power of "the facts" to inform.[53]

Unleashing Valdemar's pointless message from beyond, Poe's story does not immediately collapse in on itself like the house of Usher, as we might have expected. When he returns seven months later to have another chat with his mesmerized patient, the hypnotist's dual role as scientist and witch doctor quickly gives way to a third kind of performance once "P" begins to revive Valdemar from the trance: "It was now suggested that I should attempt to influence the patient's arm, as heretofore. I made the attempt and failed. Dr. F—— then intimated a desire to have me put a question. I did so as follows: 'M. Valdemar, can you explain to us what are your feelings or wishes now?' " (1242). This is the intoning of a vaudeville act, a carnival sideshow à la "The Cabinet of Dr. Caligari" where "P" and his subject rehearse their routine in front of a gaping audience of stupefied spectators. When "P" fails to "re-compose" the patient, the grotesque comedy becomes an even more riveting theatrical spectacle. As Valdemar's hideous voice once again bursts forth, we see the now revived corpse (seven months old) rot away before our very eyes: "Upon the bed, before that whole company, there lay a nearly liquid mass of loathsome—of detestable putridity" (1243).

The joke—if such a gruesome finish can be called a joke—is on us. By confirming from beginning to end the mesmerist's power to "arrest death," the tale dramatically enacts the parallel process of narrative suspense by which Poe mesmerizes his audience to defer the ending of his story. Just as Valdemar is acted upon by "P," so the reader is acted upon by Poe. For the duration of the narrative we are suspended in fiction's twilight region between life and death. Once the motive for telling the story (suspense) is consummated, both fiction and fictional reader dissolve into the nothingness from whence they came. Yet if the reader serves as the mesmerized subject, he or she also represents, in the process of reading, the mesmerist himself. Sustaining the narrative by curiously asking the same questions that "P" asks to sustain the corpse ("Are you sleeping?" "Are you alive?" "What are you feeling?"), we become Poe's intimate accomplices in this vaudeville performance, indispensable helpers probing "the facts" in "the case" of M. Valdemar.

In a more complex way the writer relies on his readers to help him forge his fiction in "Von Kempelen and His Discovery" (1849), Poe's last and greatest hoax, which represents the culmination of his efforts to come to terms with an audience. Published just seven months before his death, the story adopts alchemy rather than hypnotism as a controlling metaphor for the writer's craft. Despite alchemy's mythic connotations, the hoax was a direct response to a moment in history with specific economic consequences: the 1848–49 California gold rush. Regarding the quest for gold as a mockery of his own futile quest for artistic self-sufficiency and integrity, Poe used the events in California to insist on the primacy of the imagination over material gain: "I shall be a *littérateur*, at least all my life; nor would I abandon the hopes which still lead me on for all the gold in California."[54] But as Poe suggests in another letter explaining the intent of the hoax, the artist's realm of the imagination does not occupy an ideally pure world elsewhere but instead emerges directly from the material conditions of his creative medium: "I mean it as a kind of 'exercise,' or experiment, in the plausible or verisimilar style. Of course, there is *not one* word of truth in it from beginning to end. I thought that such a style, applied to the gold-excitement, could not fail of effect."[55] If the hoaxer is to "check" the excitement of the gold fever, Poe's letter goes on to claim, he must do so by simulating a popular "style" to draw his readers into the inner workings of his own equally exciting art.

Poe's stylistic experiment depends on his narrator's awkward efforts to reconstruct Von Kempelen's discovery from the news of the day, a laborious process analogous to the reader's own struggle to decipher Poe's text. Like the narrators of Poe's other hoaxes, the first-person speaker of "Von Kempelen" is less a full-fledged character than an anonymous rhetorical presence imitating a variety of prose styles: scientific report, personal reminiscence, anecdotal rumor. After the fashion of "The Premature Burial," the narrator must wade through a barrage of citations from learned journals before he can approach his celebrated subject: "After the very minute and elaborate paper by Arago, to say nothing of the summary in 'Silliman's Journal,' with the detailed statement just published by Lieutenant Maury . . ." (1357). Once he has traced Von Kempelen's discovery back to its true source (Sir Humphrey Davy's private diary), the narrator dispenses with scientific documentation to offer us a sketch of "the now immortal" alchemist based on his brief personal interaction with the man. He then yields to the temptation to narrate a widely circulated ("well authenticated") rumor describing Von Kempelen's sudden arrest and the seizure of a trunk hidden under his bed, which is later found to contain pure gold. The narrator concludes his rambling account by "speculating" on the disastrous economic consequences for the forty-niners of Von Kempelen's transmutation of lead into gold, a process which will remain a mystery until the imprisoned alchemist "chooses to let us have the key to his own published enigma" (1364).

Poe's reference to the alchemist's "published enigma" provides us the key to unlock the hoax, his own published enigma. As Burton R. Pollin has ingeniously demonstrated,[56] what appears at first glance to be a scatterbrained concoction of inconsequential items, obscure in-jokes at best, is in fact a tissue of highly significant allusions to Poe's life and work, a kind of elaborate cryptogram that urges us to share its secrets. My aim is not to duplicate Pollin's skillful elucidation but simply to present a few examples in order to show that hidden behind the hoax's ramshackle exterior lie a lifetime of Poe's most intimate concerns. In effect, Poe is leaving us his obituary, if only we could decipher it. A brief comment debunking the claims of "a Mr. Kissam" to Von's Kempelen's discovery actually veils the hoaxer's animosity toward a gullible young admirer named George Eveleth, who corresponded with Poe for three years about his own cosmological speculations, theories which rivaled Poe's *Eureka*. The hoax's references to the *Home Journal* and *The Literary World* conceal compliments to two of the only newspaper editors who ever appreciated Poe's talent, N. P. Willis and Evert Duyckinck, while an allusion to the German *Schnellpost* obliquely acknowledges Poe's debt to Alexander von Humboldt. Brought to light and pieced together, these details, along with dozens of others in the story, firmly establish the specific biographical and journalistic context from which Poe's art emerges. Masquerading under the guise of commonly held information, the facts of Von Kempelen's alchemy are instead highly charged particles of Poe's personal experience which gain significance only after they have been decoded by a special kind of reader capable of grasping the key to the author's published enigma.

Poe saves his most intimate details for the sketch of the reputed "misanthrope" Von Kempelen, an obvious figure for the artist himself. The narrator mentions that he initially met his subject six years ago at "Earl's Hotel," a coded reference to the scene of one of Poe's last public performances (at the Earl's House in Providence), which took place six weeks before he wrote the hoax. This intoxicated affair was particularly significant for Poe because it indirectly led to the painful breakup of his courtship of the wealthy widow Helen Whitman, his last-ditch effort to dig up gold. Delving into Von Kempelen's more distant past, the narrator informs us that the alchemist is said to come from "Presburg," a telling pun which poignantly underscores Poe's sense of himself as a child of journalism unattached to country or parents. The first-person speaker goes on to remark that Von Kempelen's family "is connected, in some way with Mäelzel, of Automaton chess-player memory," to which a bogus editor's note (by Poe) adds that "the inventor was either Kempelen, Von Kempelen, or something like it" (1361). Here Poe suddenly returns to a theme that had haunted him for thirteen years, ever since he had exposed the popular hoax exhibited by the entrepreneur J. N. Mäelzel and originally invented by a Wolfgang Von Kempelen—"a pure machine," we should recall, "unconnected with human agency." Descended directly from the inventor of this dreaded yet desired machine, Von Kempelen and his alchemic craft express Poe's realization that his writing operates like an anonymous generator of words paraded before the public by intermediary showmen like Mäelzel, who stands for the hoaxer in Poe. Yet if Poe is compelled to act as his own promoter, he also plays the part of the dwarf concealed inside the automaton's cabinet of mirrors, an assumed presence whose only connection with the outside world hinges on the chess moves that mysteriously appear on the chessboard one by one. Only by veiling his personal experience behind a patchwork of popular misconception, pseudoscience, and common rumor can the magazinist afford to make contact with his public.

The hoaxer's identification with Mäelzel's automaton helps us to understand the significance of Von Kempelen's alchemy, a metaphoric version of Poe's own "experiments" with style. Writing this hoax, Poe discovers, along with his readers, how to transmute the intimate facts of his life into creative riches. Late in his account the narrator offers us the final conclusion to be drawn from the scientist's discovery: " '*pure gold can be made at will, and very readily, from lead, in connection with certain other substances, in kind and in proportions, unknown*' " (1364). Those "certain other substances, in kind and in proportions, unknown" are Poe's readers themselves, catalysts who sustain the alchemic process by appreciating what is originally valuable in Poe's art, deciphering the journalist's verisimilar style, and sifting through the hoaxer's welter of news items to restore, without violating, the years of personal experience that precipitated the fiction in the first place. Unlike "The Man That Was Used Up," or "Valdemar," here Poe's readers do not consume the artist, dissipate his identity, nor do they conspire with the writer to be held in suspense solely for the duration of the narrative. Von Kempelen's alchemy is an ongoing process, a never-ending series of mutations and transmutations, with the text as the middle term between the experience of the writer and the reader. Yet we should remember that the alchemist has not set this magical process in motion without a sacrifice. Imprisoned and misunderstood by an unsympathetic public that cannot quite grasp the true import of his discovery, the scientist finally refuses (like the man of the crowd) to divulge the secret of his "published enigma." The self is now encoded in a written form, Poe cautions us, but that form is still subject to our mockery and our ignorance. Turning the common dross of his journalistic medium into intimately personal, though public, imaginative gold, Poe thus not only realizes most profoundly the value of his art but suggests as well the high price he has paid to achieve it.

2

Hawthorne's *The Blithedale Romance* and the Death of Enchantment

From the 1830s to the 1840s, as Poe gradually struggled to get away from himself by writing tales which covertly acknowledged some otherness outside the first person, Nathaniel Hawthorne was publishing a series of stories which masterfully drew on New England history and the eighteenth-century English sketch tradition to establish the kind of measured perspective on his writing that Poe could only desperately approximate late in his career. As I have argued, Poe's desire to relieve the pressure of personality entails a logic of self-betrayal, whereby the first-person narrator must expose his plotting as a fiction in order to verify his identity for the reader. In this process of self-betrayal, formal perfection substitutes for moral insight, as the first person's guilt becomes displaced onto the mechanics of tale-telling itself. The abstract moralizing that usually introduces a Poe tale is often so at odds with the specific events that follow precisely because the author can offer only the semblance of some external vantage point that would protect him from his work. As we have seen, Poe's attempts at ironic detachment tend to collapse into self-parody and confession, returning the plotter back to the prison of his "I."

In Hawthorne's early stories, on the other hand, otherness for the most part is taken for granted. History provides Hawthorne with the clearest context to get outside himself by projecting his imagination into and onto the past experience of other young New Englanders: Robin Molineux, Reuben Bourne, Young Goodman Brown, and so on. It is not simply that these tales are all cast in the third person, a form particularly well suited to historical subjects. More important, Hawthorne's willingness to keep himself out of his fiction, to differentiate clearly between omniscient narrator and character, suggests a degree of self-assurance that we don't find in Poe. Hawthorne seems more self-assured than Poe because he seems more sure of a self, particularly what it means to stand in relation to others. New England's past, critically viewed, becomes the primary mediating term for this relationship between self and other.

When we turn from Hawthorne's third-person historical tales to the numerous first-person sketches he published in the 1830s, we notice again Hawthorne's ability to maintain some controlling perspective on his work. Unlike the isolated first persons of Poe, Hawthorne's dramatized storytellers rarely talk only to themselves and consequently seldom try to originate the literary forms by which they express themselves. Hawthorne's dependence on established literary genres serves to contain the first-person narrators in these short works and keep them distinct from their author. Instead of agonized arabesques depicting mirroring and murder, we find more serene first-person performances patterned after the eighteenth-century English sketch tradition. "My Visit to Niagara," "Sunday at Home," "Snow-Flakes": the tone of these travel, domestic, and nature sketches is relaxed and congenial. Hawthorne takes a single subject for his theme and modestly treats it in a desultory fashion, striving mainly to keep his readers' interest from flagging. For the typical Poe narrator, rigidly plotted form generated by the pursuit of the other is essential to distract the first person from his loneliness. But Hawthorne's literary personae feel more comfortable with loosely organized sets of observations that barely constitute plots at all. A story like "Chippings with a Chisel," for example, begins with a narrating "I" who participates in the adventures of his stone-carver friend, but then quickly dissolves into a series of unrelated vignettes about assorted character types in the village. Hawthorne seems much less concerned than Poe about sustaining a single coherent story line, a convincing chain of cause and effect. Although he often engages in humorous self-deprecation in these sketches, Hawthorne rarely questions the credibility of his sources—an obsession with Poe that often betrays the storyteller's doubts about his own sanity. Plot and identity remain separate issues for Hawthorne because he has invested less of himself in his narration than Poe, who insists on the rigorous logic of cause and effect as a way of legitimizing himself.

Even when we move from these relatively slight sketches to Hawthorne's more meditative first-person pieces—works such as "Night-Sketches," "The Haunted Mind" and "Foot-prints on the Sea-Shore," which would seem to hold the promise of more intimate self-disclosure—we discover, more often than not, that Hawthorne's "I" is still largely derived from literary precedents which tend to assume a trusting "you" reader as a given. In the two most overtly romantic and confessional of these works, "Fragments from the Journal of a Solitary Man" and "P's Correspondence" (both presented as written documents), the first person's Byronic musings are framed by the levelheaded commentary of a narrator "friend" who serves to explain the solitary "I" by putting his suffering and "insanity" into a social context. In his 1851 preface to *Twice-Told Tales* Hawthorne himself emphasizes the assurance of society that underpins his stories: "The sketches are not, it is hardly necessary to say, profound . . . They have none of the abstruseness of idea, or obscurity of expression, which mark the written communications of a solitary mind with itself . . . It is, in fact, the style of a man of society. Every sentence . . . may be understood and felt by anybody. . . ."[1] Unlike the "written communications of a solitary mind with itself" (a perfect description of Poe's stories), Hawthorne's tales are told by social beings, "overflow[ing] with talk, and yet . . . never tedious when a friend or two are there" (224). And when actual friends are absent, then nature herself offers "companionship" (569) to defend against solitude.

Hawthorne's grounding in American history, his reliance on past literary convention, and his understanding of the self as a social construction all serve to define a fictional identity that stands removed from the author himself. This is not to say that Hawthorne's short stories are less self-reflexive than Poe's, or that Hawthorne has less doubts than Poe about the status of the American artist. Despite such reflection and such doubts, however, Hawthorne resists the temptation to make his plots, and plots alone, stand directly for the self. Even in a devilishly complex first-person tale like "Alice Doane's Appeal"—containing a story within a story, both riddled with Hawthorne's early anxiety about the place of the imagination and the relation between historical "truth" and Gothic "fiction" (215)—the narrating "I" (a budding writer of romances) remains at some distance from his chaotic materials, interested less in his plots themselves than in simply creating a powerful effect on his two young lady friends, who clearly represent Hawthorne's rather specific sense of his audience. Appealing to a tangible social world outside the story, Hawthorne's fictional "I" is thus most frequently a passive moral observer of and commentator on events rather than a directly engaged participant (see, for example, the allegories "A Virtuoso's Collection," "The Hall of Fantasy," and "Earth's Holocaust").[2]

Those of Hawthorne's stories that take art as their explicit subject, and thereby appear to afford the greatest opportunity for self-reflection, also manage to avoid the pitfalls of solipsism, either by being cast in the form of third-person parables ("The Artist of the Beautiful") and/or by being set in the past to provide additional ballast and authority ("Drowne's Wooden Image," "The Prophetic Pictures"). Despite his occasional self-deprecatory claims to the contrary, what emerges in these tales about artists is a strong sense of Hawthorne's confidence—somewhat hesitant at times and masked by a self-protective diffidence—in the power of art and an associated confidence in his own powers as a storyteller. That nature can be made to mirror art (see "The Prophetic Pictures") is not primarily a cause for paranoia and dread, as in Poe's "Usher," but instead testifies to art's magic. If "The Prophetic Pictures" ends on a dark note, it still celebrates the artist's ability to transfigure reality, to perform as a kind of god. What Poe requires entire stories to enact Hawthorne can toss off with a matter-of-fact observation such as "familiar objects appear visionary" (509). Sprinkled throughout his short stories, such Romantic tropes about the power of the imagination will give way to a more uncertain sense of the relation between art and reality once Hawthorne embarks on a book-length plot (*The Scarlet Letter*), which will require, in turn, the explicit articulation of his own theory of "romance." As Hawthorne himself will make clear in "The Custom-House" introduction to *The Scarlet Letter*, this theory is derived less from literary convention than from his personal experiences as an ambitious author struggling to come to terms with American society, past and present, as well as his own troubled familial identity. Until he becomes possessed by this autobiographical impulse, Hawthorne remains shielded from his fiction, even in his most intimate first-person sketches.

Two brief comparisons between specific tales will help clarify the contrast between Poe's confessional narratives and Hawthorne's contemporaneous works. In each case I am less interested in claiming direct literary influence than in placing two seemingly similar stories side by side to suggest crucial differences between their two authors. Like Poe's "The Man of the Crowd" (1840), Hawthorne's "The Old Apple-Dealer" (1843) dramatizes the difficulty of interpreting another's isolation. In both stories the first-person narrator invests an old man with particular moral significance, drawing generalizations about human alienation from the decrepit figure's outward misery. In both stories the stranger under scrutiny is compared to a mysterious text which then must be correctly "read" by the first person as a type representing our own suffering. In both stories this process of decoding promises to lead to a kind of doubling, by which the stranger will "become a naturalized citizen of my inner world" (714), as Hawthorne's narrator puts it. And both stories conclude this apparent doubling with a moment of apprehension and insight ("I have him now" remarks Hawthorne's narrator), when the first person seems to discover something important about himself during the course of his analysis of the other.

Despite all of these formal similarities, however, "The Man of the Crowd" and "The Old Apple-Dealer" leave the reader with quite different impressions. Poe's story charts the gradual breakdown of the first-person observer's secure perspective, followed by the frantic pursuit of the old wanderer through the streets of London. Hawthorne's sketch, on the other hand, generates no such great urgency of plotting and leaves no doubts about the objective reality of the figure under pursuit. Keeping the apple-dealer fixed in a single location (a railroad station), Hawthorne's first person can leisurely study his subject from an equally fixed, unexposed post of observation, from which he describes the old man's pathetic attempts to sell apples to railway passengers. While Hawthorne, too, stresses the desolation of his subject, the stranger at least assumes a specific role (apple-dealer) that allows him to engage in social intercourse with others, however feebly. As we have seen, Poe's naming of his stranger "the man of the crowd" destabilizes and confuses identity by threatening to collapse the distinction between the first person and the object of his pursuit. But Hawthorne's fixing of narrative perspective and social role helps to maintain a constant relation between self and other. As a result, the anticipated doubling between narrator and apple-dealer never really takes place: Hawthorne's first person is too sure of himself to forget how different he is from his subject. He can sympathize with the old man without completely identifying with him. This sympathy, in fact, is mixed with a subtle measure of condescension, particularly toward the end of the story when the first person directly bids farewell to his "old friend" and then appeals to God and heaven as conventional explanations or compensations for the old man's suffering.

Just as the old apple-dealer has "hardly individuality enough to be the object of your own self-love" (716), according to Hawthorne's narrator, so, too, does the narrator himself possess little individuality, disclosing virtually nothing about himself during his analysis of the other. Unlike Poe's story, where pursuing the stranger leads the first person to betray the self, in Hawthorne's tale the "I" and other remain separated from one another, both abstracted to a plane of generality in which the search for "the moral picturesque" (714) tends to outweigh any more pressing personal motives for self-expression.

We can see Hawthorne's avoidance of self-disclosure even more clearly when we contrast his "Monsieur du Miroir" (1836) with Poe's "William Wilson" (1839), an obvious but instructive juxtaposition. Whereas "The Old Apple-Dealer" was first published three years after "The Man of the Crowd," "Monsieur du Miroir" was published three years before "William Wilson"; as in my previous comparison, literary influence is not the issue but rather the formal and thematic similarities between stories that help to underscore key differences between the two writers. This pairing is also a bit fairer that the previous one. While "The Old Apple-Dealer" is a relatively slight sketch to set against one of Poe's masterpieces, "Monsieur du Miroir" certainly is not. "Monsieur du Miroir" and "William Wilson," in fact, are two of the most powerful, profound, and controlled explorations of the perils of self-reflection in all of nineteenth-century American literature. Both stories confront self-reflection head on by using the figure of the double (Poe) or the mirror image (Hawthorne) to literalize the dynamics of self-haunting. In both tales the identities of first person and other remain distinct only by virtue of the storyteller's greater power of speech (as opposed to the double's low whisper and the mirror image's silence). In both narratives such crucial distinction becomes threatened by the dreadful possibility that the second self is "originating every act which it appears to imitate" (403), as Hawthorne's first person remarks. Lastly, in both stories this crisis of mimesis, whereby imitator preempts original, leads to a direct encounter of sorts that holds the expectation of some general moral insight.

But here is where the similarities end. As in our previous pairing of stories, the differences between authors fall into three related categories: Poe's more urgent insistence on plot as a way to contain identity; the relative ease with which Hawthorne can talk about the paradoxes of individuality without disclosing particulars about himself; and the general attitude toward selfhood each writer manages to suggest in his story. Like "The Man of the Crowd," "William Wilson" is a story of mutual pursuit, organized chronologically in a series of escalating confrontations between self and double. Told and retold retrospectively, the tale is offered by the first person at the end of his life as a confession to justify what he hyperbolically calls (but never details) "my later years of unspeakable misery, and unpardonable crime." As in most of Poe's tales, the plot becomes a search for origins, for only by tracing the moment of doubling back to its source, and by then replaying the attempted reintegration of self and other by means of murder, can the first person hope to be at peace with himself. Such peace clearly eludes him, however, since, as I have argued, Poe's first persons have a vested interest in failing to recognize themselves in their doubles. Such recognition would lead to the complete blurring of identity between author and fictional plotter. In "William Wilson," Poe's most elaborate and calculated treatment of the problem of originality, the "I" remains infuriatingly blind to the significance of his own story. What substitutes for significance is sheer plotting, the mechanical linking of discrete events to form a chain of logical cause and effect that only outwardly appears to make sense.

"Monsieur du Miroir," by contrast, virtually has no plot at all. Instead of moving toward a single climactic confrontation between first person and double, Hawthorne's sketch is loosely organized around the image of the mirror itself, which flits in and out of the narrator's gaze as he talks. The story steadily accrues by meditation and association, not by the confining chronology of retrospective confession that drives Poe's tale. Without any rigid story line to follow, Hawthorne's first person is free to move, paragraph by paragraph, through a series of brief puzzles presented by his mirror image: its origin, speech, dress, and narcissistic fondness for water. Released from the exigencies of plot, Hawthorne's sketch takes on a more relaxed, slyly bemused air which treats the theme of self-reflection much more philosophically that "William Wilson." It is no coincidence that Poe's most explicit story about doubling is also his most explicitly autobiographical, containing specific references to the author's upbringing in England, his education at the University of Virginia, his early proclivity for drinking and gambling—all personal experiences that Poe halfheartedly tries to disguise by his first person's wildly exaggerated, off-putting rhetoric of criminality.

Hawthorne, on the other hand, divulges relatively little about himself as he calmly considers Monsieur du Miroir. The first person's calculated diffidence leads him into no personal intimacies, so that in the end the speaker remains as elusive to us as his mirror image remains to him. Falling in love, showing anger, catching a fleeting glance while traveling—all of these self-reflexive experiences in "our daily intercourse" apply equally well to reader as well as author; the effect is to establish commonality between first person and reader, not to insist on the absolute individuality of the "I," as Poe continually struggles to affirm in his story. While William Wilson sees his mocking double as unique to him, Hawthorne's first person understands that we are all haunted by our own Monsieurs du Miroir. Even when Hawthorne's sketch modulates into a more somber tone midway through, promising to disclose "stranger things to come," the first person's "confidence" is still dedicated to speaking "frankly" on matters of strictly general interest. Brief allusions to a "heavy youth... wasted in sluggishness" and "bewitching dreams of woman's love" have a conventional ring to them, serving mainly as Byronic shorthand reinforcing the alienating consequences of self-consciousness. Despite its darker, more puzzling implications, self-contemplation curiously has a reassuring effect on Hawthorne in the story. By the end of the sketch, Hawthorne's first person appears able to come to terms with himself, directly addressing his mirror image in the second person as "friend," just as he finally addresses the old apple-dealer as "friend" at the end of that sketch.

Hawthorne is clearly more at home with himself as an author than Poe could ever be. Whereas Hawthorne's "I" ends his encounter with Monsieur du Miroir by warily attempting an embrace that bespeaks a mutual respect, William Wilson is either trying to run away from his reified alter ego or else trying to kill the tormenting antagonist once and for all. Both flight and murder must take place in public, for it is only in view of others that the guilty first person can be exposed for the hollow imposter he feels himself to be. This sense of imposture dominates the story's ending, for it is William Wilson's double, not the first person, who has the last word in the tale. Hawthorne's narrator and his mirror image, on the other hand, most often meet by chance, not by deliberate design, and shun appearances in public, preferring instead the "wise cheerfulness" (403) of each other's company apart from others. Although Hawthorne's first person at one point claims to "withhold our confidence" from self-reflection's "delusive magic" (402), one needs to have confidence in order to be able to withhold it; more at ease with his second self than Poe, Hawthorne can occasionally afford to withdraw from his silent companion without feeling compelled, as William Wilson is, to contest relentlessly the mocker's right to exist. In other words, Hawthorne's haunting is intermittent; the image comes and goes in ways that suggest the author's essential independence from it. Monsieur du Miroir does not betray the first person into paranoia, self-revulsion, and murder but is simply a mysterious fact of life to contemplate with a curious mixture of awe and bemusement.

Content with themselves, Hawthorne's first-person narrators in the sketches and tales of the 1830s and 1840s share little of the paralyzing dread that afflicts Poe's nervous self-betrayers. It is only when Hawthorne abandons shorter fiction in the late 1840s and begins to ponder the concept of romance a bit more systematically that he starts to speak more directly in a voice less conditioned by literary convention than his previous sketches. What emerges is a distinctly different kind of "I," more anxious and urgent, more prone to self-criticism. The preface to his collection *Twice-Told Tales* (1851) provides one of the clearest indications of this new kind of "I." Hawthorne's earlier preface to *Mosses from an Old Manse* (1846) closely follows the English sketch tradition by not "betraying anything too sacredly individual" (1147) and by insisting that his tales, aided by Providence, "blossomed out like flowers in the calm summer of my heart and mind." Nature and art share a perfect correspondence which leaves the author with little responsibility for his own writing. In the 1851 preface, however, Hawthorne's self-presentation has changed considerably; as he begins to "criticise his own work as fairly as another man's" (1151), he discovers that authors' "opinions of their own productions would often be more valuable and instructive than the works themselves" (1151). Casting his twice-told tales in the harsh sunlight, he admits that the collection itself is devoid of substance, "look[ing] exceedingly like a volume of blank pages" (1152). And as he sums up his literary persona with a degree of impatience (a "mild, shy, gentle, melancholic, exceedingly sensitive, and not very forcible man" [1153]), Hawthorne likewise threatens to expose this familiar persona for the conventional fiction that it is. Taking self-scrutiny even further, Hawthorne wonders out loud if he wrote some of the stories in the collection simply "to fill up so amiable an outline, and to act in consonance with the character assigned to him" (1153). Assigned by whom? we might ask. In the process of partially debunking his conventional persona, the author becomes more interested in understanding how he came to construct that literary self. Art no longer grows naturally, as is implied in "The Old Manse," but rather is the product of a particular mind working for particular ends. It is only when Hawthorne shifts from writing short stories to publish a longer work of fiction, a "romance," that the artist's imagination itself becomes a disturbing notion in need of some explicit definition and justification.

It is thus Hawthorne's growing self-critical stance, as a retrospective analyst of his own work, that leads to the emergence of a new sort of fictional "I." As we shall see, this "I" will culminate in the first-person narrator of *The Blithedale Romance*, Hawthorne's only extended departure from third-person narration. For the remainder of this chapter I will be concentrating on *The Blithedale Romance* because it is this particular novel, rather than the earlier first-person short stories and sketches, which dramatizes most intricately and insistently Hawthorne's stake in his work. This authorial investment, I argue, is dangerously intensified by Hawthorne's continuing commitment to "romance" as a serious and prolonged exploration of the possible relation of his art to reality. To counter his increasing doubts about this relationship, Hawthorne will turn to a first-person surrogate, Miles Coverdale, whose own attempts to sustain a coherent narrative sometimes border on the ridiculous. But before interrogating the first person's performance, I will begin by briefly looking at Hawthorne's initial two novels in order to understand the connection between the author's growing anxieties about romance and the changing form of his fiction.

As *The Scarlet Letter* neared completion, Hawthorne wrote an introduction to the work intended to explain his motives for writing the novel.[3] The autobiographical account of the romance's genesis that Hawthorne offers in "The Custom-House" has important implications for the narrative method in the romance itself. While the preface discusses the relation between creator and creation in terms of his immediate experience as a Custom-House surveyor and aspiring romancer, the relation between the author and his fiction within *The Scarlet Letter* is strictly a function of the narration, that is, how the story is told. And this narrative stance, as we shall see, suggests a great deal about the way Hawthorne conceives of persons and interpersonal relations. In his subsequent fiction this pattern will be repeated. A theory of romance sketched out in each preface helps to gloss the narrative style within each work. The narration, in turn, implies a particular concept of selfhood, a concept which will change dramatically from *The Scarlet Letter* to *The Blithedale Romance*.

Hawthorne's account of the writing of *The Scarlet Letter* rests on three crucial events: his politically motivated dismissal from his Custom-House post; his imagined discovery of the tattered scarlet letter, bequeathed by his "official ancestor"[4] Jonathan Pue; and the inspirational effects of romance's "neutral territory" (I, 36), the magical commingling of "The Actual" and "The Imaginary," which Hawthorne likens to a commingling of moonlight and firelight. In the case of all three experiences, the author assigns himself a passive role, assuming the part of a bemused and diffident onlooker governed by a set of circumstances not of his own making. He attributes his firing to an act of "Providence" (I, 40) which enables him to find his true vocation as a writer. He locates romance's neutral territory in his own study, "a familiar room" where the influence of "the little domestic scenery" (I, 35), combined with the forces of nature (moonlight) conspire to excite his imagination.

It is the author's initial encounter with the letter, however, which most vividly gives a literal, natural basis to a figurative process. Claiming that he did not possess the scarlet A but was "involuntarily" (I, 32) possessed by it, Hawthorne observes that "some deep meaning, most worthy of interpretation ... streamed forth *from* the mystic symbol" (I, 31; italics mine). He even goes so far as to insist that the letter and its accompanying sheets of foolscap "are still in my possession" (I, 33)—tangible relics of a distant past. Asserting that "the main facts of that story [*The Scarlet Letter*] are authorized and authenticated by the document of Mr. Surveyor Pue" (I, 52) allows Hawthorne to assume from the start "my true position as editor" (I, 4): a scribe who does not invent his fictional materials but simply arranges and embellishes, or "dress[es] up" (I, 33), what has already been given to him. Despite or because of the air of mystery and ambiguity which the scarlet letter appears to generate on its own throughout the romance, Hawthorne needs to believe that his governing symbol possesses an actuality outside of his private imagination.

When we turn from the Custom-House sketch to *The Scarlet Letter* itself, we begin to understand the significance of Hawthorne's version of the novel's germination. Having given himself over in the preface to "an autobiographical impulse ... taken possession of me" (I, 3), having anchored the origins of his fiction in his personal experience as writer and Custom-House surveyor, Hawthorne is able to take his authority for granted in a very specific way while narrating the romance proper. The unrelenting intensity of *The Scarlet Letter* is due in part to the way in which the story seems to be telling itself. Rarely does Hawthorne enter the narrative to remind us that he is responsible for it. When he does intrude—for instance, to offer informed historical commentary about the Puritan community or to express incredulity about a wolf tamely approaching Pearl in the forest (chap. 18)—he does so in his guise as the tale's editor, not its creator. Instead of calling attention to its author, the action is organized by means of a series of revelations in which the omnipresent scarlet letter does the narrator's work for him. Hawthorne can remain silent about his characters' motives because the letter itself serves to disclose their secret hopes and fears. Whether or not a red A is actually burned on Dimmesdale's breast in the end, for example, is less important than the fact that such a possibility establishes an immediate correspondence between the minister's internal state and the "visible presence of the letter" (I, 258–59). Although the letter's ontological status may remain in doubt, it clearly functions from Dimmesdale's "inmost heart outwardly" (I, 258) to manifest and authenticate his guilt. What the letter may signify in any particular case is not as crucial here as *how* it makes significance possible, mediating between private and public experience, as well as between the author and his story, with an absolute, unexplained precision that Hawthorne assumes as a given. Just as he had described the burning effects of the letter on his own imagination in the preface, so Hawthorne uses the letter in the romance as a kind of transparent window to open up the imaginations of his fictional creations.

At the core of this narrative method is a belief in what Hawthorne repeatedly calls "the Interior of a Heart" (I, chap. 11). For all the letter's celebrated ambiguity, and for all the emphasis on secrecy in the narrative, the romance presumes that characters possess stable selves, and that although these selves, or personal "spheres," may be hidden from one another, each character is fixed with some essential identity from within. We can appreciate Dimmesdale's tormenting hypocrisy, for instance, only insofar as we can recognize a well-defined "contrast between what I seem and what I am" (I, 191), as the minister himself describes his own condition. By permitting the scarlet letter to symbolically articulate the discrepancy between an individual's public and private selves, Hawthorne can dramatize Dimmesdale's hypocrisy without directly commenting on or explaining his character's "interior kingdom" (I, 217). Only after the romance's final ambiguous revelation following Dimmesdale's confession (I, chap. 23) does Hawthorne suddenly reenter his narrative to confess, along with the reader, that his symbol "has done its office":

> Some affirmed that the Reverend Mr. Dimmesdale . . . had begun a course of penance . . . by inflicting a hideous torture on himself . . . Others again . . . whispered their belief, that the awful symbol was the effect of the ever active tooth of remorse . . . The reader may choose among these theories. We have thrown all the light we could acquire upon the portent, and would gladly, now that it has done its office, erase its deep print out of our own brain; where long meditation has fixed it in very undesirable distinctness. (I, 258–9)

That curious pronominal shift from third person ("some affirmed") to first-person plural ("we") is a sign of things to come.

The preface of Hawthorne's next work, *The House of the Seven*

Gables, suggests the extent to which a profound realignment in Hawthorne's relation to his imaginative materials has taken place following *The Scarlet Letter*. Like "The Custom-House" sketch, the preface to the *Seven Gables* sets out to suggest to the reader what it means to write a romance. But while the earlier preface tried to give the creative process a basis in external, historical fact, here Hawthorne is more willing to admit his own active role in originating the fiction. While "The Actual" and "The Imaginary" in "The Custom-House" are conceived as interdependent varieties of experience, the analogous generic distinction between "Novel" and "Romance" that Hawthorne proposes in this preface serves to drive a wedge between the two realms: the Novel must maintain a "minute fidelity" (II, 1) to experience, whereas the Romance (with a capital R) is not so bound. Instead of insisting that his unifying symbol is in his actual possession, Hawthorne takes quite the opposite tack by emphasizing that his Pyncheon house, shrouded by "legendary mist" (II, 2), is built out of "materials long in use for constructing castles in the air" (II, 3).

Hawthorne's desire to define the romance as an invention of his imagination dissociated from the real world leads the author to a puzzling uncertainty about the status of his characters. As in *The Scarlet Letter*, Hawthorne affirms his commitment to representing "the truth of the human heart" (II, 1), yet the nature of that truth is quite another matter. Are the "circumstances" of such truths of the writer's own choosing *or* creation"; and therefore are "the personages of the tale ... of the author's own making, *or* at all events, of his own mixing" (II, 1, 3; italics mine)? Such crucial equivocations between making and mixing—creating out of thin air as opposed to selective editing—correspond to problems of characterization and narration that emerge in the romance itself. Taking credit for his work compels Hawthorne to confront certain epistemological and ontological difficulties that he had managed to avoid in *The Scarlet Letter*. While the dismissed Custom-House surveyor can sit back and watch nature's moonlight and domestic firelight merge together in his parlor, here the author compares his role to a stage manager who must manipulate his own "atmospherical medium as to bring out or mellow the lights, and deepen and enrich the shadows, of the picture" (II, 1).

Hawthorne's increasing tendency to treat his romance as a constructed artifice surfaces early in the *Seven Gables*. When the author

begins to introduce us to the first of the present-day Pyncheons in
the second chapter of the book, we cannot help but recognize a
new kind of narrative presence. After exclaiming, "Far from us be
the indecorum of assisting, even in imagination, at a maiden lady's
toilet!" (II, 30), Hawthorne proceeds to pry into Hepzibah's private
sacraments, teasing his readers by asking questions whose answers
he already knows: "Will she now issue forth over the threshold of
our story? . . . Can it have been an early lover of Miss Hepzibah?
No; she never had a lover—poor thing, how could she?" (II, 31,
32). Explicitly identifying himself as a "disembodied listener" (II,
30), Hawthorne makes us aware that behind the story being told
there is someone telling it. Given the playful mockery directed at
Hepzibah, a mockery which will erupt far more brutally during the
prolonged taunting of dead Judge Pyncheon in chapter 18, it now
makes some sense to talk about a particular narrator in the romance
distinct from its author. Openly passing judgment on his actors,
pronouncing Hepzibah miserable or Holgrave naive, the narrator
reveals a degree of impatience with those conventions of characterization which assume that fictional creations are autonomous
agents possessing free wills. Although the characters themselves
remain the primary center of interest throughout the *Seven Gables*,
this narrative presence, sometimes uncomfortable, sometimes condescending, generates a secondary focus of interest for the reader,
who is intermittently reminded that the interaction between the
Pyncheons and Maules is being orchestrated and observed by some
higher authority. Spending an entire chapter alone with a dead
man, we cannot help but wonder about the narrative source controlling the fiction.

Hawthorne's self-consciousness about managing his "atmospheric medium" complicates his ability to represent the interior
of a human heart. In the relatively unobtrusive narration of *The
Scarlet Letter* the human heart is mysteriously revealed by the letter
itself. The *Seven Gables*'s counterpart for this all-powerful token of
mediation is the daguerreotype, which also serves to pierce through
surface appearances to arrive at the truth hidden within. But while
the letter is assumed to offer immediate transcendental insight,
Holgrave's photographs can only approximate the truth. Like the
ghostly "disembodied listener" Hawthorne inserts into his narrative
to help us evaluate his characters, the daguerreotypes stand *between*
appearance and reality. Although the photographs depend, in part,

on nature's sunshine, they are more opaque representations of the truth than the transparent, supernatural scarlet letter because they are more subject to the clotted materiality of the present. After Holgrave takes the judge's picture, for example, he must then convince Phoebe verbally that he has indeed captured the man's inner essence.

Working more by persuasion than by unmediated revelation, Holgrave's photographic art is thus analogous to his mesmerism. Both are equally "imperfect sort[s] of intercourse" (II, 206) that require the sympathetic surrender of another person. In *The Scarlet Letter* Hawthorne conceives of sympathy as an inherent character trait possessed by each individual. But in the *Seven Gables* sympathy becomes a magical process that takes place between subject and object, mesmerist and mesmerized. And as Hawthorne grows more interested in representing relations among persons whose identities are not fixed, his faith in a stable self becomes more difficult to sustain. In this sense Holgrave's climactic decision not to keep Phoebe under his spell is a key indication of the subsequent direction Hawthorne's next romance will take. By refusing to commit the unpardonable sin—the violation of the sanctity of the individual—the mesmerist restores his victim's integrity, but he does so at the cost of fully entering into the life of another. An obvious figure for the romance writer, Holgrave all along has exercised "the witchcraft of Maule's eye" to "look into people's minds" and "draw people into his own mind" (II, 189). But in the end this "privileged and meet spectator" (II, 217) abdicates his special demonic power to resume his status as just another character among equals. The sacred truth within a human heart is preserved only by keeping it a mystery from other hearts.

As Hawthorne grows more prone to self-conscious intervention, more willing to call attention to his role as romance writer, then, he also becomes more anxious about the way his art threatens to compromise the sanctity of the individual. When we turn from *The House of the Seven Gables* to *The Blithedale Romance*, we can see how this anxiety is transformed into the very subject of the romance. What remains submerged in the first two novels as an uneasy narrative presence blossoms into a full-blown first-person narrator, the bachelor Miles Coverdale, whose struggle to understand his fellow utopians serves to enact the process by which ro-

mances get written. Blithedale's poet laureate and reluctant
utopian, Miles Coverdale clearly bears a certain resemblance to the
generic Paul Pry bachelor figures who narrate some of Hawthorne's
early stories, such as "Sights from a Steeple." But insofar as Coverdale is overtly identified as a poet, his voyeuristic tendencies and
his persistent habit of mixing fantasy with reality may have more
to do with his problems as an author than with his derivation from
an established literary genre or his defects as a character.

Most critics account for *The Blithedale Romance*'s bewildering
incongruity by blaming Miles Coverdale for the confusion, thereby
directly linking the oddities in the plot, its distracting "Gothic
flimflam," as Irving Howe has called it, with the deficiencies of the
tale's teller. According to this standard line of inquiry, the narrator's
personality dictates the "radical incoherence" at the heart of the
narrative's form.[5] Once we refrain from measuring Blithedale's
minor poet by the standards of psychological realism, however, it
becomes possible to see how Hawthorne may be less interested in
using his first person to display a particular mind than in exploring
the extent to which any individual can or cannot gain access to
other minds. Coverdale's failure to gain access to others, I will
argue, leads him to construe the Veiled Lady subplot, a secret family
romance which far from falling back on "encumbering mechanisms
of enchantment," as commentators most often claim,[6] serves to
dramatize the novel's overriding concern: how connections are to
be made (between people, between things) in a world where social
relations—or relations of any kind—can no longer be taken for
granted.

Elaine Scarry has recently remarked that "Imagining is, in effect, the ground of last resort. That is, should it happen that the
world fails to provide an object, the imagination is there . . . as a last
resource for the generation of objects."[7] In the case of *The Blithedale
Romance*, the imagination's task is not to invent objects themselves
but rather to understand the hidden connections that may exist
among them. Shaken from his early confidence in the power of
art, questioning what he has formerly assumed as givens, Hawthorne takes the difficult process of making sense of the world as
his primary subject in *The Blithedale Romance*. Abandoning revelation as a mode of insight, Hawthorne concentrates on the problem
of mediation itself: how the truth about others can be known at

all. In the absence of the scarlet letter or the magic daguerreotypes, the first-person narrator must now try to delve into the human heart without the help of such transcendental devices.

As Coverdale pries for the sake of his plot, a sequence of cause and effect which will help him make sense of his experience, our attention becomes sharply divided between what is being represented and how such a representation is made possible. At times the first person is simply one participant among many in the Blithedale community. But each time the isolated minor poet obtrudes to remind us that he is contriving his narrative "fancy-work" (III, 100), the reality of the Blithedale drama tends to dissolve into a fiction peopled by the figments of his imagination. This split in Coverdale between character and narrator stems from an ambivalence on Hawthorne's part which makes his relationship to his first-person agent exceedingly complex. At the same time that he seeks to disengage himself from his creation by inviting us to attribute Coverdale's voyeuristic behavior to personal quirks in his character, Hawthorne also wants to use Coverdale to help define his own responsibilities and methods as a writer of romance. In *The Scarlet Letter* Hawthorne's urge to account for the romance's origins is largely confined to "The Custom-House" so that the tale itself is kept free from autobiographical intrusion. But in *The Blithedale Romance* it becomes very difficult to distinguish between the author's notions of making fiction and his first person's equally self-conscious commentary, once Hawthorne allows his tendency to explain himself seep into the body of the narrative.

Commenting on this kind of slippage from impersonal to personal discourse in the novel, Michel Butor helps us to appreciate Hawthorne's extended plunge into first-person narration:

> Dans le roman, ce que l'on nous raconte, c'est donc toujours aussi quelqu'un qui se raconte et nous raconte. La prise de conscience d'un tel fait provoque un glissement de la narration de la troisième à la première personne. Il s'agit d'abord d'un progrès dans le réalisme par l'introduction d'un point de vue ... Lorsqu'on s'aperçoit que ... cette ignorance est un des aspects fondamentaux de la réalité humaine, et que les événements de notre vie ne parviennent jamais à s'historiser au point que leur narration ne comporte plus de lacunes, on est obligé de nous présenter ce que nous sommes censés connaître, mais aussi de nous préciser le comment

de ce savoir-là... on rencontre fréquemment des romans où le narrateur est un personnage secondaire qui assiste à la tragédie ou la transfiguration d'un héros, de plusieurs, dont il nous raconte les étapes. Par rapport à l'auteur, qui ne voit qu'alors le héros représentera ce qu'il rêve, et le narrateur ce qu'il est? La distinction entre les deux personnages réfléchira à l'intérieur de l'oeuvre la distinction vécue par l'auteur entre l'existence quotidienne telle qu'il la subit, et cette existence autre que son activité romanesque promet et permet... [le] narrateur [est le] point de tangence entre le monde raconté et celui òu on le raconte, moyen terme entre le réel et l'imaginaire....[8]

In the novel, what is narrated to us is therefore also always someone who speaks about himself and about us. To become aware of such an act triggers a sliding of narration from third to first person. It is therefore an advance toward realism through the introduction of a point of view... When one perceives that... this ignorance is one of the fundamental aspects of human reality, and that the events of our lives never manage to organize themselves into a history that does not admit gaps, then one is not only obliged to present us with what we are supposed to know but also to specify how it comes to be known... one frequently encounters novels where the narrator is a secondary figure who assists in the tragedy or transfiguration of one or more heroes whose development he recounts to us. With regard to the author, who does not see that the hero represents his dreams, and the narrator the person who he is? The distinction between the two figures reflects in the interior of the work the distinction experienced by the author between the everyday existence to which he submits, and that other existence which his activity as a novelist promises and permits... [The] narrator [is the] point of tangency between the narrated world and the world of narrating, the middle term between the real and the imaginary. (my translation)

Associating the first-person form with an author's "prise de conscience" about his narrative responsibilities, Butor's analysis has two important implications for my discussion of *The Blithedale Romance*. First, Butor points out how first-person discourse creates two distinct dramas in the novel, "the world of narrating" and "the narrated world," each of which is purchased at the expense of the other. Seeing the first person as a "middle term," or mediator, between these two worlds helps to explain the frequently noted incongruity between what may actually be happening at Blithedale, and what Coverdale imagines is happening. Second, Butor suggests the extent to which an author's decision to write in the first person affects the representation of social relations in the fiction. Depriving his narrator of the privileges of insight, Hawthorne compels his first person to share a fundamental ignorance with his other characters, whose inner lives remain hidden from view. Instead of being revealed from within, intention is now inferred from without, induced from those particulars of gesture and word which individuals present to one another.

Without discussing his shift to the first person per se, in his preface to the romance Hawthorne addresses the two main issues that Butor raises in his discussion of the form. Like his two previous introductory prefaces, Hawthorne's brief introduction to *The Blithedale Romance* is deceptively simple and therefore warrants a closer examination. To begin with, we note that the author abandons the generic distinction between Romance and Novel proposed in the preface to *The House of the Seven Gables* in favor of a distinction based on geographical location. "The Actual" and "The Imaginary" have become so polarized, so hardened, that now Hawthorne reifies their differences in spatial terms: the "old countries" provide their writers with a ready-made enchanted "Faery Land," whereas America is a land bound by "every-day Probability" (III, 2). In the absence of such an enchanted atmosphere, the American romancer's "beings of imagination are compelled to show themselves in the same category as actually living mortals; a necessity that generally renders the paint and pasteboard of their composition but too painfully discernible" (III, 2). Unfairly matched against reality, the author's characters thus betray themselves as illusions to the degree that they pretend to be real. In Hawthorne's first two romances his belief in the truth within the human heart serves to bridge the difference between appearance and reality. But once that essentialist notion of inner truth is taken away, all that remains are two-dimensional versions of the self. Rather than vainly trying to approximate "the real world," Hawthorne chooses to swerve from it by now insisting that his characters are "entirely fictitious" (III, 2). Yet the author has already admitted that he cannot free himself completely from the demands of the actual; the point is not to ignore the pressures of present-day reality but to establish a new kind of common ground or neutral territory that fabulists in the "old countries" take for granted, and that Hawthorne himself had taken for granted in his first two romances.

Hawthorne's crucial metaphor for this new relation between world and imagination is "a theatre, a little removed from the highway of ordinary travel" (III, 1). To gain "an available foothold between fiction and reality" (III, 2), Hawthorne treats his Brook Farm experience as a stage "where the creatures of his brain may play their phantasmagorical antics, without exposing them to too close a comparison with the actual events of real lives" (III, 1). Hawthorne's comparison of the Blithedale community to a theater troupe reveals a great deal about his conception of social relations in the romance. Instead of supposing that characters' words and actions are externalized expressions of inner truth, Hawthorne posits a theater to suggest a more modern understanding of identity as personality, the playing out of social roles. In *The House of the Seven Gables* even a figure as adaptable as Holgrave is assumed to possess a stable essence. Despite his theatrical gift for "putting off one exterior, and snatching up another," the Daguerreotypist (notice the capital D) "had never lost his identity," nor "violated the innermost man" (II, 177). But in *The Blithedale Romance*, as we shall see, a person's "interior kingdom" or "sphere" gives way to spheres of influence, a complex set of master/slave power relations whereby characters define themselves by trying to persuade other characters of their natures. Turning romance into drama allows Hawthorne to give his characters a wider range for self-expression than in *The Scarlet Letter* or the *Seven Gables*. Yet as these individuals become more and more differentiated from one another, the principles governing the way people interact become increasingly more difficult to comprehend. Standing alternately on the Blithedale stage (as an actor) and observing that action from afar (as a solitary spectator), it remains Coverdale's special duty as a first-person narrator to articulate those relations, to manage the romance's atmospheric medium.

Neither a mirror of reality nor a complete abandonment of it, the Blithedale "theatre" shifts attention away from an individual's "inmost me" to focus on the pragmatics of personality—the effects persons produce on one another while acting as a group. Here is how Hawthorne, in the preface to *The Blithdale Romance*, introduces "the creatures of his brain": "The self-concentrated Philanthropist; the high-spirited Woman, bruising herself against the narrow limitations of her sex; the weakly Maiden, whose tremulous nerves endow her with Sibylline attributes; the Minor Poet, beginning life with strenuous aspirations, which die out with his youthful fervor"

(III, 2–3). Although at first glance this cast of characters may appear
to approach an allegorical configuration, the author's description
of his creations reads more like a playbill from a popular
nineteenth-century melodrama. There is nothing deep inside these
characters except what they have put there themselves by self-
presentation, the art of managing impressions.

As I will be arguing, this attempt to understand social relations
in terms of theater is double-edged, giving the romance the feel
of a realistic novel while at the same time widening the gap between
Blithedale's "actuality" and its narrator's "imagining." Emphasizing
the dynamic interplay among the group's various actors, Hawthorne treats identity as a mutual process of give-and-take. Zenobia,
for example, reacts to Coverdale differently than she responds to
Hollingsworth, so that the carefully nuanced "self" she presents to
each man depends on her sense of the particular audience for that
self. Details that mark Zenobia's personality, such as the fresh flower
she wears daily, do not reveal her essence (as the scarlet letter served
to disclose Hester's inner dimension); rather, they help manufac-
ture her social identity, the face she wears in public. Deploring the
romance's Gothic trappings, later novelists such as James and Howells called attention to this more modern form of representation,
Hawthorne's newly found ability to create a concrete "person" or
"more definite image" out of a "multiplicity of touches."[9] For these
writers such portrayals seem more "realistic," more substantial, and
less subjective because characters are socially defined; hence it is
the book's dramatic dialogue, rather than Coverdale's brooding
commentary, which these realists single out for praise.

Yet the fact that identity is disclosed solely through role-playing
makes *interpreting* such behavior problematic. Denied entry to the
interior kingdoms of his companions, the first-person narrator is
compelled to construe his characters simply by accumulating and
glossing their surface expressions. Coverdale "measure[s]" Zenobia's "inward trouble" (121) by the animosity of her speech, or tries
to catch the "intimacy of a mysterious heart" (90) by a sudden glance
or gesture. Hawthorne's analogy between romance and drama thus
has important consequences for our understanding of Miles Coverdale in particular, whose role as Blithedale's minor poet—
"turn[ing] the affair into a ballad" (33), as Zenobia calls it—corresponds to his role as a self-conscious narrator. By explicitly identifying his first person as an aspiring writer intent on transforming

his experience into art while still in the process of living it, Hawthorne suggests how his narrator's ability to construct a coherent plot, an explanatory sequence of cause and effect, directly depends on his ability to pry into the life of others. This intimate association between Coverdale's voyeurism and his plotting, in turn, allows Hawthorne to explore the possible relation between the "reality" of the romance's narrated events and the "imaginary" act of narration itself.

As Michel Butor observes, first-person narration simultaneously divides "the real" from "the imaginary," and affirms some continuity between the two worlds. Playing the part of mediator for the sake of his fellow utopians within his story as well as for his readers outside it, the artist Coverdale remains an easy target for literary critics, who label him an "unreliable" narrator given to delusion, lying, or, at best, confusion.[10] But to claim that Coverdale makes a mockery of Hawthorne's concerns by mixing up what appears to be actual with what may be simply imagined is to miss how successfully the first person's artistic mismanagement serves to dramatize those concerns. The notion of "unreliability," for example, tends to presuppose the possibility of absolute reliability, a perfect matching of world to fiction.[11] Beneath the distorted facade of the first person's fantastic account, these critics assume, there exists the true version of events, which can be reconstructed by the knowing reader. But reliability is never strictly intrinsic to a particular text or narrator; rather, the concept describes a relationship *between* reader and text: the degree to which a given reader is willing to rely on, or put his faith in, someone else's words, whether they be attributed to an author, narrator, or some other invisible source. Any act of reading demands our reliance, if only to the extent that we trust that the words on the page bear some meaningful connection to our understanding of "reality." Essentialist definitions of reliability that ignore the reader's role in the relationship by focusing exclusively on the text itself thus miss the point that such "unreliable" texts would quite literally also be unreadable.

One critical article on *The Blithedale Romance* takes the notion of first-person unreliability to an absurd extreme by arguing that Zenobia does not actually drown herself but is killed by Coverdale, who then concocts his elaborate story to cover up his crime.[12] Ignoring the first person's function as artist/narrator, this kind of conjectural reading treats Coverdale as a character whose motives can be explained in strictly psychological terms—in this case murderous jealousy. To discredit Coverdale as an untrustworthy storyteller, these critics need to build a psychologically realistic profile of their subject. Such psychologizing, however, threatens to violate the main point of Hawthorne's preface, namely, that fiction can offer only the illusion of mimesis, not mimesis itself, and that the search for an ideal congruence therefore is bound to fail. As Coverdale, from his hidden treehouse, strains to make sense of a cryptic conversation he has overheard between Zenobia and Westervelt, he notes that "real life never arranges itself exactly like a romance" (104); to bring this insight to life in the fiction, Hawthorne takes as his subject the difficulties involved in trying to participate in Blithedale's experiment and represent it at the same time.

Instead of inventing extratextual scenarios that presume to disclose "what really happened" and the narrator's motives for veiling that truth, we need to examine more closely how Coverdale's status as Blithedale's minor poet affects his interaction with other characters in the community. The simple fact is that there is no way around the first-person narrator, no clearly superior perspective from which to judge the validity of his mystifying account or fill in its gaps. His is the only story we have; once the concept of unreliability is introduced to evaluate a first-person narrative, then how is anything to be believed at all? No wonder such critics often feel compelled to move outside the text in order to establish alternative grounds for belief.

In denying us the comfort of any objective evidence or Archimedean perspective, Hawthorne also denies us any authentic picture of Coverdale's "mind." Dorrit Cohn has recently shown that despite all appearances to the contrary, a first-person narrator, conditioned by an inevitably imperfect memory, "has less free access to his own past psyche than the omniscient narrator of third-person fiction has to the psyches of his characters."[13] Coverdale himself muses on this problem near the story's opening and conclusion as he sits by the dimly glowing fire of his parlor and tries to relive an already expired set of experiences. And if Coverdale's past remains veiled from his retrospective view in the present, then his narrating self remains equally opaque to the reader, who must rest content with what the first person chooses to give him, because he cannot be given anything else. Although it would be foolish to deny that

Coverdale has certain personal limitations which help define him as a character, the first person's struggle to understand his own story may have more to do with the demands made on him as Blithedale's narrator—a self-imposed mission which is continually being confirmed by the other members of the group.

The complex relation between Hawthorne and his first person thus varies in accordance with Coverdale's own doubleness in the romance. At those moments when the minor poet becomes aware of his role as narrator to muse on the problem of storytelling, I would argue, Hawthorne is intimately relying on Coverdale to help him work out the difficulties of romance writing. Yet we cannot simply equate author and narrator, for in making his first person conscious of his narrating, Hawthorne also makes him self-conscious, that is, he imagines a particular "self" for his creation apart from the writer's own "inmost Me." However closely Coverdale's personal compulsions may appear to correspond to his author's, Hawthorne clearly means to keep his autobiographical impulses at bay by encouraging us to regard his first person as just another "imaginary personage" (1) whose painful experience should not be directly compared with "the actual events of real lives" (1), including Hawthorne's own.

To recall the preface's warning, the history of Brook Farm is one affair, the fiction of Blithedale another. In this way Hawthorne hopes to treat the problem of the artist in the book primarily in terms of Coverdale's character; the first person is thus sacrificed as an egocentric clown on occasion for comic effect in order to prevent his author from turning the romance into a naked confession. But the minor poet's difficulty, we shall see, extends beyond his personal idiosyncracies, and even beyond his special duties as a narrator. In the pages that follow I will generally refrain from analyzing in isolation the frequently discussed quirks in Coverdale's personality—his sexual fears and attractions, his effete dandyism, his envy of Hollingsworth and malice toward Priscilla—because I think these psychological dimensions of the narrator represent self-defensive evasions on the part of Hawthorne himself, who encourages us to erect a separate identity for his first-person agent behind which he can hide. Instead, I will be concentrating on Coverdale's efforts at representation, his attempt to provide some comprehensible artistic form for the Blithedale community. Although

the teller's tale and his self-ironic "character" remain entangled
throughout the book, it is the first person's role as literary plotter
that specifically enables Hawthorne to cast his own anxieties as a
romance writer into sharp relief without losing himself in his fiction.

These anxieties emerge from the very start of the romance.
The book's first chapter, with its emphasis on theatrical spectacle
and veiling, provides a key transition between the theoretical concerns of Hawthorne's preface and Coverdale's more immediate
preoccupations as the community's poet laureate. The contrast
Hawthorne makes in the preface between old-world romance and
American fiction, in fact, bears a striking resemblance to a distinction between two kinds of showmanship that Coverdale makes while
describing "the wonderful exhibition of the Veiled Lady" (5). Formerly, Coverdale remarks, during the time his story takes place,
the Veiled Lady was displayed with "all the arts of mysterious arrangement . . . in order to set the apparent miracle in the strongest
attitude of opposition to ordinary facts" (6). "Now-a-days," on the
contrary, during the time his story is being narrated, "in the management of his 'subject,' 'clairvoyant,' or 'medium,' the exhibitor
affects the simplicity and openness of scientific experiment" (5).
Instead of trying to create an enchanted atmosphere or "Faery
Land" remote from reality, the modern-day showman manages his
medium by pretending to match that reality. Like an American
writer's novels, the contemporary mesmerist's "subject" is thus compelled to betray the paint and pasteboard of its arrangement.

Analogizing two contrasting styles of writing fiction with two
contrasting styles of performance, the romance's opening pages
help to explain Coverdale's dilemma as a narrator. The story he
has to tell is indeed enchanted, but his method of presentation will
work against that enchanted past by trying to rival current reality,
the reality of putting together a work of fiction. Separated by twelve
years, the moment of narrating and the events within the narration
are at odds with one another. The entire first chapter, moreover,
enacts this very dilemma by calling attention to the first person's
awkward attempts at narrative management, thereby revealing the
paint and pasteboard of his plotting. As many critics have pointed
out, the romance opens on a very bewildering note which violates
all kinds of narrative conventions. Instead of beginning the way
most storytellers begin, namely, introducing characters one by one
and placing them in a causal sequence of events, Coverdale starts

by recounting a meeting with an unidentified old man and then immediately digresses to describe a performance "in the mesmeric line" (5) which contains a mysterious prophecy left unspoken. This strange digression, in turn, is followed by oblique references to two more mysterious figures, one a "solid character" (7), the other an elusive "mask" (8). About to be "mix[ed] . . . up irrevocably with the Blithedale affair" (8), Coverdale declines to articulate the relation among these various characters or their relation as a group to the mesmerist's spectacle. Like the Veiled Lady's own "prophetic solution" (6), this beginning also bears "the true Sibylline stamp, nonsensical in its first aspect, yet on closer study unfolding a variety of interpretations" (6).

Such artistic ineptitude serves to remind the reader that narration is not a self-evident, organic process but rather a contrived affair. Hawthorne thus immediately establishes Coverdale's presence as an imposing narrator, but he does so at the expense of his person, whose status seems quite confused, to say the least. By suggesting the first person's cognitive weaknesses, the opening chapter allows us to examine, in virtually clinical detail, how narratives can be ordered to appear more or less coherent. From the very start, then, we are not only being told Coverdale's story but the story of his story as well. In this way Hawthorne exposes the formal underpinnings of the romance while risking the complete unraveling of the events contained within. During his initial interaction with the Veiled Lady, for instance, Coverdale asks her to predict the success of "our Blithedale enterprise" (6), a crucial phrase which refers both to the experimental founding of the community (in the past) and to Coverdale's writing of the book (in the present). Linking the minor poet's hopes for aesthetic harmony with Blithedale's hopes for social harmony, the entire first chapter thus functions as a kind of invocation to the Muse of Romance, whose "enigma of identity" (6) as both the Veiled Lady and Priscilla will parallel the first person's own doubleness as narrator and character throughout the fiction.

Infused with Hawthorne's doubts about romance, his sense that the cold materialism of the present is crowding out enchantment, the book's opening chapter obscures or veils the narrated world—characters and chronological events—to emphasize Coverdale's active role as a retrospective narrator embarking on his own solitary "Blithedale enterprise." It is important to recognize that this second

kind of enterprise, that of forming a text, is strictly a solitary process. Although the romance opens with a social encounter (Coverdale's meeting with old Moodie), the predominant impression
that remains with the reader by the romance's conclusion is the
intense, inescapable condition of isolation which surrounds the figure of the first-person narrator. Those times when we are most
aware of Coverdale's presence in the text—when he calls attention
to his symbol-making prowess, confesses that he plays but a marginal part in his story, or openly questions the validity of his own
conjectures—we are also most vividly reminded of Coverdale's
loneliness. Repeatedly using the same theater metaphor that Hawthorne himself uses in his preface, Coverdale compares his position
in the narrative to a single spectator watching a play whose location
is constantly shifting. Sometimes the action seems to be really out
there, as when Zenobia catches Coverdale spying on her from his
hotel room in town and draws the shade, in effect closes the curtain
on him. But at other times Coverdale acknowledges that the creatures of his brain are acting on a "mental stage" (156) that constitutes his own "private theatre" (70). Whether the play is internal
or external, whether he is peering out from his hermitage to survey
the Blithedale landscape or listening to a quarrel between Zenobia
and Hollingsworth, the first person is unable to participate in the
action by virtue of trying to comprehend it.

Hawthorne sometimes would have us believe that Coverdale is
lonely by choice, mistakenly enjoying his alienation from other
characters as a watered-down version of Emersonian self-reliance.
But the bachelor's solitude is more importantly also a function of
his narrative duties. To maintain a vision of Blithedale, and thereby
chronicle its course, the minor poet must exempt himself from the
community. The first person can tell Blithedale's story only by
refusing to live it. And his refusal to live the story, in turn, leads
the first person to distort it. Narration-isolation-distortion: Coverdale himself comments on this unavoidable sequence during an
extended meditation on his "mode of observation":

> It is not, I apprehend, a healthy kind of mental occupation, to
> devote ourselves too exclusively to the study of individual men
> and women. If the person under examination be one's self, the
> result is pretty certain to be a diseased action of the heart . . . Or,
> if we take the freedom to put a friend under our microscope, we
> thereby insulate him from many of his true relations, magnify his

peculiarities, inevitably tear him into parts, and of course, patch him very clumsily together . . . Thus . . . I did Hollingsworth a great wrong by prying into his character, and am perhaps doing him as great a one, at this moment, by putting faith in the discoveries which I seemed to make . . . He—and Zenobia and Priscilla, both for their own sakes and as connected with him—were separated from the rest of the Community, to my imagination, and stood forth as the indices of a problem which it was my business to solve . . . In the midst of cheerful society, I had often a feeling of loneliness . . . Of course, I am perfectly aware that the above statement [an analysis of Hollingsworth's egotism] is exaggerated, in the attempt to make it adequate . . . The paragraph may remain, however . . . as exemplifying the kind of error into which my mode of observation was calculated to lead me. The issue was, that, in solitude, I often shuddered at my friend . . . in my wood-walks, and in my silent chamber, the dark face frowned at me again. (69–71)

As Poe's first-person narrator discovers in "The Man of the Crowd," treating others as discrete objects of analysis entails a certain degree of caricature. The plotter first isolates a small number of characters from an endless tangle of relations (a process which demands that he isolate himself), selects and highlights some of their most prominent individual features, and then sees how these isolated individuals interact with one another. Coverdale, in fact, gives us a miniature model of his narrative method in the romance when he gazes out of his hotel room in town to view the world without. Irked by his quarrel with Hollingsworth, the minor poet decides to leave Blithedale, remarking, "I was beginning to lose the sense of what kind of world it was, among innumerable schemes of what it might or ought to be" (140). "Returning into the settled system of things, to correct himself by a new observation from that old stand-point" (141), Coverdale seeks to regain the "solidity" of the "actual world."

The drama that ensues remains one of the romance's key episodes. Calling himself "a devoted epicure of my own emotions" (146), Coverdale first experiences a self-satisfied charm remarkably similar to the mood enjoyed by the narrator of "The Man of the Crowd" before he begins his own catalog of the urban masses outside his hotel window. Coverdale's hotel room, like his hermitage, "symbolized my individuality, and aided me in keeping it inviolate" (99), a protected post of observation set against everything outside

the self. When he turns outward from idle introspection to connect
with the world at large, however, his protection begins to break
down, leaving the first person with little "for common-sense to
clutch" (153).

Coverdale awakens to reality in several stages, each progressively more problematic. The first stage is hearing. Released from
the tyranny of the eye, the minor poet can freely connect "each
characteristic sound" (146) of the city to invisible scenes which his
imagination suggestively conjures up: the arrival of hotel guests;
the march of a military band; the applauded spectacle of a mechanical diorama exhibited nearby. Once he opens his eyes, however, his imagination becomes constrained by the visual field, which
happens to be the rear of a row of houses. Presented with this
undifferentiated cityscape, Coverdale determines to locate some
individuality:

> Here, it must be confessed, there was a general sameness. From
> the upper-story to the first floor, they were so much alike that I
> could only conceive of the inhabitants as cut out of one identical
> pattern, like little wooden toy-people of German manufacture . . .
> After the distinctness of separate characters, to which I had re-
> cently been accustomed, it perplexed and annoyed me not to be
> able to resolve this combination of human interests into well-
> defined elements . . . Men are so much alike in their nature, that
> they grow intolerable unless varied by their circumstances. (149–
> 50)

Accustomed to "making my prey of people's individualities" (84),
Coverdale thus begins to focus on a single boarding house, piercing
through the windows of its blank facade to infer the life within.
He first sees a young man making himself up in front of a mirror,
and then, in "the next story below, two children, prettily dressed,"
softly kissed by "a middle-aged gentleman."

Based on this action, the man immediately is transformed by
Coverdale into "a papa," shortly to be joined by "a mama." Roles
and relations among individuals thus suddenly fall into a self-
evident design, as description inevitably crosses over into interpretation; out of an undifferentiated group of persons—boy, girl, man,
woman—a family has been created. Moving from one "story" to
the next, Coverdale first narrows his vision to focus on discrete
objects and then unites these isolated objects to form a configu-

ration—a plot—which makes provisional sense of the world. In this way a man "in a white jacket" creeping from the house's basement with a broken dish becomes a guilty "Irish man-servant" (151), while a solitary dove is similarly "invested" with its own "fantastic pathos" by the first person.

Coverdale's fabrication of his world soon takes a more coercive turn. Haunted by his premature departure from Blithedale, he returns to the same window the next day to distract himself from a growing sense of regret at having "left duties unperformed" (154). As he moves from story to story, Coverdale suddenly comes across some "airy drapery," and then, "as if I had all along expected the incident," he encounters Zenobia, looking "like a full-length picture" (155), complete with Westervelt lurking in the background. If the storyteller shirks his responsibility to his characters, then these "goblins of flesh and blood" (157) are compelled to seek him out, shaping themselves against his intentions. As Coverdale peers out of his window, Zenobia, Priscilla, and Westervelt form an artificial tableau that anticipates the kind of transformations from humans into art objects which so preoccupy Hawthorne in his next romance, *The Marble Faun*. Unable or unwilling to change his cast of characters midway through his narrative, the first-person spectator falls victim to his own "method" of construing reality by framing it:

> There now needed only Hollingsworth and old Moodie to complete the knot of characters, whom a real intricacy of events, greatly assisted by my method of insulating them from other relations, had kept so long upon my mental stage, as actors in a drama. In itself, perhaps, it was no very remarkable event, that they should thus come across me, at the moment when I imagined myself free. (156)

Rather than disguising the fact that he is imaginatively imposing himself on the world, Coverdale in this way freely admits it, letting his exaggerations and misconceptions stand in order to suggest the price one must pay to transmute experience into art. As the minor poet himself intimates, his "speculative musing" (194) is a response to the world, a way of coping, not a reflection of it: "By long brooding over our recollections, we subtilize them into something akin to imaginary stuff, and hardly capable of being distinguished from it" (105). Those critics who find Coverdale "unreliable" would do well to consider how reliable the first person remains whenever he is discussing his problems as a narrator: his lapses in memory; his imperfect symbolizing; his wild surmising; his failure even to catch the denouement of his own plot. Returning to Blithedale half an hour too late, Coverdale ponders the consequences of missing Zenobia's climactic fight with Hollingsworth:

> And what subjects had been discussed here? All, no doubt, that, for so many months past, had kept my heart and my imagination idly feverish. Zenobia's whole character and history; the true nature of her mysterious connection with Westervelt; her later purposes towards Hollingsworth, and reciprocally, his in reference to her; and, finally, the degree in which Zenobia had been cognizant of the plot against Priscilla, and what, at last, had been the real object of that scheme. On these points, as before, I was left to my own conjectures. (215–16)

Trying to act as his own interpreter (an inevitability for any first-person narrator), Coverdale thus continually preempts the role of the doubting reader and thereby reasserts the very narrative authority he is always disclaiming for himself. Coverdale's "realism" as a narrator, however, his representation of the difficulty of storytelling itself, cannot help but distract us (and him) from the story he is trying to tell.

Coverdale's awareness of his own fictional methods, his sense of himself as Blithedale's sole artistic conscience, seems to me to constitute the central issue of the romance. But here, too, Hawthorne raises more questions than he is willing to answer, merging the first person's postures as passive onlooker, godlike seer, and jealous intruder. Soon after Westervelt first arrives at Blithedale to quicken the intrigue, Coverdale compares his own subordinate role to "the Chorus in a classic play, which seems to be set aloof from the possibility of personal concernment" (97). Caught midway between Blithedale's action and the unknown higher agency controlling it, which he calls "Destiny . . . the most skilful of stage-managers" (97), the first person defines himself as a "calm observer" or privileged commentator who has been singled out by fate to survive the tragic drama in order to "detect the final fitness of incident to character, and distil, in his long-brooding thought, the whole morality of the performance" (97). The passive role of spectator thus quickly shades over into a more assertive stance, as Coverdale invokes an authority above and beyond himself to vindicate his prying. When Coverdale is later rebuked by Zenobia in town, he explicitly associates his spying with a divinely inspired mission:

> She should have been able to appreciate that quality of the intellect and the heart, which impelled me (often against my own will, and to the detriment of my own comfort) to live in other lives, and to endeavor—by generous sympathies, by delicate intuitions, by taking note of things too slight for record, and by bringing my human spirit into manifold accordance with the companions whom God assigned me—to learn the secret which was hidden even from themselves. (160)

Viewed in its dramatic context, such a statement represents Hawthorne at his most evasive, trying to have it both ways by fusing Coverdale's worst qualities as a character—his "vulgar curiosity" (160), petty egotism, and self-righteousness—with a profound realization concerning the nature of artistic mediation. Depriving his narrator of the gift of omniscience, Hawthorne can thus closely examine how his first-person agent must consequently run the risk of inference and distortion if he hopes to retrieve some semblance of that gift.

In this way Hawthorne seeks to repossess the kind of narrative authority that had slipped away from him in the first two romances by dramatizing the consequences of that very loss. Pretentious as it may appear, Coverdale's posture as a "mesmerical clairvoyant" (46) suggests how knowledge has to be earned in the absence of any direct access to the hearts and minds of others. To recall Michel Butor's terms, the conscientious novelist "is not only obliged to present us with what we are supposed to know but also to specify how it comes to be known." Coverdale's visionary prying performs precisely this function. In order to find the "moral" of the story, "the final fitness of incident to character," the plotter pretends to assume a godlike authority over the Blithedale enterprise. While "incident" is the province of an unknowable "Destiny," "character" remains the unique property of each individual in the drama. Since he neither controls the romance's "real intricacy of events" (156) nor possesses the secrets of the actors within, his plotting—construing the hidden relation between "incident" and "character"—

comes to depend on sheer guesswork. When he leaves Blithedale to return to town, Coverdale himself wonders "whether the whole affair had been anything more than the thoughts of a speculative man," a prospect that inevitably tends to "rob the actual world of its solidity" (146).

By making Coverdale the sole medium through which Blithedale is represented, Hawthorne gives us little to choose between the minor poet's delusions and his insights. Both are necessary forms of speculation imposed on "the actual world" which intensify the first person's isolation. Yet Coverdale's alienation is part of a larger problem of alienation at Blithedale that extends beyond the first person's unique responsibilities as a narrator. As I shall argue, the minor poet represents only a special case of that pervasive egotism which enslaves every character in the romance. Troubled by his own society's preoccupation with "self," Hawthorne uses his first-person agent to get at this greater theme, for first person is a form particularly well suited to dramatize the dangers of an all-consuming "I." But to make the struggles of the egocentric narrator/artist his exclusive subject would risk falling into the same kind of massive solipsism that the romance sets out to examine; while Hawthorne realizes that his thematic intentions must necessarily be mediated by his narrative form, he refuses to allow himself to be self-reflexively trapped by this first-person form. For Hawthorne such a tempting surrender to self-reflexivity (found in so many modern texts) must be resisted as a vain indulgence. Coverdale's narration, then, remains simply the most prominent manifestation of an affliction that plagues all the other members at Blithedale, as will become evident once our attention turns away from the poet onto his fellow actors in the drama.

Individuals remain so remote from one another in *The Blithedale Romance* because they are all so busy establishing their own personal spheres. With varying degrees of awareness, Zenobia, Hollingsworth, Priscilla, and Coverdale are limited by the particular role or version of self each plays in the Blithedale "theatre" to the exclusion of all others. The romance's prefatory playbill makes this clear: if Coverdale acts as the community's "Minor Poet" throughout the romance, Hollingsworth remains a "self-concentrated Philanthropist" intent on dominating both the "weakly Maiden" and the "high-spirited Woman." It is the most self-consciously theatrical member of the group, Zenobia, who eventually realizes how par-

ticipating in the Blithedale drama simply serves to aggrandize each
individual's ego. Throughout the romance Zenobia is acutely aware
of the inevitable artifice involved in forming an alternative society,
"a new arrangement of the world" (13) analogous to the first person's efforts to reorganize reality. Repeatedly reminding the minor
poet in particular that he is turning the affair into a ballad, Zenobia
frequently causes "our heroic enterprise to show like an illusion, a
masquerade, a pastoral, a counterfeit Arcadia, in which we grown-
up men and women were making a play-day of the years that were
given us to live in" (21). When Coverdale finally attempts to justify
his prying by alluding to his "uncertain sense of some duty to
perform" (170), Zenobia quickly reduces his pretentious sympathy
to "self":

> Bigotry; self-conceit; an insolent curiosity; a meddlesome temper;
> a cold-blooded criticism, founded on a shallow interpretation of
> half-perceptions; a monstrous scepticism in regard to any con-
> science or any wisdom, except one's own; a most irreverent pro-
> pensity to thrust Providence aside, and substitute one's self in its
> awful place—out of these, and other motives as miserable as these,
> comes your idea of duty! (170)

After she has been jilted by Hollingsworth, Zenobia levels a
similar but more damning charge against the Philanthropist:
"Are you a man? No; but a monster! A cold, heartless, self-be-
ginning and self-ending piece of mechanism! . . . It is all self! . . .
Nothing else; nothing but self, self, self! . . . You have embodied
yourself in a project" (218). Hollingsworth's particular blindness, Zenobia implies, lies in his inability to distinguish between
his philanthropic scheme and himself: personal identity becomes "embodied" and thus trapped by a mere idea or system,
which then seeks to absorb everything outside itself by breaking
down the "repellent self-defensive energy" (46) of other individuals. While the first person at least acknowledges that his narrative fancywork is partly a product of his imagination,
Hollingsworth is too self-engrossed to realize that his visionary
project for prison reform is also a symbolic scheme as insubstantial as the Blithedale enterprise itself.

It is not just Coverdale's "poetical" performance, then, that
breeds monstrous isolation in himself and others but the confining

roles that all the members of Blithedale assume to help fix their
identities for a community still in the process of being formed.
Whether these identities are largely self-imposed (as in the case of
Hollingsworth) or imposed by social convention (Zenobia's sense
of her limitations as a woman), the Blithedale enterprise—both the
community and Coverdale's plot—depends on the harmonious in-
tegration of its parts. Herein lies the particular significance of the
romance's Veiled Lady subplot, which is not only crucial for understanding the first person's relation to Priscilla, Zenobia, Westervelt, and Hollingsworth but also for understanding their relation
to one another. As I have suggested, the invocation to the Veiled
Lady in the romance's first chapter serves to orient Coverdale to
his task as narrator. When she reappears a few chapters later, now
under the guise of Priscilla, she fulfills the same office for the other
utopians. Before the mysterious girl arrives in the arms of Hollingsworth, Blithedale's "Knot of Dreamers" can vaguely speculate
on the prospects for their experimental enterprise. One unidentified member asks, "Have we our various parts assigned?" (16)—
a crucial question whose theatrical implications do not emerge until
Priscilla enters the scene through the "medium" (49) of Hollingsworth. His abrupt knock on the door generates the initial "dramatic
suspense" (25) by which Coverdale and the other characters will
subsequently become "entrapped" (29) in a narrative framework
or "Destiny" not of their own making. Blithedale's "first incident"
(29), the introduction of the strange "unsubstantial girl" (26) triggers the kind of speculation out of which plots are contrived: in
characteristic fashion Coverdale immediately fantasizes that she is
a mute snow-creature; Zenobia pointedly asks, "What does the girl
mean?" (28); while Hollingsworth concludes that "Providence has
sent her to us as the first fruits of the world . . . As we do by this
friendless girl, so shall we prosper!" (30). Possessing the Veiled
Lady's "prophetic solution" (the success or failure of the Blithedale
enterprise), Priscilla thus becomes "an object of peculiar interest"
(35) inspiring Coverdale/Hawthorne to construct a center of coherence for the Blithedale community—a surrogate family similar
to the miniature family construed by the first-person narrator from
his hotel window.

     People can weave a plot out of the seamstress's life because she
is so lifeless herself. As Coverdale reminds us with tedious repet-
itiveness, Priscilla is "unformed, vague, and without substance" (72)

when she first enters Blithedale, a "figure in a dream" (168), "out of the realm of Mystery" (115), who is as "impressible as wax" (78). According to "The Silvery Veil," a legend inspired by Zenobia's looking into Priscilla's eyes, the girl is in fact simply the "candlelight image of one's self" (108). The "enigma" of her identity thus allows people to invest her with their own significance, until they "absorb" (167) her life into their own egos. At the same time that she becomes the primary target for Coverdale to vent what he calls his "petty malice" (126), she also more importantly gives the frustrated bachelor a greater part to play—a "purpose in life" (133) that Hollingsworth accuses the artist of lacking. In order to solve Zenobia's question ("What does the girl mean?") Coverdale is obliged to turn the affair into a ballad complete with "supernatural machinery" (33). A will-less spirit for unveiling the truth about others, Priscilla defines Coverdale's particular duties as a narrator, while he in turn finds her "serviceable" (74) as a "delicate . . . instrument" (75) for fabricating his plot. If Coverdale is Hawthorne's sole medium, then Priscilla, or rather the Veiled Lady, becomes Coverdale's medium.

We are now in a better position to appreciate Coverdale's final, infuriating confession, which he rightly claims is "essential to the full understanding of my story" (247). Critics usually read Coverdale's blushing admission as simply a grotesque dislocation of desire from Zenobia to Priscilla, another sign of the first person's self-deceived lying. But as Zenobia suggests to Miles late in the romance, the poet's freedom "to make an opera-glass of your imagination" (170) will inevitably lead him to fall in love with the Veiled Lady/Priscilla, who is the only possible locus of desire for the romancer. Created in the image of her maker, Priscilla remains the artist's perfect subject, giving body to Coverdale's narration in direct proportion to her own lack of substance. In sacrificing Priscilla's personality for the sake of his plot, Coverdale thus admits his final allegiance to the act of narration, "the fancy–work with which I have idly decked her out!" (100). Invested with mystery, the seamstress allows the first person to spin his own translucent veil, the fancy-work by which he seeks to engage the Blithedale enterprise. Coverdale loves the heroine of his romance because without her there would be no story to tell, no role for the poet to perform within the utopian community.

Priscilla is the central instrument of mediation not only for Coverdale but for Blithedale's other men as well, who all use her

to further their competing schemes. Of particular interest here is
Westervelt, who serves to parody Coverdale's melodramatic efforts
to forge a plot. Before we actually meet the Professor, we feel his
presence through the medium of Priscilla whenever she responds
to a "distant voice" (75). Westervelt thus initially represents a powerful invisible agency in the romance, a counterplotter or master-
mind who continues to exercise the kind of spiritual influence over
Coverdale's characters that Coverdale himself can only pretend to
possess. Speculating that Westervelt's "evident knowledge of matters, affecting my three friends, might have led to disclosures, or
inferences that would perhaps have been serviceable" (96), the first
person looks for a "connecting link" (86) among his characters by
moving back and forth—from Priscilla to Westervelt to his secret
"wife" Zenobia to old Moodie—in order to imagine a source, some
buried past, that might explain the community's bonds of "familiar
love" (19). Without such a family romance, Coverdale (and Hawthorne) could not plot Blithedale's social dynamics.

Once Westervelt bodily enters the narrative, however, his claim
to omniscient authority is ruthlessly debunked as spirit-rapping
humbug common to the lyceum lecture circuit. Upstaged by Hollingsworth at the Village Hall, the Professor's "artifice" is brought
"more openly upon the surface" (199) during a performance that
echoes the book's opening chapter and Hawthorne's preface to the
romance preceding it. This final exhibition of the Veiled Lady
brings all of Hawthorne's own anxieties to the surface, allowing
him to share the same "horror and disgust" (198) his first-person
agent expresses during the spectacle. Before Westervelt begins his
entertaining spectacle, Coverdale overhears another member of the
audience recite a series of "stranger stories than ever were written
in a romance" (198), all of which coldly demonstrate how one human being could retain "a miraculous power . . . over the will and
passions of another," until "the individual soul was virtually an-
nihilated" (198). Reciting these weird tales as if they were simply
in "the category of established facts" (198), the unidentified storyteller thus immediately anticipates Westervelt's own performance, "a delusive show of spirituality, yet really imbued
throughout with a cold and dead materialism" (200). While the
Professor professes to link, by his sympathy, "soul to soul . . . into
one great mutually conscious brotherhood" (200), his modern-day
spiritual act is actually a cynical display of domination for its own

sake, the brutal violation of the Veiled Lady's selfhood. As soon as Westervelt's paint and pasteboard are revealed, however, his associationist sentiments are also exposed for what they really are: a mere conjurer's trick or cover for sheer power play. Undermining the sanctity of the individual, attractive theories of community thus become repulsive as soon as they are put into practice.

Insofar as Hawthorne and Coverdale demystify the basis for Westervelt's manipulation, author and narrator—being virtually identical here—unravel their own mutual show of plotting. The Veiled Lady romance works only if we assume that there are indeed some buried links among the characters, an association that just barely eludes the first person's grasp. Otherwise all the mysterious talk of "veils," "mediums," and "spirits" which Irving Howe and others so deplore would remain little more than a set of metaphors to schematize the nature of social and artistic mediation. Throughout the romance Coverdale has conceived of Blithedale's interpersonal relations in terms of a master/slave paradigm: Hollingsworth is a "bond-slave" to his all-consuming "visionary edifice" (55); Zenobia is a "bond-slave" (217) to Hollingsworth; while Priscilla is everybody's "bond-slave" or "servant" (33, 87, 115). Yet the Village Hall episode suggests the more frightening possibility that people can be slaves without clearly knowing their masters. Despite Coverdale's best efforts to weave a plot around the Veiled Lady, the principles governing the dynamics of the group remain hidden from view.

The problem is not that Westervelt's power is "miraculous" but that it is not miraculous enough, that there is no authentic transcendent agency controlling the community's affairs. Once the basis for social relations is no longer presumed as a given—neither a supernatural "fate" nor an enchanted family—the coherence of the Blithedale enterprise becomes problematic. What are these utopians doing together, and why does Hawthorne feel the need to give them something (a plot) in common?

An unsigned review of *The Blithedale Romance* which appeared the year the book was published (1852) addresses precisely this question:

> The analysis of the characters is so minute, that they are too thoroughly individualized for dramatic cooperation, or for that graduated subordination to each other which tends to give a har-

monious swell to the narrative, unity to the plot, and concentrated force to the issue. They are simply contemporaries, obliged, somehow, to be on familiar terms with each other, and even when coming into the closest relationship, seeming rather driven thereto by destiny, than drawn by sympathy . . . the main tendency is toward isolation—for the ruling faculty is analytic.[14]

A mere aggregation of "contemporaries obliged, somehow, to be on familiar terms with each other": such a devastating description applies equally well to the first person's inept plotting and the halfhearted efforts of Blithedale's various members to arrange themselves into a unified cooperative body. Intuitively collapsing the distinction between the act of narrating and the narrated action, the anonymous reviewer has seen how the book's aesthetic incoherence corresponds to the community's social incoherence. Threatened by annihilation, the modern-day "individual soul" either retreats into its own inviolable sphere or seeks to dominate other souls in order to expand the territory of the self. As a result, the Blithedale "theatre" turns into an arena for conflicting interests where people use one another for their own selfish purposes. The more Hawthorne and Coverdale try to imagine and analyze individual identity (what makes Hollingsworth so appealing to the women, for instance), the less able they are to understand the group, which becomes bound together solely by the supernatural machinery of Coverdale's imaginary fancywork. The mockery Hawthorne heaps on his first person's narrative folly can only partially disguise what is at stake for Hawthorne himself in the plotting; for the passive-voice construction of the romance's key question ("Have we our parts assigned?") suggests the author's own inability to comprehend who is in fact assigning these atomized roles and how they are being assigned.

In Hawthorne's first two romances, ordering interpersonal relations by way of a plot is not such a problem, because characters are already presumed to be organized by some authority outside the text. In the case of *The Scarlet Letter*, the Puritan community is defined by Hawthorne's sense of his past, while the secret family within that community is formed by the primal act of adultery that takes place before the narrative begins. As soon as we discover what the scarlet letter stands for, Hester, Dimmesdale, and Pearl are naturally drawn together to comprise a single social unit. Similarly,

the Maules and Pyncheons in *The House of the Seven Gables* relate
to one another as they do because of the pressure of genealogy,
which serves to confirm the nature of their interaction. In *The
Blithedale Romance*, however, there is no omniscient agency outside
the first person's present narration to help determine what his
characters have in common with one another; any common ground
or familiarity among individuals (literally "a great and general family" [128]) remains solely a function of Coverdale's self-conscious
plotting. And in Hawthorne's last completed romance, *The Marble
Faun*, this self-consciousness will become so intense that the only
experience which the creatures of the author's brain are able to
share with one another is the experience of art itself.

From one romance to the next, relations among persons become more and more an artificial function of plot for Hawthorne
because he finds more immediate forms of intimacy increasingly
threatening. Intimacy's threat to the "individual soul" is most apparent in *The Blithedale Romance* during the traumatic confrontation
between Hollingsworth and Coverdale, a scene largely made up of
dialogue which James the realist praised as "nothing better in all
Hawthorne."[15] The episode (chap. 15) is important for several interrelated reasons. First, it represents Coverdale's most intense engagement in his story as a character, not a commentator, who faces
his rival schemer without the benefit of any thick narrative screen.
Second, this "crisis" between the two men directly precipitates Coverdale's leave-taking from Blithedale, a departure which in turn
leads to the romance's long hallucinatory middle section—which
critics so often dismiss—from the first person's fantastic musings
in town to his return to Blithedale in the midst of a bewildering
masquerade. Third, and most important, the interaction between
blacksmith and minor poet most clearly shows the dangerously
oppressive power of personal presence. From the start of the romance, Coverdale has identified Hollingsworth as a "solid character" (7); it is during this scene, as the two men build a stone wall
between them, that Hollingsworth's solidity openly menaces the
first person's own sense of self.

Their interaction begins benignly enough. As is his wont, the
minor poet amuses himself by frivolously projecting into the future
to speculate that Blithedale's utopians will all become "mythical
personages" one day in an "Epic Poem" (129). Dismissing Cover-

dale's "fantastic anticipations" (130) as "nonsense" (129), Hollingsworth replies that the community's social experiment has no value
other than to offer the bachelor "a theme for poetry" (131). Only
by convincing Coverdale that the Blithedale enterprise has "no
substance whatever" (132) can Hollingsworth make a case for the
substance of his own imagined design for social reformation. Yet
it is not the rationality or practicality of Hollingsworth's scheme
which Coverdale finds so beguiling; rather, it is the way the philanthropist makes his appeal to him on personal grounds, arguing
that his project would give the idle poet some necessary "purpose
in life" (133). When this calculated appeal fails, Hollingsworth turns
to an even more intimate form of persuasion, pleading with Coverdale to join him simply to become "my friend of friends, forever"
(135). But Coverdale manages to oppose Hollingsworth's "tremendous concentrativeness and indomitable will" (135) by interpreting
his companion's appeal to friendship as a threat to his own "individual being" (135). On the verge of being subdued, Coverdale
musters "a strenuous exercise of opposing will" (136) to affirm the
distinctness of his identity.

     Coverdale is able to maintain his individuality against Hollings-
worth's "system" (131) because he conceives of their power struggle
in physical terms, as if his corporeal self were literally in danger
of being engulfed by another's body. Recounting their crisis, the
first person persistently describes the dynamics of domination and
submission as a material process:

> As I look back upon this scene, through the coldness and dimness
> of so many years, there is still a sensation as if Hollingsworth had
> caught hold of my heart, and were pulling it towards him with
> an almost irresistible force. It is a mystery to me, how I withstood
> it . . . Had I but touched his extended hand, Hollingsworth's mag-
> netism would perhaps have penetrated me with his own concep-
> tion of all these matters. But I stood aloof. (133–34)
>
> I never said the word ["No!"]—and certainly can never have it to
> say, hereafter—that cost me a thousandth part so hard an effort
> as did that one syllable. The heart-pang was not merely figurative,
> but an absolute torture of the breast . . . It seemed to me that it
> struck him, too, like a bullet. (135)
>
> And that was all! I should have been thankful for one word more,
> even had it shot me through the heart, as mine did him. (136)

The pair's disagreement about Blithedale's substantiality or in-substantiality is thus paralleled by the substantiality of their own intimate interaction, which achieves an overpowering kind of immediacy as soon as Coverdale gives it a literal basis. But even reified as magnetic "force," Hollingsworth's self-concentrated will still remains a mystery. Turning his back on the philanthropist to save himself, the first person implicitly turns his back on this sort of physical immediacy to save his plot. He leaves his characters, in other words, in order to gain some perspective from which to understand them. In the absence of such a disembodied perspective, individuals continue to dominate one another in ways that defy any transcendent explanation, just as Zenobia is ultimately fatally overwhelmed by Hollingsworth.

The threat of Hollingsworth's bodily presence to others (and to the philanthropist's own well-being) is part of a larger pattern of embodiment and disembodiment that affects every character in the romance. After bidding farewell to his Blithedale companions, Coverdale lingers perversely for a moment to take leave of the community's swine, four "greasy citizens" that become a part of this curious pattern: "They were involved, and almost stifled, and buried alive, in their own corporeal substance ... they dropped asleep again; yet not so far asleep but that their unctuous bliss was still present to them, betwixt dream and reality" (144).

Involved in their own corporeal substance, the Blithedale pigs suggest how self-engrossed individuals like Hollingsworth or the materialist Westervelt remain trapped by the roles they project for themselves. Coverdale, on the other hand, can dematerialize himself in order to "live in other lives" (160), just as he experiments with seeing the world through the eyes of old Moodie and Westervelt at various points in the romance. At the risk of giving up "my poor individual life, which was now attenuated of much of its proper substance, and diffused among many alien interests" (157), Hawthorne's first-person narrator thus denies his own personal sphere of influence so that he can mediate among the veiled egos of others. During his early sickness, for example, the minor poet quickly finds the Blithedale enterprise to be "an unsubstantial sort of business, as viewed through a mist of fever" (43). Yet as he becomes disembodied and reincarnated, ritually dies and is reborn, the "bodily faint-hearted" (44) narrator first experiences prophetic dreams, followed by "feverish fantasies" (45) that invite him to possess his characters' secrets. "A little beside himself" (45), as Hollingsworth skeptically remarks, the first person leaves his body to achieve a "species of intuition—either a spiritual lie, or the subtle recognition of a fact—which comes to us in a reduced state of the corporeal system" (46).

Faced with substantial, unmanageable characters like Hollingsworth, on the one side, and ethereal apparitions like the Veiled Lady, on the other, Coverdale must evasively maneuver between spiritual lies and all too solid facts if he hopes to comprehend the Blithedale enterprise. The romance's pairing of spiritualism with lying and materialism with oppressive, confining everyday actuality creates an impossible set of alternatives for Coverdale. The first person must either fantasize by himself or become trapped by an overpowering set of rigid master/slave relations. Despite the plotter's best efforts, the mental world, the province of the self, remains at odds with the physical or social world. As Leo Bersani has suggested, Coverdale's inability to establish some clear common ground between substance and insubstantiality derives from the problematic way that Hawthorne has conceived of romance in his preface.[16] Setting up a dubious dichotomy between "day-dream" and "fact," the author compels his first-person agent to negotiate between the two realms. A victim of Hawthorne's self-evasiveness as well as a representative of his deepest fears, Coverdale is doomed to graphic failure because Hawthorne's notion of romance makes "The Actual" and "The Imaginary" so discontinuous to begin with.

At bottom *The Blithedale Romance*'s peculiar incongruity or radical incoherence stems from Hawthorne's uncertainties about his own society, a sense which would eventually lead him sadly to confess to his old friend Franklin Pierce: "The Present, the Immediate, the Actual has proved too potent for me."[17] Lacking the kind of stable center of coherence given by the inherited scarlet letter and the Pyncheon house, Hawthorne now explicitly embraces the problems of the artist himself as his primary subject, "an apology for the absence of a hero," R. W. B. Lewis has noted, for any writer faced "with the shadowless fragmentations of the immediate scene."[18] In the case of *The Blithedale Romance*, these fragmentations amount to a complex set of power relations whose principles remain beyond the author's apprehension. Caught between his reverence for a vanished past and his hope for a still unrealized future, Hawthorne thus confronts the changing present with extreme ambivalence: although he can accept the modern notion of identity as personality, he also seems unwilling, unlike later literary realists, to dramatize social interaction without arriving at some first cause or hidden relation to control Blithedale's "theatre." Role playing is simply not good enough for the same reason that Hawthorne ultimately is not completely satisfied with self-referentially enacting the first person's problems as a narrator in the present. In both cases the individual ego—whether it belongs to a character like Hollingsworth within the fiction or to the artist without—threatens to overtake and petrify the imaginations of others, to rob them of their independent life. Hence Coverdale's Veiled Lady plotting, whose search for some shared experience expresses Hawthorne's conservative fears that contemporary harsh realities, both social and artistic, will spell the death of romance's capacity for enchantment.

Hawthorne's oppressive sense of the present makes itself felt most sharply during the romance's two odd interpolated stories, "The Silvery Veil" and "Fauntleroy," which are also the two most glaring signs of the narrative's lack of unity. Designed to "tie together the loose ends of the plot," the two tales "serve to conceal a larger incoherence," as Richard Brodhead has noted.[19] While the story Hawthorne inserted into the *Seven Gables* perfectly matches text to context, so that Holgrave's enthralling of Phoebe powerfully coincides with his ancestor's bewitching of Alice Pyncheon, *The Blithedale Romance*'s interpolated stories emerge out of contexts that are only peripherally linked to the content of the tales. Once again the act of narration and the narrated world are at odds with one another. By hinting at previously undisclosed facts that might help uncover the romance's true relations, each story serves to gloss a narrative which can no longer provide the terms to gloss itself. Whereas the stories themselves serve mainly to bolster a sagging plot structure, their dramatic contexts—a night of group entertainment at Blithedale and a crowded tavern in town—suggest the value of communal storytelling itself, its ability to bring isolated individuals together. There thus seems to be a fatal kind of crosspurpose at work in both Zenobia's and old Moodie's tales; for in addition to offering information and hard facts, the stories also function to restore enchantment to the romance. "The Silvery Veil" and "Fauntleroy" are literally meant to be read as "fairy tales" (186) set radically apart from Blithedale's contemporary scene. In the act

of telling, however, Hawthorne's awareness of the present gradually overwhelms the fairy tale, which is despiritualized into gross
materiality as soon as it is bodied forth, in much the same way that
"the wizard" Westervelt is despiritualized when he enters Blithedale
midway through the narrative.

Beginning on that clearly make-believe, "once-upon-a-time"
tremulous note, each "legend" ineluctably collapses into the present, as the author's ability to sustain enchantment becomes satu-
rated with doubt. Slipping from romance to realism, the "cheerless
fireside" so common to fairy tales abruptly becomes for Fauntleroy
"in truth, but only a rusty stove" (186). Names themselves undergo
telling transformations: the "Veiled Lady" suddenly turns into
"Priscilla" in the middle of Zenobia's story (and Theodore into
Coverdale by implication), while "Fauntleroy," his fairy-tale rich
"elder child," and poor younger "ghost-child," similarly give way
to the more mundane family trio "Moodie," "Zenobia," and "Priscilla." These striking nominal transformations correspond to
equally striking shifts in narrative perspective, particularly in the
case of old Moodie's tale. Like most fairy tales, "Fauntleroy" begins
in third-person omniscience that would seem to exclude the first
person's presence. But by the end of the legend Coverdale is back
in the picture again, obtrusively speculating on its meaning. This
shift from third to first person thus replays in miniature the course
of Hawthorne's literary career. As the first person imaginatively re-
constructs a private dialogue between Zenobia and her father, we
are left to wonder if old Moodie himself provided the "details of
the interview" or if Coverdale simply invented them for the sake
of "picturesqueness" (190). Indeed, when, a few pages earlier, the
narrator self-consciously catches himself in the midst of a fanciful
description of Westervelt to admit that "this was all absurdity" (188),
we would do well to consider who is supposed to be speaking now—
old Moodie, Coverdale, or Hawthorne? The epistemological problem of reference grows even more acute when the narrator goes
on to confess that Westervelt's character once "was even less understood than now, when miracles of this kind have grown so absolutely
stale, that I would gladly, if the truth allowed, dismiss the whole
matter from my narrative" (189). Reiterating the concerns of the
romance's preface—the contrast between the cheap, exploitative
theatrics of the present, as opposed to the enchanted, shared "mir-

acles" possible even in the recent past—that anxious, weary "I" surely belongs to Hawthorne as much as to Coverdale.

What makes *The Blithdale Romance* so fascinating—"the breakdown of Hawthorne's art, and its most remarkable achievement," to borrow Taylor Stoehr's fine phrase[20]—is the fact that despite Hawthorne's best efforts at self-concealment, at hiding behind Coverdale, his first-person agent allows him to doubt his own solutions, to confess his inability to restore enchantment to its proper place. While attempting to substantiate the imagination, to show how it possesses an actuality of its own, Hawthorne conversely means to dramatize how "the real world" is itself a symbolic structure that could be formed and reformed. But the sheer fictionality of the Veiled Lady and her cumbersome secret family serves to remind us that Blithedale's social and aesthetic coherence is provisional at best, depending as it does on the solitary musings of a speculative man. Seeing Hawthorne the romancer in Coverdale the minor poet, we can appreciate the author's willingness to have his literary experiment with the first person fail in precisely the same manner that Blithedale's social "experiment" (195) falls apart. And so we leave the lonely, middle-aged bachelor to stare into the smoldering embers of his fire, exquisitely aware of his own shortcomings. Left to his own devices, the first-person narrator tries to extract some significance from his experience in words which express Hawthorne's hope for the future of *his* Blithedale enterprise:

> Yet, after all, let us acknowledge it wiser, if not more sagacious, to follow out one's day-dream to its natural consummation, although, if the vision have been worth the having, it is certain never to be consummated otherwise than by a failure. And what of that! Its airiest fragments, impalpable as they may be, will possess a value that lurks not in the most ponderous realities of any practicable scheme. They are not the rubbish of the mind. (10–11)

3

The Jamesian Critical Romance

Turning to the first person to help him work out the meaning of romance, Hawthorne invents in Miles Coverdale a slippery stand-in who simultaneously manages to convey with uncanny accuracy the difficulties of storytelling and to make a perfect fool of himself in the process. Dramatizing the failure of Blithedale's enterprise—both the community and the plot—at the expense of his personal dignity, the minor poet allows Hawthorne to preserve his own shaky artistic integrity, but only by permitting the author to hide behind his surrogate's clownish ineptitude. In his landmark study *Hawthorne* (1879), Henry James recognized the doubleness of Coverdale's position, the complex relationship between the figure of the first person and the form of the romance. Discussing Hawthorne's participation in Brook Farm, James remarks:

> Miles Coverdale, in *The Blithedale Romance*, is evidently as much Hawthorne as he is any one else in particular. He is, indeed, not very markedly any one, unless it be the spectator, the observer; his chief identity lies in his success in looking at things objectively, and spinning uncommunicated fancies about them. This, indeed, was the part that Hawthorne played socially in the little community at West Roxbury. [1]

Yet when James turns from the writer's life to discuss the novels themselves in greater detail, this relatively untroubled equation between the author's "part" and his first person's identity is called into question: "The standpoint of the narrator has the advantage of being a concrete one; he is no longer, as in the preceding tales, a disembodied spirit, imprisoned in the haunted chamber of his own contemplations, but a particular man, with a certain human grossness" (128–29).

How can "a particular man with a certain human grossness" still remain "not very markedly any one"? The answer lies in James's understanding of Coverdale's unique status in the novel as "the spectator," so that what he sees strictly determines who he is. While James tends to evaluate the other characters in the novel according to the standards of psychological realism, he links Coverdale's "success" to his function as a narrator who can look at things "objectively" and spin "fancies" about them. Realizing in the minor poet Coverdale the special claims that authorship makes on the author, James thus appreciates how the first person's identity cannot help but be "lightly indicated" (129), his bodily presence obscured by the story he is trying to see and tell. His perspective may therefore be "concrete" even though he himself is not.

A portrait of the artist as medium, Coverdale is less a complex personality for James than the typification of a certain attitude toward other people. James sums up this attitude when he voices the complaint of Hawthorne's contemporaries that the author came to Brook Farm as "an intellectual vampire, for purely psychological purposes" (85). Playing the part of "half a poet, half a critic and all a spectator" (129), Coverdale thus stands for a host of artist/vampire figures who crop up just as often in James's fiction as in Hawthorne's. As has been amply documented, both Hawthorne and James are fascinated by the tendency of the imagination to feed vicariously off of others, until experience simply becomes the raw material for art;[2] in this respect, Coverdale clearly served as a model for the "lightly indicated" first-person narrators James turned to during a period of crisis and experimentation late in his own career. As I will be arguing, the nameless agents narrating *The Aspern Papers,* "The Figure in the Carpet," and *The Sacred Fount* all carry the implications of Coverdale's voyeurism to its logical extreme by showing how the urge to pry into the lives of others exempts these first persons from living themselves.

Despite the obvious affinity here between James and Hawthorne, however, these late first-person narrators of James perhaps have more in common with Poe's undifferentiated speakers than with Coverdale (a character whose very name, after all, essentially corresponds to his behavior). This connection between Poe and James may seem a bit surprising, since James professed to scorn Poe throughout most of his career.[3] Yet in *Hawthorne*, to return for a moment to that early study, James curiously mixes his contempt with praise in a key passage which significantly is the only extended discussion in the critical biography of an American writer other than Hawthorne. Calling Poe's judgments "pretentious, spiteful, and vulgar" (62), James nonetheless goes on to quote with approval the criticism Poe levels against Hawthorne for relying on allegory. What bothers both Poe and James about allegory is its tendency, in James's words, to spoil "a meaning and a form" (62). Or, as Poe observes "if allegory ever establishes a fact, it is by dint of overturning a fiction" (63). Overtly directing the reader to some abstract reference outside the narrative, allegory for Poe and James thus violates a text's air of self-sufficiency and self-containment, the impression that it is a world unto itself. This illusion of self-enclosure, the comments of Poe and James imply, can be sustained only if the author carefully attends to the stringent requirements of his fictional form.

Elsewhere in his study James emphasizes Hawthorne's "extreme amenity of form" (128) while attempting to apologize for his own habit of referring to Hawthorne's novels as "charming"—a condescending adjective that James admits to being "vague [and] unanalytic" (128). But the phrase "amenity of form" may simply be James's polite way of chiding Hawthorne for his uneconomical plotting, that is, his relative inattention to the rigorous logic of tale-telling. That is, "romance," for Hawthorne is primarily a conceptual category, not a literary form; it seeks to describe a fluctuating relation between the author's fiction-making and his sense of reality, but it does so without insisting that the artist's imagination must conform to some strict epistemological order. While he does, in the *Seven Gables* preface, allow that romance "must rigidly subject itself to laws," these laws, in turn, must obey a higher authority, "the truth of the human heart." Hawthorne thus moves from problems of fictional form to return to the more nebulous sphere of personal psychology, a domain that largely depends on the assumed inviolability and autonomy of the individual ("truth under circumstances . . . of the writer's own choosing"). Although representation is certainly a problem for Miles Coverdale, riddled as he is by failed conjecture and personal rebuff, the first person's attempt to find some enchanted center of coherence at Blithedale is a leisurely affair; unconcerned with his narrative's maddening missing links and flagrant loose ends (symptoms of the disintegrating relations within the community itself), Coverdale is not driven by the kind of singularity of purpose that spurs Poe's obsessed first persons, who are intently bent on perfection. Given the amorphous nature of his subject, James thus cannot help but use vague and unanalytic critical terms to describe Hawthorne's plots.

As we shall see, James, like Poe, is more sensitive than Hawthorne to the disciplining pressure of literary form, what William Carlos Williams called "the harder structural imperatives" when he singled out Poe's method for praise. In particular, I am interested in the way that both Poe and James realize how first-person plotting can, in effect, define a self and not vice versa. For both Poe and James, moreover, the alternative to form's coercion would seem to be sheer formlessness, a dreaded state that threatens to dissolve the first person's sense of self altogether. To anchor that identity, the Jamesian narrator must therefore pursue himself by latching onto another, not a two-dimensional double, as in the case of Poe, but a richer mystery of equally singular focus which could simultaneously help embody the otherwise anonymous "I" and originate the perfect plot. To help establish a context for these highly schematic first-person narratives of detection—the relationship they bear structurally to Poe's tales of analytic retrogradation and thematically to Hawthorne's treatment of artistic voyeurism in *The Blithedale Romance*—I will first turn to James's 1907–9 critical prefaces to examine his own remarks about the difficulty of making fiction, especially his understanding of the formal demands that storytelling makes on the storyteller.

I

Thirty-two years after the initial publication of *Roderick Hudson*, Henry James seized the occasion of the novel's appearance in the New York Edition to reappraise his youthful work. Looking back on his first large-scale endeavor, the mature novelist is filled with a curious mixture of pride and embarrassment. Noting that "experience has to organise . . . some system of observation—for fear . . .

of losing its way,"[4] James fondly recalls the exhilaration he initially felt as an ambitious but terrified young writer bravely facing the novelist's "perpetual predicament": the struggle to invent or find a fictional form that could accommodate, through "surrender and sacrifice," a hopelessly entangled set of relations which in reality "stop nowhere" (AN, 5). As soon as James begins to examine the particulars of the book's execution, however, the author's pleasing memories of his once enthusiastic aspirations quickly give way to a more self-critical discussion of the novel's glaring weaknesses. What might appear to constitute the book's most intensely felt elements, in fact, are precisely those which the accomplished novelist finds most dissatisfying: the pale opening scenes set in New England, Hudson's abrupt fall and disintegration, and the sculptor's passion for his compatriot Mary Garland. Choosing a subject too close to home—the fate of the American artist in Europe—the young James lets himself become overwhelmed by its immense personal implications. Despite the professed grandeur of his hero's sufferings, "poor Roderick" ultimately remains "beyond our sympathy," James retrospectively realizes, because the novel's organization fails to achieve that "certain factitious compactness" (AN, 15) which could give the artist's catastrophic experience a more balanced sense of proportion.

What "really save[s]" *Roderick Hudson* and keeps the novel from immediately sinking into vapid self-indulgence, according to James, is the attending presence of Hudson's companion, Rowland Mallet, whose consciousness remains the "principle of composition" or "point of command" that governs the entire drama. If the artist Hudson is a dismal failure, the critic Mallet is a smashing success. The first in a long series of Jamesian spectator figures, Mallet serves to frame and enclose Hudson's experience and to act as a "clear medium" representing the sculptor's condition with greater objectivity than the sculptor could himself. Dividing his sensibility into two distinct parts—passionate artist and passive witness—James uses Mallet ironically to counterpoint a romantic subject which does not possess the means to restrain itself. Mallet's sympathetic mediation thus comes to assume narrative control in the book, filtering, shaping, and revising the artist's agony in much the same way James described the novelist as hammering out and arranging experience into some design of "factitious compactness" (AN, 15). Applauding his beginner's luck by intuitively choosing Mallet as a center of coherence, the mature James reaffirms his lifelong commitment to a literary form that could remain both objective and intimate.

If we turn from James's own explanation of *Roderick Hudson* to the novel itself, however, we see that Hudson's failure as a fictional creation and Mallet's success as a filtering medium are not separate issues, as James might have them, but directly depend on each other. The sculptor falls to pieces so rapidly because his author quickly loses interest in him, as if James suddenly realized midway through the book that Mallet, not Hudson, was his true subject. "Poor Roderick" is thus sacrificed to make Mallet's probing critical intelligence come to life. By endowing Mallet with a personality in his own right, whose desires and motives interfere with Hudson's (their mutual love for Mary Garland, for instance), James lets the sculptor dissolve into a thin caricature of the suffering romantic artist. Hudson becomes too thickly screened, or depersonalized, by Mallet's "systematic" apprehension. Even though Mallet does not actually tell the story, his analytic presence comes to govern the novel's action. What we may gain in objectivity about the artist we lose in intimacy, while our deepening intimacy with the critical observer is purchased at the expense of his objectivity. As soon as Mallet begins to act as an independent character as well as a surrogate narrator, his "clear medium" starts to grow clouded.

While James's allegiance to Mallet underscores the novelist's need for some disciplining perspective to put the artist's own sense of self into a more comprehensive context, the fatal cross-purposes at work in *Roderick Hudson* point to the hazards of introducing such a narrative perspective. As James's discussion of form in the novel's preface suggests, the fundamental problem is that representation can never be presentation; a story can never tell itself but must be actively organized and arranged by someone, whether it be a disinterested, godlike outsider (like the narrative stance assumed by Flaubert in his fiction), an intrusive omniscient author (like Fielding or Trollope), or the consciousness of a character acting in the fiction. With only partial success, James invokes Mallet's critical presence in order to have it both ways, to work simultaneously from within and without.

Narration is more than a technical issue for James. In the critical prefaces the novelist repeatedly returns to the difficulty of compressing life's endless "canvas" (AN, 5) into a more constricted medium because such an act of ordering bears directly on a more crucial set of concerns: the nature of an engaged writer's immersion in his writing; the possibility of expressing experience in fiction; and the relation between how a story is made and who makes it. The various technical aspects of composition James addresses in his prefaces—"picture" versus "scene"; the art of revision; the struggle against "lurking forces of expansion" (AN, 42); the unavoidable gap between intention and execution; the dangers of "the mere muffled majesty of irresponsible 'authorship' " (AN, 327–28)—suggest the mysterious way in which fictional representation is intimately linked to fundamental questions of identity and authenticity. Narration, Steven Gilman notes, is "precisely that element of fiction which coerces and degrades it into a mere alternative to life, *like* life, only better of course, a dream (or a serviceable nightmare), a way out, a recompense, a blueprint, a lesson."[5] Quoting Gilman, Lionel Trilling goes on to make explicit what remains implicit throughout James's criticism: "A chief part of the inauthenticity of narration would seem to be its assumption that life is susceptible of comprehension and thus of management. It is the nature of narration to explain; it cannot help telling how things are and even why they are that way."[6] The "story of one's story" (AN, 313) recounted in each of the critical prefaces, then, traces James's search for a narrative form to reproduce "the authenticity of concrete existence" (AN, 311–12) without distorting or explaining it, as the figure of Rowland Mallet tends to explain Hudson away.

To appreciate the difficulty of James's self-imposed task, we need only glance at *The Awkward Age*, a late work curiously resembling *Roderick Hudson*, which radically tries to circumvent fiction's inevitable distortions by dispensing with narration altogether. In his preface to the work James complains about the storyteller's convention of creating his fictional world by authoritative commentary, what he calls the habit of " 'going behind.' " Objectivity becomes compromised whenever the novelist succumbs to the urge to enter into his plot through explanation and amplification, "to drag out odds and ends" as "aids to illusion" (AN, 111). Why not allow characters to speak for themselves and let the hidden dramatist's overriding commitment to architecture alone structure the action? But novels are not plays, James realizes, however closely they may approach the pure presentation of drama. As in the preface to *Roderick Hudson*, James once again calls attention to the "sacrifice" by which the authorial "critic" or "outsider" translates "real things" into the illusory "terms" of fiction (AN, 103). Carefully "covering ... my tracks" in *The Awkward Age*, James succeeds in achieving "guarded objectivity" for the novel, only to cut off his rich emotional experience of composing the book from the book itself. What James gains in objectivity he loses in intimacy, since his experimental attempt at narrative self-erasure removes "any conceivable or calculable form" for the writer to "cast myself" (AN, 108). The result is a brilliant performance of great power in which the author disappears into his character's talk, just as this ever-expanding talk comes to represent and finally replace each actor's sense of self. James's willing sacrifice of contact with his story thus rehearses the subject of the novel—the designed dissolution of personal intimacy and individual consciousness into pure acts of speaking and witnessing. But while the characters at least have their own speech in the fiction, their author virtually has none.

Trying to account for the "general and complete disrespect" (AN, 108) with which the reading public greeted *The Awkward Age*, James admits in the preface that his "ingenious labour" might have been a bit too ingenious, his secret plan too "artfully dissimulated" (AN, 108). In the absence of any tangible figure or central perspective helping to organize the novel's action from within, James retrospectively notes that the reader may fail to connect with the fiction. He anticipates this failure in the book itself by attributing surface details of his character's features and gestures to the perception of some presumed spectator who invisibly oversees the novel's drawing room conversations ("The acute observer we are constantly taking for granted would perhaps have detected in her ... "[7]). While Rowland Mallet is given too much corporeality in *Roderick Hudson* to be able to maintain an objective point of view, the bloodless spectator who haunts *The Awkward Age* is perhaps of too ethereal a substance for us to share vicariously in the unnarrated dialogue he coldly registers.

This is James's predicament: to make his presence intimately felt in the fiction (and thereby acknowledge his responsibility for creating it) without allowing the narrative presence to dominate the novel's action. Refusing to take the authority behind his act of authorship for granted, James refuses to assume the godlike stance of a puppeteer above and beyond the world of his fiction. His well-known disparagement of Trollope best expresses his distrust of irresponsible omniscience.[8] But try as he might to confine the action of his dramas to surface presentation, James also recognizes (in the preface to *The Awkward Age*) that some interpretive "going behind" or contextualizing is inescapable. As the examples of *The Awkward Age* and *Roderick Hudson* show, characters in fiction can neither constitute themselves nor interact with one another without some outside organizing perspective to objectify each individual consciousness. Throughout his critical prefaces James repeatedly refers to consciousness as a "vessel," a term which suggests how for James the imagination must be given some tangible shape.[9] Only insofar as they are formally contained are James's agents free to realize their personhood. Without such formal containment, relations remain endless and endlessly tangled. To find narrative boundaries for the novel thus becomes a way to bind and identify the discrete selves within as well as to help demarcate the author's own self without.

For James this relation between self and fiction is rendered most problematic in the first-person form of narration, the clearest alternative to omniscience. Merging consciousness and narration, first-person discourse might appear to offer the perfect escape from the torments of execution. By delegating responsibility for recording the "authenticity of concrete existence" to an agent acting in the fiction, the writer is no longer compelled to coerce and explain from the outside. Yet it is precisely this tendency to dissolve "certain precious discriminations," most notably inside and outside, which bothers James about this "form foredoomed to looseness" (AN, 320). In his critical preface to *The Ambassadors* he goes on to discuss why he does not allow his "central figure" Strether "all the subjective 'say,' as it were, to himself" (AN, 320). Although the decision to deny Strether his subjective "say" by writing in the third person may strike us as inconsequential, since James is always so close to his center of consciousness anyway, it is this very closeness which raises two interrelated problems.

The first "menace" (AN, 320) concerns the relation between Strether and his own experience. Making Strether "at once hero and historian," simultaneously "subject and object" (AN, 320), would invite chaos by forcing the central unifying figure to simultaneously play two contradictory roles, namely, organizing narrator (recall Rowland Mallet) and suffering actor (Roderick Hudson). Allegiance to the plot would grow confused and diffused with allegiance to self, James suggests, because self-narration permits no agency outside the "I" to set its limits and thereby define this "I."

Boundaries cannot be constructed from within; the first person's attempt at self-authentication produces what James elsewhere calls a "usurping consciousness" (AN, 90) which blindly and irresponsibly sprawls in the fiction without any controlling authority. To sustain a context for his experience, therefore, Strether must be "encaged and provided for" (AN, 321) by James's own act of narration, which preserves discriminations by centering the intermediary figure in the fiction while maintaining an objective perspective outside it. Distinct from author ("I") and reader ("you"), the third-person Strether ("he") serves to maintain the boundaries of the text, the fictional world of the novel whose relationship to the artist's "real" world is the main issue raised by the critical prefaces.[10]

James relies on third-person contextuality not only to preserve the integrity of his central figure but also to preserve the distinction between himself and his fiction—a distinction in jeopardy precisely because he is so intimately engaged in his writing. Just as Strether must adopt a peculiarly diffident attitude toward his experience as a means of seeing his way through life's muddlement without succumbing to it, so must his author guard against first-person narration's "terrible *fluidity* of self-revelation" (AN, 321): the collapse of his own experience of writing into the "I" of his fictional deputies. These agents serve the author's purpose only insofar as their minds remain discrete objects of analysis isolated from James's own emotions. Once a storyteller admits an "I," according to James, he is plunged into "the darkest abyss of romance" (AN, 320), unbounded subjectivity. Fiction is sustained by the faith that it refers to a world outside the self, a middle ground between writer and reader; merging self with fiction, first-person narration removes this ground for objective mediation.[11]

James's explicit identification of first-person form as "romance" helps us to see that the discriminations he seeks to preserve in the novel are primarily epistemological. His famous preface to *The American* defines the preferred genre of his literary predecessors Poe and Hawthorne not by its subject matter but by its uncertain subjectivity: whereas "the real represents to my perception the things we cannot possibly *not* know . . . [the] romantic stands . . . for the things that . . . we never *can* directly know; the things that can reach us only through the beautiful circuit and subterfuge of our thought and desire" (AN, 31–32). Fiction written in the first person is intrinsically romantic for James because it fatally lacks any authorial context, giving us instead "experience disengaged, disem-

broiled, disencumbered, exempt from the conditions that we usually know to attach to it" (AN, 33). The "disengaged" quality that
James finds in romance applies equally well to the first-person form,
for in both cases any positive apprehension of the external world
remains subordinated to subjective thought and desire. Trying both
to verify an identity and to situate that identity in some ordered
sequence of action (a plot), the first person brings imagination into
intimate contact with existence, yet also obscures any authentic
knowledge of that life.

Unlike first-person narration, third-person storytelling automatically provides a means of discriminating between an "encaged"
character's awareness of events and the language used to convey
that awareness. In his critical preface to *What Maisie Knew*, James
ponders the crucial question raised by that book's title. Maisie can
experience corruption yet remain in a state of unadulterated innocence because as the author's "vessel of consciousness" she is
allowed "many more perceptions" than "terms to translate them"
(AN, 143, 145). "Constantly attend[ing] and amplify[ing]" Maisie's
vision, the author's "own commentary" becomes a kind of guardian
to the girl more responsible than those actual adult guardians who
remain "embalmed in her wonder" (AN, 146). Observation is therefore not contaminated by narration. We certainly may doubt the
success of James's experiment, since the incongruity between Maisie's "infant mind" and his own dense prose is perhaps too radical
to constitute knowledge of any convincing sort. But the preface's
insistence on distinguishing the author's terms of telling from his
agents' experience suggests how important it is for James to hold
the writer's special medium in reserve. "Life being all inclusion and
confusion," he notes in preface to *The Spoils of Poynton*, "and art
being all discrimination and selection," the novelist redeems
"clumsy Life" by a "sublime economy" which systematically trans-
mutes "splendid waste" into hardened representation (AN, 120–
21).

Simultaneously shaping a story and acting in it, the first-person
narrator tends to blur crucial discriminations between "art" and
"life." Rather than equating the terms, James means to keep them
rigorously analogous—two distinct but inseparable kinds of experience.[12] This analogy is elaborated throughout the critical prefaces
in two ways. First, James connects his worldly affairs as a writer
with his art by obsessively tracking down each narrative's originat-

ing "germ" or first cause—an overheard anecdote or actual conversation from which his novels grew into discrete objects. Second,
James associates his adventures during the act of composition (its
"thrilling ups and downs" [AN, 319]) with the life of his fictional
characters by dwelling on a predominant emotion common to both
(usually joy, bewilderment, or pain). But the question of form in
the novel, as we have seen, consistently leads James to epistemological and ontological problems. As he recounts each "story of
one's story," the boundaries he hopes to maintain begin to break
down, for the critical prefaces *themselves* constantly remind us of a
shadowy "I" that lurks behind every work of fiction he wrote. Identifying his own procreative labors with the passions and labors of
his characters, the novelist-turned-reader speaks in his own voice
to "track my uncontrollable footsteps, right and left, after the fact"
(AN, 328). To "live and breathe and rub shoulders" with his "bleed-
ing participants," James suggests in his last critical preface (to *The
Golden Bowl*), the writer must account for "the creative power otherwise so veiled and disembodied" (AN, 328, 327). Occupying the
common ground between novels and novelist, the critical prefaces
become a kind of conscience for James's texts, exposing the authority and anguish—the compositional "lapses and compromises,
simplifications and surrenders" (AN, 126)—hidden within.

As in Hawthorne and Poe, the first person in James thus
emerges most clearly as a *critical* presence monitoring the relation
between self and fiction; whereas the 1907–9 prefaces perform this
analytic function retrospectively, James finally admits, while discussing *The Golden Bowl*, his "accepted habit" of inserting into the
shorter works themselves[13] a peculiar sort of intermediary "witness
or reporter . . . who contributes to the case mainly a certain amount
of criticism and interpretation of it." Like the elusive figure of the
author in his prefaces, this "imagined observer" is "not strictly
involved, though thoroughly interested and intelligent." The interplay between the story's "minor" poet and the events in the
fiction becomes a way for James to dramatize his own strained
interaction with his materials (AN, 327–28). With varying degrees
of self-exposure, the author thus risks unveiling his creative power
in these confessional works in order to test the limits of narration,
that is, to display and exaggerate, however ironically on occasion,
the dangers his art posed for any authentic engagement with life.

Once the "impersonal author's concrete deputy or delegate"

(AN, 327) enters a story as its narrator, however, the tale he tells may simply turn out to be his author's own. In the absence of clear epistemological boundaries, James threatens to fall headfirst into his fiction; to express the novelist's interest in his work, his "confessed agent" must therefore remain an "unnamed, unintroduced, and . . . unwarranted participant" (AN, 327). This absolutely crucial insistence on anonymity for his first-person commentators enables James to protect his own impersonality in the face of the form's terrible fluidity of self-revelation.[14] Acting as the "convenient substitute or apologist for the creative power" (AN, 327), the Jamesian "I" thus functions as a sort of nameless generic narrator who registers the effects of that creativity without revealing the author directly. As we shall see, James is particularly sensitive to the way in which first-person discourse is always motivated, how it continually gestures to its own emergence as discourse.[15] But such motivation must be drained of personality and denied a psychological basis if the author is to shield himself from his critical intelligence at work in the fiction. To the degree that his first-person narrators are deprived of personhood, they live solely by their acts of analysis; and to that degree they bring extravagantly into relief the problems such analysis raises in trying to mediate between experience and imagination.

Turning from theoretical issues to empirical evidence, it should come as no surprise to discover that despite his misgivings James did, in fact, write a number of first-person tales, and that the narrators of several of these stories are explicitly identified as critics whose sense of self in each case strictly depends on the objects of their analysis.[16] Directly anticipating the "I" who haunts the critical prefaces, these fictional first persons of the late 1880s and 1890s use the same vocabulary to describe their literary quests that James would later use to define his compositional procedures—terms for detection (hunting, sniffing, looking for clues, following leads) and plotting (theorizing, appropriating, building). In the pages that follow, I will be analyzing a sequence of three such first-person narratives that help pave the way for James's late phase: *The Aspern Papers* (1888), "The Figure in the Carpet" (1896), and *The Sacred Fount* (1901).

In all three stories, the narrator is a solitary bachelor who obsessively interprets telltale traces of a hidden source of creativity that promises to give him access to some esoteric knowledge: a poet's private papers; a novelist's secret figure; a community's sacred fount. Defined solely by this all-consuming search, the nameless "I" telling each tale possesses no personal identity apart from his function as commentator; all the storyteller's energies are condensed into a single compulsive act, the Poe-like obsession to keep on narrating and explaining in the midst of great confusion. Insofar as these first persons play the part of critics, they remain exempt from experience by virtue of trying to gloss it and give it some form. From one story to the next, I will be arguing, these narrators become more and more "unindividualised" (AN, 329)—to use James's own term—just as the secrets that they are trying to detect grow increasingly elusive and intangible. As the secret under scrutiny becomes more metaphorical (changing from a bundle of letters to life's "sacred fount"), the first person's plotting also becomes progressively more internalized, until the "sacred fount" can achieve any sense of actuality in the fiction only through the representation of its pursuit. As the act of narration begins to supplant its own object, moreover, criticism and authorship, as forms of writing, become virtually identical. (For example, is the narrator of *The Sacred Fount* a figure for the possessed novelist or the equally possessed reader?) And as artist and critic come to resemble one another, I argue later in this study, James's notion of marriage becomes more and more central to each tale, a subject seemingly unrelated to the author's formal concerns. As we shall see, however, marriage for James represents a state of perfect union simultaneously containing identity and difference that both transcends and depends on the first person's own act of telling. Although James's relation with his first-person bachelors varies in intimacy from tale to tale, in all of these works marriage remains a crucial force shaping the narration.

II

By way of introduction, it may be helpful to examine briefly "The Author of Beltraffio," a first-person story from James's middle period (1884) which tentatively raises the same problem that would so preoccupy James in his later first-person narratives: the conse-

quences of confounding art with life. Like the later works, "The
Author of Beltraffio" is narrated by an anonymous bachelor whose
identity comes to depend on the action he observes and interprets.
This "young American of critical pretensions"[17] visits the house of
the author Mark Ambient in order to become intimate with the
"greatest of living writers" (16). For Ambient's young admirer, the
writer's latest novel, *Beltraffio*, is "the most complete presentation
... of the gospel of art," an "aesthetic war-cry" championing "art
for art" (4). Under the spell of the author's work, experience has
meaning for the worshiping first person only insofar as it resembles
art: "That was the way many things struck me at that time, in
England—as reproductions of something that existed primarily in
art or literature. It was not the picture, the poem, the fictive page,
that seemed to me a copy; these things were the originals, and the
life of happy and distinguished people was fashioned in their image
(8)." Like Poe's Gothic house of Usher, Ambient's cottage, "glorified
and translated" by the narrator's aesthetic sensibility, becomes a
self-sufficient "palace of art" (8). To know Ambient personally, the
narrator naively assumes, would give him access to the transcendent
realm of his writing.

Once inside the writer's "palace of art," however, the narrator/
critic encounters a number of disturbing "signs" which call into
question his romantic assumptions about the primacy and purity
of the creative imagination. The stage is explicitly set for a series
of inward doublings after the fashion of "Usher": first-person companion, the artist Ambient, and Ambient's weird sister, identified
as his "ghost[ly]" "imitation" (25). But what we get instead is a
slightly sordid domestic comedy. As he grows familiar with the
mundane details of Ambient's life, the outsider is led to the "shock-
ing surmise" (11) that this "being organised for literature" (41) is
not even master of his own palace. Ambient is, in short, a "hen-
pecked" husband subject to the will of an unsympathetic wife who
refuses to believe that she is "living in one of his [Ambient's] books"
(17), as the narrator who lives only for art would have it.

For the remainder of his story the young critic focuses on the
power struggle between husband and wife to possess the sole product of his marriage, a beautiful but sickly boy who, Mrs. Ambient
fears, is being poisoned by his father's immoral aestheticism. Persistently likening the child to "some perfect little work of art" (21),
the narrator seeks to reconcile the couple and save the fragile boy

by giving the wife the manuscript of her husband's new novel. As he relinquishes the role of passive observer to assume a more active "obtrusive and designing" (58) role in his own narrative, however, the first person's "vision" of concord dissolves; for instead of becoming more appreciative of her husband's art, Mrs. Ambient reacts by shielding the boy from his father altogether, finally letting the innocent victim die to keep him from growing up under the writer's influence. Only after their son is gone does the grieving wife begin to read and understand her husband's work.

Caught in a stark conflict between pagan and Christian values, the plotting narrator/critic thus sets in motion a strange sort of economy which will reappear, with increasing complexity, in James's later first-person parables. One kind of evanescent work of procreation, the son, is "sacrificed" (71) so that the unfeeling wife can be "converted" (73) to another kind of beauty, her husband's literature. The fruits of worldly marriage are destroyed to enable another form of intimacy to flourish: the passionate intercourse between writer and reader. Despite the narrator's folly in thinking that perfect art can dictate a perfect life, and despite his inability to comprehend the relation between husband and wife, the young bachelor/critic does manage to effect some kind of compensation or aesthetic conversion after all, horribly ironic as it may seem.

Contrasting two forms of union, sexual and aesthetic, as well as schematizing their interplay, "The Author of Beltraffio" suggests possibilities about the relation between art and experience that James would explore more fully in many of his subsequent stories. In "The Beast in the Jungle," for instance, James suggests how life and love may be obsessively renounced not for art but only for an idea falsely resembling art, while a tale like "The Lesson of the Master" offers a more ambiguous, though perhaps equally false, set of choices for an aspiring young writer who must decide between an all-consuming dedication to literature and an equally passionate commitment to marriage. James's first-person tales present a special case of this conflict by denying the narrator/critic access to *both* art and experience so that he may tell his story. But in "The Author of Beltraffio" the narrator's stance in relation to this tension between life and letters is worked out only inchoately. The modulation from comedy to tragedy is too sudden and the wife's measures too drastic for the action which precedes her fatal decision. Similarly,

if the price she pays to become her husband's reader strikes us as
too high, so the first-person's own role in the affair seems insuf-
ficiently developed. A clear target of satire, he also plays the part
of a quester hoping to gain a privileged understanding of the artistic
process. But the concrete object of his quest remains unspecified
throughout the story. Beginning with *The Aspern Papers*, however,
written four years after "The Author of Beltraffio," James would
more carefully define the first-person narrator's role as a professional critic who mediates between the artist's secret world and the
public world of social experience.

The Aspern Papers follows the pattern of "The Author of Beltraffio": a prying first-person bachelor probes into the domestic
situation of a famous writer in order to learn secondhand how
passion can be transformed into art. Unlike James's earlier story,
however, the godlike artist of *The Aspern Papers* is absent from the
tale, being long dead, while the specific object of the critic's search
is ever present but hidden—a set of private love letters from the
poet Jeffrey Aspern to his still living mistress which the narrator
hopes to edit and publish for the world to share. Again, the assumption is that the revelation of the artist's biographical details,
his personal life, will shed light on his immortal writing. While the
"young American of critical pretensions" in "The Author of Beltraffio" goes about his business openly, the more experienced literary investigator of *The Aspern Papers* works by subterfuge. The
first person's artifice, in fact, is essential to his story. As we have
seen, narration in the first person is intrinsically duplicitous, creating a confusion of identity between the roles of engaged actor
and disengaged observer. Acting as an "editor"[18] in his story, as
well as the bold editor or narrative arranger of it, the scheming "I"
of *The Aspern Papers* presents one face to his fellow characters and
another to the readers who eagerly follow his secret machinations.
Near the beginning of his story, the first person freely admits his
own doubleness, remarking that "hypocrisy, duplicity are my only
chance" (12) if he is to possess the papers that he desires with self-
proclaimed "monomania" (5). To foreground this hypocrisy, James
introduces one Mrs. Prest, adviser and accomplice, who, along with
James's readers, is immediately taken into the first person's "confidence" (3), a word which powerfully resonates from the very first
sentence throughout the remainder of the tale.

The editor's confidence game proceeds by ingratiating himself
into the Venetian household of two lonely and obscure American

spinsters, Miss Tina and Miss Juliana Bordereau, niece and aunt, respectively, the elder of whom was long ago loved (and perhaps jilted) by the critic's hero, the great American original Jeffrey Aspern. The facts of the woman's affair with Aspern are limited to vague rumors supported by speculative readings of the poet's love lyrics themselves—a situation the curious narrator hopes to remedy by publishing the artist's private papers. In order to "become an intimate" (3) of Aspern's former lover, the first person decides to gain the niece's trust and sympathy, to exploit her "susceptibility to human contact" (21). His "experiment" (35) in confidence depends on "making my entertainer believe me an undesigning person" (20). This pose would enable him to pretend to "make love to the niece" (14), as he jokes to his confidante, Mrs. Prest. Assuming a "feigned name" (14), the imposter gradually discloses to his readers the details of his masquerade, how he contrives to respond "ingenuously" (17) to Miss Tina, or to "feign amazement" (20) at will. The first-person critic can so confidently counterfeit unpremeditated sincerity only insofar as he can clearly distinguish his function as narrator from his role as an artless character; his amorous "triumph," the bachelor reasons, is "only for the commentator—in the last analysis—not for the man, who had not the tradition of personal conquest" (21).[19] As I will be arguing, however, this crucial distinction between "commentator" and "man" becomes difficult for the first person to sustain; for his commitment to commentary (editing the letters, narrating the story) grows progressively entangled with his feigning of personhood as he pursues his plot to restore the dead poet's words.

Calling attention to his own compositional resources, riddling his speech with double entendres and literary allusions, or improvising the character of an imaginary servant on the spot, the narrator revels in his own deceit. Early on the hollow showman comes to play a clownish version of Milton's Satan, an identity that is reinforced by his self-consciously "extravagant" (88) pledge to "work the garden" (15) so that he may then "take possession" (25) of Juliana's house and the "tangible objects" (12) of Aspern's love hidden within. Seen in this light, the editor of *The Aspern Papers* is little more than a glib and seductive intruder who cultivates confidence by low cunning. Yet the narrator's ability to charm his victims for the sake of art also serves to charm his readers, who cannot help but be attracted by his power to invent a convincing role for himself that might bring us closer to Aspern's secrets. Like

Mrs. Prest, we can be "expected to draw amusement from the drama of my intercourse with the Misses Bordereau" (38). However base, his plan displays his talent for making fictions. He himself defines his activity as hatching a little "romance" (47)—the same significant term that James uses to describe the story in his critical preface.[20] With a fanatic single-mindedness that rivals Satan's, but with more self-mockery and bemused wit than Satan could ever muster, the first-person critic-turned-hypocrite dissimulates for what he takes to be a higher good:

> My eccentric private errand became a part of the general romance and the general glory—I felt even a mystic companionship, a moral fraternity with all those who in the past had been in the service of art. They had worked for beauty, for a devotion; and what else was I doing? That element was in everything that Jeffrey Aspern has written, and I was only bringing it to light. (43)

Instead of simply dismissing the narrator's vain "romance," as many readers tend to do,[21] we need to consider more closely what the poet Aspern means to his devoted editor. In a late-Victorian world where art is in the process of replacing religion (recall the conflict in "The Author of Beltraffio"), the literary critic plays the part of priest. The antiquarian sees himself as an "appointed minister" (6) paying homage to the memory of the great poet, who is no less than a "god" (5). When Mrs. Prest chides her friend for acting as if the bundles of letters contained "the answer to the riddle of the universe" (5), she is not far from the truth: it is this sublime element of make-believe or "as if" which enables the literary detective to go about his work with such devotion.[22] The inspiration of the first person's quest for meaning, as well as the object of his histrionic craft, Aspern fulfills a romantic ideal of originality: "[A]t a period when our native land was nude and crude and provincial . . . when literature was lonely there and art and form almost impossible, he had found means to live and write like one of the first; to be free and general and not at all afraid; to feel, understand and express everything" (50).

The editor's mission to publish the dead writer's "sacred relics" (43)—to resurrect, as it were, his literary remains—becomes a way for the critic to bring the lost poet back to life. To rescue the artist from history, moreover, the first person must recreate his god in his own image. Defining himself as "a critic, a commentator, an historian, in a small way" (89), the narrator tells Tina that he writes to "measure" (90) the "poets of the past," who cannot "speak for themselves" (89). At key moments in his narrative he even playfully imagines that Aspern is directly addressing him. The "revived immortal face . . . of the great poet" serves as a spiritual "prompter" (42), while the singer's "charming" (7) voice, echoing and mingling "in a dying fall" (5) with the first person's own fallen speech, remains the most intangible but significant trace of Aspern's haunting presence. During these dreamy moments of self-absorption, when the writer is imagined as authorizing the critic's plotting, first person and lost hero virtually merge.

Criticism, James implies, is simply a species of romance that may tell us more about the critic than the particular literary object under investigation. But the first person's narration is saved from doubling in on itself by the substantial presence of the two elderly women, who come to embody the dead poet's passion in ways that the first person could never foresee. While the existence of the hidden documents remains an open question throughout the tale, subject to the first person's (and our own) belief in things unseen,[23] the Misses Bordereau positively refuse to conform to the critic's literary theories. As is his wont, he initially views the women as mere conduits facilitating his fraternal, nonsexual intercourse with Aspern. Miss Tina leads to Miss Juliana, the ancient lover "who had inspired a great poet with immortal lines" (88); she, in turn, leads to the sacred letters, the tangible source of unmediated aesthetic contact with the dead artist. Having an unbounded faith in his own literary imagination, the narrator goes so far as to hypothesize early on that Juliana's "miracle of resurrection had taken place for my benefit" (23).

Given the first-person commentator's tendency to convert the world around him into romance, his strategy is initially clear: to incorporate the two women into the little plot about Aspern that he is hatching. His confidence game, then, becomes primarily an act of appropriation, to "take possession" (an ominous phrase which recurs with increasing frequency [25, 33, 54, 69]) of the house, the spinsters, and the treasure within. His vocabulary is borrowed from medieval romance—a comic mixture of terms for military conquest ("laying siege," "plan of campaign," "spoils") and metaphors for courtship ("my suit," "another arrow for my bow," a "breech" in their "citadel"). As in *The Spoils of Poynton*, the impulse to appropriate material "things," protagonists in themselves, tends to govern the logic of personal relations. The poet's letters, in this case, dictate the collector's every move. But just as the first-person narrators of Poe and Hawthorne meet resistance from forces beyond their control (Poe's readers, Coverdale's fellow utopians), so the grasping imagination of James's confessed agent must confront a reality not of its own making. While the critic's approach depends on his ability to interpret others' intentions without revealing his own, niece and aunt repeatedly frustrate the anticipated course of his plot; with their "common . . . property" for making "unexpected speeches" (53), the two begin to cast doubt on his early assurance that "the sense of playing with my opportunity was much greater after all than any sense of being played with" (42). Like Hawthorne's Coverdale, the first-person narrator of *The Aspern Papers* discovers that he cannot enter into the minds of other people. Masked by her "baffling green shade" (28), Juliana "remain[s] impenetrable . . . she had a fuller vision of me than I had of her" (27). Unable to comprehend the concealed motives of his two fellow characters, the first person as "man" gradually gives up his highly stylized hypocrisy to assume a less aggressive role, "reading" (42) the external evidence of their ambiguous "attitude" (28) toward him.

Testing the limits of his perception, the editor realizes that the "veiled interest" Juliana takes "in my proceedings" (34) may permanently obscure the "esoteric knowledge" (44) which he credits her with possessing. The strange old woman's resistance "deepen[s] the mystery" (54) and inaugurates a cat-and-mouse game, plot and counterplot, in which the poet's mistress and his critic work on each other's confidence through the medium of Miss Tina. While the romantic pursues his dream of transcendent union with Aspern (to grasp the "hidden values" [99] buried in his letters), Miss Juliana continually puts material stumbling blocks in his path. On his metaphoric imagination she imposes a more literal set of constructions. Although he understands early on that his base plan to "pounce on her possessions" (24) may exact some sacrifice, the narrator is surprised to learn the extravagant price he literally must pay to Juliana: an astronomic sum of cold, hard cash for three months' rent in advance. Just as the bachelor narrating "The Author of Beltraffio" is shocked by the claims of the quotidian on the mar-

ried artist, so the first person of *The Aspern Papers* is shocked by
the ancient lover's cynical "vision of pecuniary profit" (71).

Miss Juliana's preoccupation with money is crucial for understanding the story. The narrator reads her demand for gold as
simply an idiosyncratic quirk of her jaded personality, but the matter is actually more complex than that. In the "little romance" that
the first person muses on, Juliana's "singer had betrayed her, had
given her away . . . to posterity" (48) by transforming their mutual
love into poetry and then abandoning her as an unnecessary en-
cumbrance. By seeking to publish the poet's love letters, the editor
participates in that original act of creative treachery, again "betraying a lady's confidence" (97) in the name of art. Yet the "ravaged" old woman means to make the poet pay for his spent passion
by taxing his surrogate. As he gradually comes to reenact Aspern's
affair, the critic is compelled to make amends for the artist's in-
discretion. A tangible form of social exchange, the gold serves to
remind the first person that the conversion of art into criticism
assumes value only by virtue of some palpable sacrifice, just as
Aspern's ageless poetry has exacted its price from Juliana in making
their personal passion immaterial. Like the miniature portrait of
Aspern that Juliana later proposes for exchange, the gold becomes
a highly charged symbol which helps to actualize the latent past
into present power. Although Juliana's bargaining is intended to
set limits on the narrator's designs, their crass commerce fore-
shadows the way James will discover how to use money figuratively
to represent the workings of the imagination. In the plots of later
novels such as *The Spoils of Poynton*, *The Wings of the Dove*, and *The
Golden Bowl*—each of which is absorbed by the relation between
spending and borrowing, loss and gain—the notions of sacrifice,
wealth, and value inextricably come to depend on one another to
form a complex imaginative economy. At once a burden and a
source of liberation, money becomes the crucial medium facilitating
the acts of exploitation and redemption that mark these late works.
Here, however, James is still clearly differentiating between the
commercial and metaphoric meanings of money, if only to see how
these two forms of payment interact whenever the professional
critic seeks to be initiated into the secrets of art.[24]

Converting her desire back into material terms, Juliana offers
the first person his vision of "mystic companionship" with Aspern,
but at the cost of a more social kind of transaction. Despite his

insistence that "Miss Tina was not a poet's mistress any more than
I was a poet" (52), once the con man begins to barter monetary
and emotional values with the two spinsters for the "hidden values"
of art, he proceeds to rehearse, in debased, comic form, the lovers'
long-lost ritual of courtship and engagement. Just as the poet once
used Juliana to transmute her love into literature, so the poet's
editor fakes "human contact" with Tina in order to acquire and
publish the writer's letters. Completely identifying with the object
of his literary quest, the narrator thus establishes the logic that
subsequently compels the aunt to demand gold as a kind of dowry
for Miss Tina, a fact which the lovesick niece herself recognizes.
The marriage dowry turns the pathetic woman into one of James's
classic sacrificial victims: the critic participates vicariously in the
artist's passion by making mock love to Tina, while the dying mistress also relives her own desire through the niece.

Out of this complex array of transferences—from the original
intimacy between Juliana and Aspern (the man), to the critical
intercourse between narrator and poet (embodied in his letters),
to the recycled amorous commerce between bachelor and old
maid—a system of compensation emerges, with the concept of marriage at its heart. By cultivating their garden, the designing editor
promises to bring niece and aunt "life" (36), which the pair, in turn,
will repay with "pleasure" (39). But the critic's "pleasure" and the
women's "life" are terms that never manage to be wedded to each
other in the story. Neither the aesthetic union nor the correspond-
ing sexual one can be consummated, as we shall see, because each
ultimately depends on the other's failure.

The problem is that as the narrator gets closer to the letters,
surrogate poet and surrogate mistress both undergo "transformation[s]" (142) that render their marriage out of the question.
The first person cannot pretend to make love to Miss Tina without
first abandoning his pleasurable fraud; as soon as he begins to be
frank with her, telling her what his readers already know, the crafty
"commentator" temporarily gives way to the "man" who can engage
the woman's emotions. Just before the "climax of my crisis" (117),
when Juliana suddenly catches the "publishing scoundrel" in the
act, he finally confesses to Tina his "real name" (111) and designing
intentions. Once the plotter succumbs to "the last violence of self-
exposure" (93) to become "a new person" (113), the confidence he
has carefully nurtured throughout his narrative threatens to dis-

solve into thin air. The first person sums up his predicament nicely when he admits that "a lodger who had forced an entrance had no *locus standi* as a critic" (34).

Miss Juliana's effort at bribing the narrator into marriage, on the other hand, succeeds only as long as she withholds the hidden relics (real or imagined) from the critic's grasp; hence his suspicion that the dying woman is "making me engage myself when in fact she had sacrificed her treasure" (93). As it turns out, Miss Tina does gain "life" after all, but only when she does "the great thing" (142) by destroying the papers which both mistress and commentator had "lived on" (131). Miss Tina moves from innocence to experience by turning the letters into ashes. "Beautified" by the "sense of her failure" (141), the niece momentarily achieves "the force of soul" (142) that startles the first person into real passion, but at the expense of his narrative function as Aspern's editor. On the verge of being seduced from art into life, the bachelor finally seems ready to "pay the price" (142) for his quest, until she tells him of her liberating act of destruction. In a gesture which anticipates the sacrifices enacted by the heroines of *The Spoils of Poynton* and *The Wings of the Dove*, "poor Miss Tina" (142) thus becomes her own person. She gains her "own voice" (142) at the very moment she renounces the narrator's love, paradoxically affirming her sexuality by burning the only means she possesses to share it with a man. In the end the editor's pleasure and the old maid's life work against each other.

There is a crucial moment earlier in the story, however, when critical pleasure and human love could, in fact, converge rather than betray each other, when two sorts of marriage could be celebrated simultaneously. After he has, in effect, scared Juliana to death by violating her inner sanctum, the publishing scoundrel returns for one last interview with Miss Tina. She gives him the miniature portrait of Aspern as a prologue to an awkwardly veiled offer of marriage. Imagining "mockery" (131) in the dead poet's smiling face, the editor responds to this "heroic" show of "confidence" (138) by denying both lover and letters in language uncharacteristically blunt. In order to disengage himself from the old maid, the bachelor must also demystify the object of his quest: "I couldn't pay the price. I couldn't accept the proposal. I couldn't for a bundle of tattered papers, marry a ridiculous pathetic provincial old woman" (137). Although he castigates himself for "not having known when to stop" (137) (a common danger of first-person narration), sympathetically identifying Miss Tina's sense of loss and "desolation" (132) with his own, his conscience is simply not strong enough to overcome his aversion to the spinster as a lover.

How do we account for the editor's rejection of Tina's marriage offer? The customary explanation concludes that the scoundrel recoils in horror because he is completely blind to the implications of his own fearful behavior, a sexually "starved and repressed" meddler who foolishly hopes "through Aspern's history . . . to experience a small share of the life he does not permit himself to live through at first hand."[25] This seems to me to put the cart before the horse, to evaluate the first person's actions on the basis of sublimated psychological motives presumed to exist from the start. I would argue that the narrator's experience cannot help but be secondhand precisely to the degree that he must remain a disengaged "commentator" and not a "man" if he hopes to tell his story. His sexual desires do not motivate his narrative act but rather originate *from* it.

We commonly think of persons as moral ends in themselves. But the nameless editor of *The Aspern Papers* can locate his moral end only extrinsically in the papers, not within himself. Stated quite simply, James's first person has no identity outside of his all-consuming quest for the dead poet's words, or, more accurately, outside of the language he invokes to represent that quest; though he finally discloses to Tina "who I really was" (114), the reader is still left in the dark, for he never gives us any personal information apart from his *locus standi* as a critic (his "real" name remains undivulged, for example). His "self" continues to function as a provisional fictive construct deriving from his plot, a fact that is underscored when the "I" concludes his narrative by gazing at Aspern's portrait and bemoaning "my loss—I mean of the precious papers" (142). In the final analysis, any temporary emotional investment the critic makes is made in the service of art's hidden values.[26]

Rather than simply viewing the first person's frustrated mission as an expression of assumed character deficiencies, his overwrought posturing and sterile bachelorhood should be seen as signs of his total allegiance to his vicarious role as commentator. Literary historian and witness, the first person, along with James, betrays to posterity "a palpable imaginable visitable past" (AN, 164). In the process of betrayal, first-person narrator, Aspern, and author all victimize people, turn them into art, and therefore depersonalize themselves. Lacking any history of its own, the first-person "self" uses the past of others. Yet the critic's feigning of manhood is masterful enough to help give his mock lover momentary "force of soul" and to bring the dead poet's words back to life. The narrator's personal experience does not contradict his literary imagination, in other words, but is partially constituted by it. As he retrospectively recounts his failure, the editor translates Aspern's charming voice, "the mere echoes of echoes" (8), into his own language; for his written romance has been tracing the poet's hidden letters "under my hand" all along: "I hold it singular, as I look back, that I should never have doubted for a moment that the sacred relics were there; never have failed to know the joy of being beneath the same roof with them. After all they were under my hand ... and they made my life continuous, in a fashion, with the illustrious life they had touched at the other end" (43). The artist's "illustrious life," moreover, remains visually represented in the only tangible item that survives the tragic loss, Miss Tina's heroic gift of Aspern's divine image. At the story's conclusion the portrait significantly "hangs above my writing-table" (143), an iconographic emblem embodying the past that inspires the critic's own equally palpable craft. Assembling and condensing his experience into a written form, the editor inadvertently replaces Aspern's lost love letters with his own; in this way *The Aspern Papers* comes to stand for the missing Aspern papers themselves.

The critic's peculiar brand of blindness does not occasion any direct insight into Aspern's art but rather enables the first person unknowingly to experience and reproduce for us a lesser version of that art, a tragicomic representation of the original passion. Here we see the particularly close connection between James's interest in the critic as analytic middleman and his reliance on the first-person narrator as an agent who not only acts in his story but is also presumed to address a community of readers outside the narrative.[27] In the case of *The Aspern Papers*, the confessing first person's sense of an audience corresponds to his duplicitous role as editor and commentator, publicly exposing the poet's love letters to posterity. To recall Michel Butor's phrase, the narrating "I," like the critic in society, is the middle term between the real and the imaginary, on the cutting edge of the fiction.

The critic's negotiating between private imagination and public opinion thus entails a special sort of betrayal. Just as Miss Tina is briefly transfigured by her sense of loss, so the confidence man manages to shadow forth the beauty of Aspern's poetry most intensely when he is most openly engaged in criminal prying. Juliana finally reveals "her extraordinary eyes" (118), the source of the poet's inspiration, at the very moment she catches him in his shameful, bungling attempt at transgression.

This intimate connection between analytic penetration and the realization of beauty points to an underlying ambivalence on James's part. Throughout *The Aspern Papers* he tries to discriminate between the narrator's critical folly and Aspern's poetic sublimity by consistently subjecting his first person to the same kind of irony the narrator himself can display only intermittently. But as authorship and criticism grow closer together in the narrative as forms of writing, it becomes more and more difficult for James to identify with his first-person literary historian and, at the same time, to dissociate himself from his agent's baser acquisitive instincts. One way James attempts to control his divided allegiance in the tale is by emphasizing the narrator's own split between "commentator" and "man." In his subsequent first-person story "The Figure in the Carpet" (1896), however, this ambivalence will become more pronounced, more difficult to contain. Treating the act of interpretation as a kind of riddle, "The Figure in the Carpet" offers us the spectacle of another curious narrator/critic who remains fundamentally at odds with the tale he is telling. The first person's estrangement, I shall argue, suggests competing impulses in James himself—impulses which he seeks to resolve under the concept of sexual union.

Like the storytellers of "The Author of Beltraffio" and *The Aspern Papers*, the anonymous first person narrating "The Figure in the Carpet" is a nervous, ambitious bachelor eagerly aspiring to learn the mysteries of art. Unlike these earlier narrators, however, this "ardent young seeker for truth"[28] is frustrated by obstacles that would appear to be internal as well as external, a function of the way he initially poses questions of interpretation. While the two previous stories emphasize the high cost of the critic's inquiry (the melodramatic death of Ambient's son and Aspern's aged mistress, respectively), "The Figure in the Carpet" treats this sort of sacrifice almost playfully. Although James manages to kill off five characters in the course of thirteen pages, death becomes simply the sheerest contingency of providence or "fate" (260) for the narrator. And since the plot largely remains beyond the first person's control, "The Figure in the Carpet" is not marked by the kind of self-conscious duplicity the editor in *The Aspern Papers* so ostentatiously exhibits. Possessing little of the publishing scoundrel's charming talent for ironic self-dramatization, this first person seems to play a relatively simple part in his own story. Yet it is his very marginality, his failure to recognize the implications of his experience, which makes James's tale so similar to Poe's impenetrable enigmas. Like Poe's "The Man of the Crowd," "The Figure in the Carpet" abandons all richness of dramatic incident or character development to pursue a single narrative thread: the interpretive quest that obsesses every figure in the story (except the silent figure in the carpet itself).

The frenzied search is conducted by a series of social transactions, or mock doublings, between persons presumed to have greater or lesser critical intelligence. Opening his tale by bragging how he had "earned a few pence" (216) and made a name for himself, the first person goes on to relate how fellow critic George Corvick delegated to him responsibility for publishing an article on Hugh Vereker's latest novel in the "organ of our lucubrations" (216), a weekly periodical aptly titled *The Middle* (popular criticism as a form of social mediation; the first-person narrator/critic as middleman). Overhearing Vereker dismiss his attempt at critical appreciation as "the usual twaddle" (226), the wounded reviewer soon has occasion to question the esteemed novelist directly about his writing. Late at night author and journalist trade metaphors about what the public has missed in his work—"my little point" (229), "the very passion of his passion" (230), "this little trick" (231), "an exquisite scheme" (231), "esoteric message" (233), "organ of life" (234), "general intention" (234)—until the narrator becomes "fired" (232) to uncover the writer's secret, now reified as "a complex figure in a Persian carpet" (240). Critical enthusiasm quickly fading into frustration, however, the first person tells Corvick about Vereker's hidden intention, who tells his fiancée, Gwendolen, and the hermeneutic game of detection is on in earnest. Though passionately engaged in the mystery, Corvick and Gwendolen fail to

decipher Vereker's "inner meaning" (243) until after Corvick leaves
on assignment for India, where he later cables Gwendolen that he
has got it. Verifying his solution with Vereker, "the supreme authority" (254), whose "literary portrait" (260) he begins to write,
Corvick promises to tell Gwendolen the secret as soon as they are
married. But, as the narrator has informed us at the start of his
tale, Gwendolyn would marry Corvick only if her disapproving
mother were to die.

Now the hand of "fate" capriciously and comically intervenes
to quicken the plot, "a series of phenomena so strangely interlaced"
(260). First Gwendolen's ailing mother finally yields to "long-
threatened failure of the heart" (261), enabling the long-desired
marriage to take place. Then, while on their honeymoon Corvick
dies in a sudden accident. Mrs. Corvick admits to possessing the
literary secret but refuses to divulge it to the prying first person,
claiming that "it's my *life*" (266). Meanwhile the novelist Vereker
dies, with Mrs. Vereker quickly following suit. Gwendolen writes
her second novel and eventually marries another critic, Drayton
Deane. After *she* dies in childbirth, the narrator asks Deane to satisfy
his feverish obsession. But Deane confesses that his wife never
mentioned Vereker's secret to him, and the two "victims of unappeased desire" (277) are finally left to ponder the narrative's
successive clues. From these linked deferrals of meaning—the critic's initial failure to "get at" (221) the novelist, Vereker's failure to
enlighten his audience, Corvick's failure to publish his solution,
and Deane's failure to get it from his wife—all that remains to
document the figure in the carpet are a few written fragments:
cryptic telegrams and letters hinting at triumph, the "heartbreaking
scrap" (263) of Corvick's literary portrait, Gwendolen's novel
Overmastered, and the narrator's own retrospective account of his
frustrating defeat.

The intense self-referentiality of "The Figure in the Carpet"
offers tantalizing possibilities for the reader—but dangers as well.
In his New York Edition preface to the tale, James claims that he
wrote the story "to reinstate analytic appreciation" (AN, 228) in his
public, but the exact nature of that appreciation is still a matter of
some controversy. The urge to treat the tale as a puzzle in need of
a solution has occasioned, over the years, a series of allegorical
interpretations that simply mirror the theoretical assumptions of
each successive generation of critics. In the early 1960s the story

was commonly seen as a parable illustrating the Intentional Fallacy (complete with unreliable narrator), while in the 1970s these New Critical approaches gave way to structuralist analyses of textual ambiguity (minus author or narrator), which in turn have recently become supplanted by various deconstructive treatments (denying the possibility of a "readable" text).[29] From one discussion to the next, the same passages in the story tend to be singled out and glossed to support a favored critical tenet. But unless we mean simply to reduplicate the text, pursuing "The Figure in the Carpet" just as the first person pursues the figure in the carpet, we must first clarify the relation between author and narrator in order to see how the tale's ambiguities may, in fact, derive from James's own ambivalence about the function of criticism.

I begin by considering what is at stake for James in the writing. A brief notebook entry he made in the process of "father[ing]" (AN, 221) his fable provides a fascinating glimpse into the narrative's inner workings:

> I seem to see a little subject in this idea: that of the author of certain books who is known to hold ... that his writings contain a very beautiful and valuable, very interesting and remunerative *secret*, or latent intention, for those who read them with a right intelligence—who see *into* them, as it were.... No reviewer, no "critic," has dreamed of it: lovely chance for fine irony on the subject of that fraternity. *Mettons* that he mentions, after all, the fact of the thing to only one person—to *me*, say, who narrate, in my proper identity, the little episode. Say *I'm* a "critic," another little writer, a newspaper man. I am in relation with him, some-how—relation, admiring, inquisitive, mystified, sceptical—whatever it may be.[30]

What interests me here is the way James sides with the critic in this literary game, excitedly pursuing the writer's unknown "renumer-ative secret" until his identification with the reader's role turns into "*me* ... who narrate." In his "proper identity" as a critic, the first person thus emerges from James's own analytic preoccupations, while the artist remains a secondary figure throughout. Those mor-alizing readers who anxiously refuse to recognize James in the tale's "little writer" are also implicitly refusing to recognize themselves. As G. A. Finch has observed, "The story would lose its inner drive and final impact were the reader any better off than the narrator";[31]

analytic appreciation can be instilled only by maintaining a state of
critical uncertainty about the figure's meaning from beginning to
end.

Yet despite the author's intimate interest in the analytic quest,
James also means to draw "fine irony" from his subject by satirizing
his first person's efforts at critical thinking. Although we ultimately
may not be any better off than the baffled narrator, much of the
comedy in the tale depends on our ability to distinguish between
the narrator's sense of the plot and the larger plot governing his
discourse. In both cases the force dominating the course of action
is death. As a character confined within his own story, the first
person sees the sudden deaths of Mrs. Erme, Corvick, Mr. and
Mrs. Vereker, and Gwendolen only as a strange series of discrete
events, mysteriously linked by some "fate." Beyond his point of
view, however, such an extreme fate points to James's own providential agency at work in the tale, which constantly teases us by
deferring the revelation of the secret figure. Calling attention to
this authorial control, James thus exaggerates the way in which
death can serve as a plot device designed simply to maintain narrative suspense. While both the author and his first person cannot
afford to invest themselves emotionally in any of these deaths if
they hope to continue the narrative thread, the difference is that
James alone is responsible for creating the coercive pattern which
will determine his confessed agent's subsequent failure.

James seeks to disengage himself from his narrator in another
related way which also stresses the difference between a primary
author and a secondary critic. Expounding on his "general intention" to his mystified young admirer, the novelist Vereker makes
a distinction between the critic's reliance on analysis and the artist's
genius for synthesis: "It stretches, this little trick of mine, from
book to book, and everything else, comparatively, plays over the
surface of it" (231). Although the insights of a novelist-turned-
reader may be just as suspect as all the other glosses offered in the
story, Vereker's claim that his artistic secret is an organic, all-
embracing experience, a "complete representation" (231), provides
a clear contrast to the narrator's early assurance that the "truth"
can be neatly extracted from a text and then presented to the public
in easily digested pellets of wisdom. Initially the first-person journalist conceives of his review as an act of "unveiling" (224) whereby
the "mystery" in Vereker's writing will be completely demystified

for good. Naively presuming to decode the creative labors of others, the tale's possessive "little writer" thus threatens to supplant the work of the author who would then be reduced to a marginal figure. The very fact that the novelist and the reviewer are both writers compels James to find a way of insisting that each must go about his business quite differently. Unlike *The Aspern Papers*, here history no longer clearly separates artist and critic; any distinctions to be made in the fiction must therefore be made by an author who acts as his own interpreter. Even with "pen in hand" (234), Vereker remarks to his reviewer, the novelist could never be "one of *you* chaps" (234), an interesting statement considering the relish with which he tries to explain his work.

We are now in a better position to appreciate the contradictory tendencies motivating "The Figure in the Carpet." Complaining, in his preface, about the "limp state" of contemporary criticism, its habit of obscuring the artist's "intended sense of things" (AN, 229), James (turned critic himself) suggests that he wrote the tale with a clear didactic purpose: not to deny the role of criticism altogether, but to educate a growing body of professional journalists and reviewers in the ways of analytic appreciation.[32] But, at the same time that he wants to teach his critics what it really means to read, he also wants to preserve a role for himself apart from that criticism, to protect his writing from those little writers. Only by insisting on a clear division of labor between novelist and critic can James keep his art an impenetrable mystery. Giving his story the feel of a sacred parable, James thus means to remain his own best explicator. Like the secret figure in the carpet itself, the entire tale is designed to provoke endless commentary, none of it definitive. And, as we shall see, it is the story's poor narrator who must pay for this tension between disclosure and concealment; the first person's function as a solitary eyewitness plotting from within not only distinguishes him from James but, more important, also sets him apart from the other critics in the story.

Taking "the little measure of my course," James's "anonymous scribe" (AN, 228) "count[s] my real start" (219) from the moment Corvick introduces the interpretive task. The birth of the narrating "I" and the emergence of the text's riddle thus occur simultaneously, both depending on the controlling "course" of James's plot. As the little writer proceeds with his story, the force of this abstract arabesque continues to overwhelm personal identity. The "self" of each character can be articulated only to the degree that he or she contributes to the solution of the puzzle. When Corvick dies, for example, the narrator reacts in an extraordinarily callous way which dramatizes his inability to halt the critical pursuit even momentarily:

> I pass rapidly over the question of this unmitigated tragedy, of what the loss of my best friend meant for me, and I complete my little history of my patience and my pain by the frank statement of my having, in a postscript to my very first letter to her after the receipt of the hideous news, asked Mrs. Corvick whether her husband mightn't at least have finished the great article on Vereker. (262–63)

The first person's "responses to life" are appallingly "inadequate," as many readers are quick to point out, although most miss the comedy in such a passage.[33] His responses are attenuated in this way by necessity, so long as "a piece of literary experience" (264) and *not* life is the sole object of his little history. As each agent in the fiction helps to plot that literary experience, moreover, he or she comes to reproduce it step by step. Like a string of pearls linked together by an invisible thread, the first person, together with his fellow detectives, make up the very configuration they would solve. The riddle involves social relations, nothing more, nothing less. The novelist Vereker himself uses this "string of pearls" metaphor to describe his secret, and James reinvokes it in *his* explanation of the story, adding the key adjective "evolutionary" (AN, 228). I have intentionally borrowed the metaphor to suggest how the readers in the tale tend to turn into the object of their quest in the process of questing after it, just as the narrator of *The Aspern Papers* rehearses the passion he hopes to find extrinsically in the letters. The figure in the carpet, that is, gradually assumes the human form of the figures who try to interpret it. When the novelist compares his secret to a bird in a cage, for example, his understanding is borne out by the narrator's realization, in the end, that he is "shut up in my obsession forever," a "dungeon" complete with "bars" (270). The critic ends up *in* the mystery rather than *on* its trail. As readers of "The Figure in the Carpet" have recently begun to realize, James's riddle is to be lived, not solved, its clues experienced, not communicated. Rachel Solomon puts it succinctly when she states that "the figure can be known only as a person is known."[34]

What commentators of the story tend to ignore, however, is that knowing is one thing for James and *telling* that knowledge quite another. On this basis we can begin to discriminate between the narrator and his fellow critics. Simply put, the first person's role as narrator precludes the possibility that he could ever understand the novelist's secret. Corvick, Gwendolen, and Deane are in the presence of the figure when they are the furthest removed from the narrator's own discourse: in India; on a honeymoon; privately sharing a life together. While these three individuals can rest to enjoy the fruits of their critical experience in silence, the narrator can never stop talking. Analysis for him simply means incessantly narrating, keeping a story going which cannot afford to be interrupted by insight. Only by erroneously assuming that the secret is a discrete piece of information to be divulged and published can the hapless first-person scribe trace the plot's design—a linear string of social transactions in which Vereker's mystery is alternately passed on and embodied. Like Poe's domestic tale "The Black Cat," the narrative of "The Figure in the Carpet" thus oscillates between represented surface and buried presence: just as the black cat turns into a bas-relief and then returns as a second (entombed) cat, so the secret "figure" surfaces momentarily in the literary "portrait" of Vereker that Corvick "quietly" (262) begins to write, only to be immediately submerged in his widow's "life" (266).

Beginning with the narrator's first interview with Vereker, spatial metaphors of depth, concealment, and burial wind their way through the tale. In the brilliant presence of the master, just before he has learned about the writer's "buried treasure" (235), the first person experiences an even deeper enigma:

> I can see him there still, on my rug, in the firelight and his spotted jacket, his clear face all bright with the desire to be tender to my youth. I don't know what he had at first meant to say, but I think the sight of my relief touched him, excited him, brought up words to his lips from far within. It was so these words presently conveyed to me something that, as I afterwards knew, he had never uttered to any one. (228)

Unlike Mrs. Corvick's "life," however, that mute meaning "far within" is available to the narrator only insofar as he persists in trying to weave it into his own narration.

This tension between the unbroken surface of the narrative and moments of veiled interiority corresponds to a more important relation in "The Figure in the Carpet" between textuality and presence, the act of writing/reading and the interaction between persons. Before he meets Vereker, the first person simply equates the writer with his writing. "I sat up with Vereker half the night" (221) initially refers to the critic's reading of the novel. Corvick, according to the narrator, also subscribes to this critical principle: "He'd call it letters, he'd call it life, but it was all one thing" (242). Once he encounters the author face to face, however, the narrator soon begins to note a difference: "I had taken to the man still more than I had ever taken to the books" (247). Vereker is *not* his books, the first person learns, and cannot be bodily translated into a written form, just as Gwendolen later recognizes that the novelist's secret passion "can't be got into a letter" (252). To interpret the tale as a dramatization of the Intentional Fallacy or, more radically, as a deconstruction of the author's person, seems to me a clear misreading. James does not seek to erase the figure of the novelist completely from the tale but simply to protect himself by preserving some distinction between an author and his work.

Trying to pry content from form, the narrator fails to get at his subject, to convert Vereker's metaphors into information, to locate meaning in any detachable thing. Yet his very failure suggests the greater mystery of social being and human desire that prompts the little writer's plotting throughout. "Immensely stirred up" by the first person's "anecdote," Corvick insists that "there was more *in* Vereker than met the eye" (257; italics mine), to which the narrator replies that "the eye seemed what the printed page had been expressly invented to meet" (247). This association between the eye and writing is crucial. Trapped within their texts, anonymous scribe and fellow reviewers, novelist Vereker, and *his* author Henry James are all figures whose identities are mediated and bound by print, the surface which the critic's "tremendous eye" (227) scans and deciphers for the public. But, as Vereker suggests, "Nobody sees anything" (227) because the author's secret remains beyond writing and reading, even though it must be experienced through "letters." The first person, Corvick, Gwendolen, and Vereker all make their "living by the pen" (248, 250, 261), but their life, their passion, who they are remain unnarratable. All that can be told in the story is the impossibility of this telling. The cardinal points of the figure in the carpet (Vereker's and James's) cannot be verbalized but only witnessed silently, even though the eyes refuse to tell the narrator what he desires to know:

> I read some singular things into Gwendolen's words and some still more extraordinary ones into her silences. Pen in hand, this way, I live the time over, and it brings back the oddest sense of my having been, both for months and in spite of myself a kind of coerced spectator. All my life had taken refuge in my eyes, which the procession of events appeared to have committed itself to keep astare. (261)

The first person's moving words beautifully evoke his hopeless position in the narrative, a "coerced spectator" whose writing testifies to a special kind of silence he can never know for himself.

The fable's analogue for this inexpressible presence is sexual union. Marriage for James becomes an act of authentication. The operative pun in "The Figure in the Carpet" is "engagement" (257), a state of being which refers both to Corvick and Gwendolen's intimacy with Vereker's books and to their desire for each other. Our young bachelor "I" makes the connection explicit: "They would scarce have got so wound up, I think, if they hadn't been in love: poor Vereker's inner meaning gave them endless occasion to put and to keep their young heads together" (243). Corvick's curious stipulation about marriage, along with Vereker's encouraging remarks (240) and the narrator's own speculations about "lovers supremely united" (265) thus serve to dramatize James's attempt to wed analysis with experience, but at the expense of his first-person narrator. Early on the first person imagines the act of reading as a game of chess, with Vereker on one side and the engaged couple on the other, united in their critical passion. This literary game entails a principle of conversion from "literature" to "life," which Gwendolen and Corvick enact together and which expresses James's hopes for a special reader: "For the few persons, at any rate, abnormal or not, with whom my anecdote is concerned, literature was a game of skill, and skill meant courage, and courage meant honour, and honour meant passion, meant life" (250).

The problem is that we can never really be those special readers because we are only reading the first person's critical account, not Vereker's novels themselves. Corvick and Gwendolen, on the other hand, are directly engaged by the novelist's work. Although from our perspective they are contained within the first person's discourse, they are not burdened by it as we are. The partners are therefore free to pursue their textual love affair apart from the narrator's incessant plotting. We recognize again how James's fundamental ambivalence has led him (and us) into a no win situation: how the impulse for disclosure, underscored by James's own comments in the preface and by Vereker's glosses in the tale itself, becomes overshadowed by the artist's urge for concealment, his skepticism about the value of any form of explication at all. James tries to find a way out of this quandary by conceiving of successful criticism as a kind of absolute sacrifice beyond all articulation, whereby understanding is purchased strictly by silence (death). The good critic dies so that art may live. As we shall soon see, if Gwendolen were to relate "The Figure in the Carpet," she quite literally would have nothing to say. The tale must therefore be told by a survivor who is incapable of participating in either art or life by the very logic of James's scheme. Delegating the responsibility for narration to his first-person agent, James can only hope that we might be able to reproduce outside his text what Gwendolen and Corvick may be reproducing from within. Given his bachelor/critic's blanket of talk, and the epistemological uncertainties that it creates, the couple's passionate union remains little more than a potential resolution which depends for its realization on our mute faith in their presence together.

Consummating love without communicating it, Corvick brings his wife "face to face" (256) with the great secret, which she can then simply, beautifully live. From the anonymous scribe's point of view, however, the "fruit of the affair" (271) is nothing but death and silence. After the partners are "united very quietly" (262), Corvick dies, "unable to deliver" his "heavy message" (271), while the "inarticulate" (266) widow later dies in childbirth. What has critical intimacy engendered to compensate for such loss?

One way to answer this question would be to pose another: why is the hapless bachelor who narrates the action condemned to be excluded from the "marriage in literary circles" (271) that he witnesses with envy? Why is he left simply to stare—at Gwendolen and at Drayton Deane ("from her husband I could never remove my eyes" [273])—a "conversational blank" who cannot grasp the implications of his own tale? I would suggest that the "exile" (260) cannot *tell* what the mystery might be unless he remain the odd man out. To participate in the critical intercourse would be to participate in its silence. Only by being foiled, failing to consummate his burning desire, does the anonymous scribe manage to transpose something of the figure into writing, a recognizable form for the world to see. The "I" thus forgoes humanness or authenticity in order to formulate a plot that contains a secret within it. It is this literary "anecdote" (247), we recall, which initially stirs up the lovers' "private understanding" (249), stirs up Deane, and ultimately stirs us up as well. A flawed critic and an incomplete human, the first person nonetheless patiently, painfully goes about tracing the novelist's figure. The story takes place between the lines, as it were, someplace where the baffled detective cannot be if he is to mark its clues and its effect on others.

The antithetical tendencies of "art" and "life" may be resolved, but only by sacrificing narration as a superficial kind of analysis which paradoxically makes profounder forms of critical penetration possible. James thus evokes an ineffable state of presence through an all too articulate mouthpiece: a solitary first-person narrator who finally serves as a kind of matchmaker engaging reader to text, just as his anecdote helped wed Corvick to Gwendolen. Yet in some sense the means James uses to "reinstate analytic appreciation" (AN, 228) in his public may work against our engagement; treating marriage as a kind of veiled allegory for the critical act seems a particularly barren form of pedagogy, since all the passion in the story is filtered through the first person's opaque representation. In his final first-person detective fiction, *The Sacred Fount* (1901), James's tendency to originate plots in abstract hypotheses about social behavior reaches an intolerable extreme for some readers. But "The Figure in the Carpet" is saved from this sort of arch theorizing by its brief though highly charged scenes of personal interaction.

James's understanding of marriage comes to life during those poignant moments when the figures in the story exchange small signs of love with one another. The real mystery of the tale takes place, between the lines, in the first person's own awkward efforts at unmediated human contact: his late-night encounter with Vereker; his attempt to pry the secret out of Corvick's ardent widow; and his final conversation with Gwendolen's widower, Drayton Deane. In each case the search for understanding and friendship

accompanies the search for the figure in the carpet. By small gestures, murmurs, and glances, pregnant pauses or silences that verge
on meaning, "nerves were exposed" (233). When Vereker and the
narrator first meet, the novelist gives the offended critic a warm
pat on the shoulder, a token of affection which he, in turn, later
bestows on his presumed co-victim of "unappeased desire," Drayton
Deane. The first person thus concludes his tale by initiating another
into the riddle of interpretation.

Making Deane feel the same passion that he has experienced,
the narrator finally means to gain his "revenge" (277), a sign of his
power to tell a moving story. But his ambiguous interaction with
Deane may, in the end, simply suggest once again his severe limitations as a narrator. What the first person takes to be puzzlement
and distress on Deane's part could, in fact, be deeper indications
of the husband's growing appreciation for the intimacy he had
known with his wife. Deane's "waves of wonder and curiosity" (277)
may be motivated less by the figure in the carpet than by the decision of his recently departed partner to keep the secret from him.
Briefly united with Corvick, Gwendolen transforms the novelist's
secret into "life," a passion which subsequently finds a more en-
during expression in her relation with Deane. Either the secret can
no longer be converted back into "information" (274) or Gwendolen
has intentionally refused to tell her new husband, thus forsaking
the critical pursuit for the experience of love. In this sense Gwendolen's claim to "life" becomes a kind of sacrifice, just as she literally
is sacrificed herself to give birth to their second child. In his "fine
ignorance" (268) of the artist's buried treasure, the widower Deane
actually comes to live it not as a critic but rather as a man. Gaining
from his wife's renunciation, Deane may be more of a victor than
the "victim" the first person imagines him to be. Yet since we are
given so little direct insight into the couple's affairs, so little opportunity for compassion, Gwendolen's sacrifice remains only a
dimly realized possibility. Whether Vereker's general intention simply cannot be spoken or is left unspoken by choice, it is clear that
the narrative has come full circle, that the narrator's opacity has
served to foreground the mysteries which still elude him—and us
as readers.

Because we can engage the text itself strictly as readers, James
is compelled to affirm those human values outside of the writing
solely by indirection. In the anecdote's "extraordinary chain of

events" (277), figures share their emotions "face to face," a key
term for presence which carries great significance in the narrative
(228, 238, 245, 256, 266, 267, 269). For instance, when Gwendolen
and the narrator initially discuss Corvick's discovery in his absence,
the first person unknowingly experiences a human riddle more
curious than the figure itself: "She thought like one inspired, and
I remember Corvick had told me long before that her face was
interesting. 'Perhaps it can't be got into a letter if it's "immense" ' "
(252). Rendered "facially luminous" (252) by her insight into the
nature of the artist's secret, Gwendolen thus enacts the very meaning of her statement: what a face may "signify" is an indivisible
gestalt that depends on the interaction between viewer and person
viewed.

James's concept of union thus emerges most vitally in the tale's
unnarrated dialogue, dramatic moments when significance is construed jointly. The secret which initially precipitates the interpretive
quest, in fact, is not solely Vereker's but is shared by novelist and
critic. Their late-night commerce serves to represent a kind of
marriage. Playfully identified as doubles (227), first person and
hero come to terms with each other by exchanging metaphors for
the artist's life and passion. Vereker's "little point" (229) is echoed
and drawn out by the narrator, who offers his own clumsy for-
mulations in "cheap journalese" (232) to get at Vereker's "intention"
(231). In this groping process of give-and-take, where both partners
try to find words to express the inexpressible, the novelist's secret
gradually assumes life. Their quickening dialogue thus "hastens
[the] difficult birth" (233) of the interpretive quest. But the sur-
facing of the figure in the carpet (240) as a clear object of mystery
is only a by-product of the intangible relation between the two
excited men, the "strange confidence" (237) that holds novelist and
critic together as persons. Their brief but passionate intercourse,
in turn, prepares the way for the more fruitful but quieter intercourse between Corvick and Gwendolen.

To appreciate the crucial role that marriage plays in "The Figure in the Carpet," we need only glance at James's treatment of
sexual union in his earlier first-person quests. In "The Author of
Beltraffio," for example, James posits two separate kinds of marriage, social and aesthetic; the fruits of one must be given up if the
other is to survive. *The Aspern Papers* similarly sets the commentator's all-consuming literary mission at odds with personal conquest,

despite the fact that the first person inadvertently comes to burlesque Aspern's original passion. For poet as well as critic, love
finally must be abandoned for the sake of "letters." Marriage is
thus represented in the two earlier stories as a threat to private
artistic consciousness;[35] although James mocks his young narrators'
foolish assumptions about the inviolability of art, he also exposes
his own anxieties about the potential of the commonplace to con-
taminate the creative process. In these stories and others of the
1880s and early 1890s ("The Lesson of the Master" and "The Private Life") James suggests that the writer's practice is a thing unto
itself which can be integrated into social reality only by some elaborate system of compensation.

In "The Figure in the Carpet", on the other hand, marriage
becomes an essential way for James to understand his own labors.
No longer do "art" and "life" betray each other, nor are they simply
one and the same; here the two experiences suddenly converge
through the first person's narration, which represents a middle
ground—"marriage" or "engagement"—a term which imposes
form on the Jamesian consciousness.[36] The marriage contract becomes a figure for the fertile imagination, which analogizes the
passions of the writer/critic with the passions of men and women
living in the everyday world. While the wife or potential wife in
the earlier stories is insensitive (Mrs. Ambient), cunning (Juliana),
or hopelessly naive (Miss Tina), now the woman's strength is central
to the first person's quest.

Possessed by her secret and self-possessed, Mrs. Drayton
(Gwendolen Erme Corvick) Deane is permanently beautified by her
union, much the same way that Miss Tina is momentarily transfigured: "Stricken and solitary, highly accomplished and now, in her
deep mourning, her maturer grace and her uncomplaining sorrow,
incontestably handsome, she presented herself as leading a life of
singular dignity and beauty" (264). Although the uncomprehend-
ing first-person bachelor finds her "tongue-tied" (260) by her new
knowledge, Gwendolen most vividly represents or lives the text's
riddle because she is the only figure in the tale who acts as commentator *and* novelist, engaging herself in the critical hunt while
she is being "reviewed" (268) by others. Tempering analysis with
consummated desire, the widow thus embodies within herself the
very marriage which James hoped to create between experience
and criticism: a state of pure presence to be entered into.

Triumphing silently over the act of narration, this univocal state of presence will become increasingly central for James. But it will also grow progressively more intangible and fragile, until it finally can be articulated only by sheer speculation. In his most prolonged venture into a first-person abyss, James assumes a metaphoric "sacred fount"—a life-giving source of passion between man and woman. Imagined to multiply unappeased desire beyond all bounds, this secret object of analysis supplies the first person with the same kind of "endless interest" that James himself would later admit to finding in his fictional characters, "compositional re-source[s]" like Maggie Verver (AN, 329). Obsessively pursuing this first cause, however, only brings the bachelor/narrator of *The Sacred Fount* to the brink of madness and dissolution; for in the course of telling his story from within, as we shall see, the plotter's "self" is exposed as more of a fiction than the fount it has helped to create.

III

In *The Sacred Fount* James painfully and extravagantly bids farewell to first-person romance. Seduced by romance's "beautiful circuit and subterfuge of our thought and desire" (AN, 32), a figure for the sacred fount itself, James's narrator assumes a "glittering crystal palace"[37] or "perfect palace of thought" (311) directly akin to the haunted palace that imprisons Roderick Usher. At once beautiful and grotesque, James's Gothic plot shares with Poe's arabesques a neurotic rage for order as it follows chains of winding corridors without end. Along the way the first person encounters ghostly bodies, fractured identities, and characters who are incessantly treated as art objects in a desperate effort to construe some know-able coherence for the weekend guests at Newmarch. At the still center of his "secret search for the infinite to be quenched" (166), James's absorbed plotter tries to explain why he is so in love with the products of his imagination:

There was a general shade in all the lower reaches.... The last calls of birds sounded extraordinarily loud; they were like the timed, serious splashes, in wide, still water, of divers not expecting to rise again. I scarce know what odd consciousness I had of roaming at close of day in the grounds of some castle of enchantment. I had positively encountered nothing to compare with this since the days of fairy-tales and of the childish imagination of the impossible. *Then* I used to circle round enchanted castles, for I moved in a world in which the strange "came true." It was the coming true that was the proof of the enchantment, which, more-over, was naturally never so great as when such coming was, to such a degree and by the most romantic stroke of all, the fruit of one's own wizardry. I was positively—so had the wheel revolved—proud of my work. I had thought it all out, and to have thought it was, wonderfully, to have brought it. Yet I recall how I even then knew on the spot that there was something supreme I should have failed to bring unless I had happened suddenly to become aware of the very presence of the haunting principle, as it were, of my thought. (128–29)

That controlling principle or supreme fiction which justifies and shapes his enchantment will come to depend on James's under-standing of sexual intimacy.

Earlier in his romance the first person explicitly asserts that to be married is to be "in presence" (42). This key insight, in turn, derives from his theory of the sacred fount: an originating relation of passion between two lovers by which one lover gains life by using up and drawing from the resources of the other. Since the first-person bachelor can never himself be "in presence" as long as he is telling his story, this intimacy remains "postulated" (28–29) from countless "tell-tale" (16) traces, but never positively known. The narration thus follows a logic akin to psychoanalysis, a hermeneutic process in which things often mean their concealed opposites, or, in Paul Ricoeur's words, "interpretation as an exercise in suspi-cion."[38] Indirectly representing such a hidden first cause solely by its felt absence affords James only the most tenuous of narrative forms: a hallucinatory fantasy betraying a minute attention to ra-tiocination and detection that threatens to lose itself, like Poe's tales of analytic retrogradation, in endless abstraction and insanity. As R. P. Blackmur noted, *The Sacred Fount* is "the nightmare nexus in James's literary life";[39] despite, or because of, the intensity with which both James and his narrator exhaust their clues and master possibilities, the novel may seem wildly out of control, an ornate exercise in self-purging. Initially conceived as a ten-thousand-word short story, the writing sprawled to monstrous proportions (seventy-five thousand words), as James tried to use the first person to come to terms with the way his own imagination worked.[40] The result is a weird, exasperating piece of fiction which is at once the weakest of James's mature productions and the most revealing.

Structurally *The Sacred Fount* manages to combine the most troublesome narrative features of *The Awkward Age* and *Roderick Hudson*. Like *The Awkward Age*, social relations are constituted strictly by drawing room conversation, dialogue which tends to expand and duplicate itself without any clear constraints.[41] While talk in *The Awkward Age* is left to its own devices, *The Sacred Fount* is additionally burdened by a novelist figure (like Rowland Mallet) whose critical perspective on the action tends to overshadow the actors within the tale. The fact that James's center of consciousness is also narrating *The Sacred Fount* complicates matters further, for it is this fascination with the imagination's subjective speculations, coupled with an equally strong commitment to characters as social entities mutually shaped by one another, which gives readers of the novel such fits, and which makes the dynamics of the sacred fount itself so puzzling.[42] At the same time that the narrator wants to establish a community of interest by talking about the sacred fount and encouraging others to talk about his theory, he also wants to keep his exquisite sense of things to himself and to screen any possible possessors of his secret from one another. Like the other members of Newmarch, he thus remains isolated within his private experience even in the midst of the most unrelenting social interaction.

Unlike the other guests, however, the first person is also Newmarch's narrator; before we can disentangle the relation between private and social experience in the tale, we need to consider the problematic ontological status of its teller. To tell a story normally presupposes a self to tell it, yet if we try to regard the narrator as a character in his own right, it becomes difficult to assign any motives for his obsessive quest apart from the sheer "constructive joy" (221) of construing the sacred fount, the source of life. James's previous first persons are at least recognizable as professional men of letters, but the speaker of *The Sacred Fount* is bereft of all identifying personal, psychological, or social conditions. Virtually the only two things we know about him are that he is male and that he is unmarried, so that even the most dedicated New Critics have difficulty disengaging James from his mad narrator by treating him as if he were a fully authenticated persona. Throughout the story the "I" remains little more than the sum total of what he sees, hears, and speaks. Rarely does he occupy any physical space at Newmarch (sitting down to dinner is one occasion) or possess any body at all. While his counterpart narrating "The Figure in the Carpet" is allowed the minimal consolation of a pat on the shoulder and face-to-face engagement, the spooky speaker of *The Sacred Fount* significantly makes bodily contact with another character only twice (touching hands with May Server and Guy Brissenden, two crucial moments of departure in the novel). We thus gradually come to identify him in the same way he comes to know others at Newmarch, namely, on the evidence of fragments: the surreal sign of a "shoe" and then "an outstretched leg" (83) here or a "caught . . . voice" (3) there. Given the attenuation of the community's corporeal substance and the unreliability of appearances at Newmarch, the closest approximation to presence in the novel, aside from marriage, is simply speech, the medium through which the sacred fount circulates. As in *The Awkward Age*, talk alone is responsible for creating a community of participants.

Out of thin air, and in the face of extreme epistemological uncertainty, the first-person speaker thus pieces together his plot: a series of social exchanges and private speculations about a set of real or imagined relations of intimacy, all linked together by the narrator's faith in the unseen sacred fount. This ebb and flow of talk about an "ultimate" (22) law of union proceeds in four stages. Initially detecting change in two characters—from stupid to clever (Gilbert Long) and from old to young (Mrs. Brissenden)—the narrator/critic constructs his theory by inviting others to confirm his suspicions. Mrs. Briss is draining life from her aging husband Guy, he conjectures to his painter friend Ford Obert, while he intimates to Mrs. Brissenden that Long is gaining his wit at the expense of some woman "reduced to idiocy" (37). Mrs. Briss herself quickly surmises that this unknown lover must be the depleted widow May Server. The very fact that the first person has expanded the consciousness of others, turning Mrs. Briss and the painter into agents in a drama of his own making, compels him to protect the more vulnerable, passive victims in his theory (May Server and Guy Briss) from his delegated detectives. Overwhelmed by this oppressive sense of responsibility, the plotter briefly tries to break free of his "private madness" (162) altogether, only to discover that his romance is now so overdetermined that he cannot escape from his own paranoid speculations. He thus ends up frantically defending his "perfect palace of thought" (311) against a former confidante as a way of defending his sanity, since self and plot—both fictions—have become one and the same in the course of narrating. Throughout *The Sacred Fount* the narrator is victimized by his own art, for in the absence of any third-person authorial context, the "I" must struggle to erect boundaries from within in order to shield the members of Newmarch from one another and to protect himself from his own overwrought imagination.

These boundaries, which are also social bridges, must be fixed from the start. As he begins his journey to Newmarch, the first-person narrator immediately speaks of "placing" people (6), quantifying their intrinsic properties (Long's intelligence, Mrs. Briss's age), and setting them against other known relations. His tendency to schematize these relations into abstract patterns provides an epistemological context for a highly formalized society in a state of flux. Signification is so difficult at Newmarch because its members are continually masking their motives from one another; as in Hawthorne's Blithedale utopia, to act "naturally" is a meaningless proposition, since human nature is always mediated by a complex web of ambiguous social interaction. In both cases the first person can penetrate the artifice of the group only by relying on an exaggerated "fine symmetry, of artificial proportion" (183). Just as Coverdale/Hawthorne use the romance of the Veiled Lady to articulate the mysterious dynamics of master-slave power relations, so James and his first person invoke an equally magical principle of sacrifice, the sacred fount, to account for and stabilize male-female relations at Newmarch. Such a rigid caricature or geometry of sexual intimacy makes comprehension possible.

Grounded in an absolute concept of sexual union, the narrator's "torch of analogy" (66)—youthful Mrs. Briss is to her worn-out husband as profiting Long is to a mysterious lover—creates an economy of reference for him to share with others, a means of processing affairs "mingled and confounded . . . not according to tradition" (15). "Experience," to recall James's preface to *Roderick Hudson*, "has to organize . . . some system of observation—for fear, in the admirable immensity, of losing its way" (AN, 3). The law of sexual intercourse that the bachelor/outsider imposes on Newmarch by a kind of executive fiat offers precisely this type of provisional organizing formula or *donnée* from which all else follows.

Although observation and narration remain two distinct ways of knowing in the novel, the narrator's acts of witnessing quickly become subordinated to the imperatives of his systematic plotting. As Naomi Lebowitz has remarked, *The Sacred Fount* is a kind of "critical preface in action,"[43] with the sacrificial theory of the fount serving as the originating germ that motivates the first person's self-authorizing discourse.

Earlier I observed that in the course of their quests James's first-person narrators enact, in debased versions, the riddles of creativity they would decipher: Aspern's love letters and Vereker's secret figure. *The Sacred Fount*'s "evidence of relations" (38) is similarly brought to life by the narrator's social interaction with his fellow Newmarch guests. But in this case the commentator is responsible for *inventing* the very object of his analysis, what he calls at one point "the missing word" (64). Because his search lacks any well-defined vision or tangible goal—a bundle of papers, or a metaphoric figure in a carpet—the first person must objectify his quest by reifying the process of narrating itself. He therefore begins to refer to his theory of the fount as an "edifice" (111) which is enlarged with each new conjecture. "Build[ing] with confidence on others" (1), his obsessive discussions about the fount imitate its own metaphoric laws of operation: just as the fount's passion is presumed to "multiply in the transfer" between "creditor" and "borrower" (53), the narrator's exchanges multiply and prolong his pleasure beyond his initial investment in his theory. In order to "pay," however, the narrator realizes that his obsession must also "borrow" (23); as he moves closer and closer to understanding the fount by identifying with its suffering victims, "poor Briss" and May Server, his language increasingly sides with the victimizers, Mrs. Briss and Gilbert Long. Translated into speech, compassion becomes a form of exploitation that will eventually undo the narrator himself.

Even more so than *The Aspern Papers* and "The Figure in the Carpet," the sheer act of speaking leads the first person into an intolerable paradox in which he is excluded from the very intimacy he desires by virtue of helping to express and sustain it in others.[44] Consolidating his imaginative gains to construct a coherent foundation for passion, the commentator neglects alternative solutions to the "riddle" (15) of Newmarch that remain beyond his grasp. The initial meeting between Briss and the narrator establishes this pattern of failure for the entire novel. Startled into "blankness" by hearing an "unknown" gentleman call his name, he quickly recovers to recognize Mrs. Brissenden's depleted husband, who had "mistaken the signs" while "in quest of his quarters" and wandered into the narrator's own room in the "bachelor wing." Helping "the hero of his odd union" to "place himself" in the married wing, the first person thus finds his domesticated double, an alter ego through whom he can experience vicariously the fount's life (21). Yet this key moment of identification also contains a crucial difference that marks an unbridgeable barrier between the two: Briss is married but the anonymous "I" is not. Acting as the married man's "protector, his providence, his effective omniscience" (171), the fount's narrator finds a pathos in "poor Briss" that his theory will allow him to observe and orchestrate—but only from the outside.

As he profits from this projected sense of pathos, the bachelor/scribe is led from poor Briss to May Server, who remains throughout "the controlling image for me, the real principle of composition" (167). Lacking any certain knowledge of the widow's secret liaison, the narrator analogizes the husband's ravaged state with her equally distraught condition in order to create "a real relation, the relation of a fellowship in resistance to doom" (146). May Server thus becomes a more exquisite version of Coverdale's Veiled Lady,[45] a silent instrument of mediation serving to contain the excesses of the narrator's imagination by providing a center for his plot, as well as for the Newmarch community. As with Priscilla, it is the drained woman's "blankness itself" which strikes her enamored admirer as "the most direct reference of all" (196). Calling his presence "a rough substitute for Guy's" (141), the surrogate lover, like his more farcical predecessor narrating *The Aspern Papers*, proceeds with "extraordinary tenderness" (129) to convert the widow's "consuming passion" (136) into the enchanted terms of art. During their scene together in the dreamlike wood—the heart of the novel—the first person realizes most profoundly the power and beauty of his romance, as well as its severe limitations.

James's narrative is so moving precisely because it acknowledges moral responsibility for making Server "a wasted and dishonoured symbol" (136) in the very act of eloquently building on "some intimacy of unspeakable confidence" (140). The passive victim's vulnerability, the "confessed collapse" that dissolves her public mask of restless sociability, derives from her peculiar kind of silence: "a supremely unsuccessful attempt to say nothing" (135). Just as her formerly vacant lover, Gilbert Long, is presumed to gain the "gift of talk" (52) by her sacrifice, so the first person now turns her "mute address" (141) into his haunting narration. "Voided and scraped of everything" but her "consciousness" (136), Server must even give up that precious possession when the "providential" (154) narrator begins to "put the words into her mouth" (141) as a way of imaginatively entering her mind. Yet the brief moments she does manage to speak for herself, the first person acknowledges that "the whole airy structure" he has erected with the aid of poor Briss might fall to pieces once she begins to deny any special relation with her sad co-victim. Listening to May insist that Briss is "strikingly in love with his wife" and that she herself has "never *been* in love" (149), the narrator decides to restore her autonomy by pressing her to desist from speaking "beautiful duplicity" (140). Since he "had not the direct benefit" of "her passion and her beauty" (151), the bachelor knows only that his fragile, disintegrating subject cannot be "kept" in motionless surrender any longer. He must therefore let go (they are holding hands) to regain "the temporary loss of my thread" (151). When the husband in question suddenly appears on the scene, as he always seems to do, like a kind of wish fulfillment, the relieved surrogate withdraws to let Briss and Server enjoy their advantage or "margin" over his plotting, which has helped to "formulate their relation" (155). Whether or not the widow's denial of intimacy simply betrays the depths of that intimacy, as the first person must assume to sustain his analytic "superstructure" (230), their very talk of marriage reminds the narrator of his proximity to, yet exclusion from, the sacred fount.

The first person can so use Server's silence because she herself "hasn't any *talk* . . . to speak of" (112). The "quandary" facing the widow (who has lost all three of her children) thus lies "in her certitude of every absence of issue" (100). It is this quandary of absent issue which compels the narrator to speak for her and to represent her losses. The matter of "issue"—whether speech or procreation, or language as a substitute for procreation—is crucial for understanding the entire novel. When, late in the narrative, Mrs. Briss and her poor husband turn their backs on the inquisitive narrator to retire to the privacy of their bedroom, they literally verify his recurring fear of acting like "the uninvited reporter in whose face a door is closed" (156). Suddenly feeling "the thickness of our medium" (199), the bachelor/scribe "aim[s] at an issue" (199) out into the fresh night air. That triple pun on "issue" neatly fixes his own predicament. Recalling yet again his solitary state, the "I" seeks "issue"—a way out of the endless Gothic corridors of house/head/plot, some relief from the suffocating torture chamber his analytic imagination has fabricated. As he subsequently will realize, such "criticism" is simply "the vision of horrors" (298). In order to break free of his own solipsistic "palace of thought" (311), the first person must arrive at some conclusive issue, a rational goal or point of origin outside himself that can be resolved by recourse to objective evidence. Hence his initial model of social relations, reified as the sacred fount: "the power not one's self . . . that made for passion" (17). To aim with passion at such an issue finally means to give birth to something. As his beautiful edifice grows larger and larger, the forlorn narrator worries that all of his analytic labor will conclude "without an issue" (184), that, like May Server, he will have absurdly sacrificed "affairs of one's own" (89) for the sake of some "ridiculous obsession" (89) that bears neither "fruit" (219) nor "flower" (205).

By the end of the romance, "the point at issue" (278) raised by his accuser, Mrs. Brissenden, is nothing less than the first person's sanity. During their midnight colloquy, which sprawls to take up the final quarter of the novel, the narrator's worst fears are realized, as his exquisite scheme suffers a nightmarish peripety or unraveling. Mrs. Briss's systematic dismantling of his plot exposes the same torments of execution that James would later dramatize in his critical prefaces. Throughout his romance the first person has exercised "a process of providential supervision as made me morally responsible" (154) for the characters his theory has shaped. But as Lady John insists, "a real providence *knows*; whereas you . . . have to find out" (176).

The first person's main problem is essentially epistemological; once he sets his plot in motion, its agents are free to act for themselves, or even to act against him in ways he cannot foresee, as his former confidante, Mrs. Briss, learns to do. "An element of our start," he confesses toward the end of the novel, "had been that I admired her freedom" (305). This original freedom enables Mrs. Briss to assume the recalcitrant role of counterplotter, a reader/author who transgresses the uncertain narrative boundaries of the

"I" by bluntly proposing a "finished system" (318) of her own: Gilbert Long is "the same ass" (305); nothing has changed, and therefore no plot, which depends on change, is possible. To salvage his beloved structure, the first person must assume that Mrs. Briss is lying, that she and Long have been conspiring behind his back all along to protect either May Server or themselves. At one point he goes so far as to conjecture that Long's stupidity has been feigned from the beginning, strictly a "fictive ineptitude" (297). Granting Long this sudden self-directed intelligence would ironically allow the first person to regain some control over his own hapless plotting. But in the face of Mrs. Brissenden's relentless opposition, he cannot even sustain the fiction that he has invested in a fiction all along. In other words, the sacred fount stubbornly refuses to relinquish its grip on reality; despite the manifold possibilities of infidelity raised by Mrs. Briss, her denial still follows the narrator's original theory by simply realigning the identities of victimizer and victim. Just as both wife and bachelor have depleted poor Briss's resources throughout the novel, the wife now drains the narrator's own well of creativity: "My wealth of imagination . . . was . . . her strength" (240). Like Gilbert Long, the "transfigured talker" (106), Mrs. Briss is also "made" a "talker" by the sacrifice of another.

Mrs. Brissenden is able to draw on the narrator's imagination because of the special kind of knowledge she possesses. Just before the rivals confront one another, poor Briss makes "the final expression of his sacrifice" (225) by bearing his wife's request for a late-night interview. Offering the narrator his hand in farewell, he leaves the first person with "things unspoken and untouched, unspeakable and untouchable, everything that had been between us . . ." (227). But the narrator's intimacy with Briss (like his equally intimate meeting with May Server) is only a pale shadow of the married man's relation with his wife. At his moment of greatest crisis, when the narrator can no longer calculate "for what issue she was heading" (301), Mrs. Briss delivers the fatal blow to his enchanted castle by suggesting that Lady John, not May Server, is Long's secret lover, and that she positively knows this simply because her husband has told her so. "I take his word" (307) she asserts, just as earlier Briss had insisted that his wife "tells me everything" (118). Whether the husband's information is true or just a smoke screen for a sordid set of affairs, or whether he has, in fact, "talked" (307) at all is largely beside the point. Mrs. Brissenden's reliance on her husband suggests a foundation for belief that transcends the many ambiguities of the situation. May Server may have "made love" (316) to Briss, as his wife claims, and/or she herself may be boldly covering up her own extramarital affair with Long. Or Mrs. Briss may have been lied to from the start, a possibility which squares with the narrator's early assumption that the victims must keep their victimizers blissfully ignorant of the truth. In any case, a sacrifice, or draining of the fount, has clearly taken place. Suddenly we are made aware of an entirely different system of discourse that has been quietly operating on the margins of Newmarch all along: an intercourse of presence in which intimacy is exchanged between sexual partners, as opposed to the obsessive solitary conjectures of the bachelor. Yet in confronting the first person with the limits of his own knowledge, Mrs. Briss paradoxically affirms what she sets out to deny, for the notion of the sacred fount itself depends on this same assumption of marriage as an absolute value. We cannot sanction her counterplot without drawing on the fount for support.

Providing an analogy for every kind of relation at Newmarch (sordid or sublime, real or imagined), the theory of the fount is thus preserved—but only at the expense of its creator, who is left speechless in the end. When the first person, ever the plotter, initially attempts to regain his self-confidence and restore his collapsing "house of cards" (261) by retrospectively tracing a *new* fount or first cause based on Mrs. Briss's surprising change in perception, she claims that she stopped believing his hypothesis "as soon as I was not with you—I mean with you personally" (287). But as the narrator himself realizes, his "person" is constituted by a "tension ... purely intellectual" and is therefore strictly a by-product of his "theory" (288). "Carried away" (262) by his feverish search for form, a perfect end in itself, the creator no longer seeks to save poor Briss and May Server, "inhumanely" (104) reduced, as they are, to wasted symbols of art. He instead tries to save "my precious sense of their loss, their disintegration and their doom" (273), a "sense" which the first person has entirely invested in his act of narration; to challenge his plot, as Mrs. Briss presumes to do, is to call his person into question.[46]

The narrator's effort to preserve "the kingdom of thought I

had won" (255) thus becomes a mock-heroic struggle to maintain his sense of self: to prevent his "I" from dissolving under pressure into meaningless chaos. From this initial state of chaos the first-person narrator has fashioned an elaborate verbal structure that conceals "its weak foundation" (311), namely, the fact that his identity is a provisional grammatical construct to begin with. Like May Server, he finds himself waging a "small lonely fight with disintegration" (167). To lose such a frantic battle means to lose, quite literally, "presence of mind" (191), to return to "that blankness" (193) that inevitably awaits the writer upon quitting Newmarch society. Faced with the possibility that there is "nothing" (296) in Gilbert Long and therefore nothing in his theory, the exhausted first person "go[es] utterly to pieces" (297), his plot reduced to a "mere heap of disfigured fragments" (311).[47] Mrs. Brissenden finally leaves him, a narrator if nothing else, with the nagging "issue" of his sanity. She pronounces him "crazy" (318), a "last word" that "put me altogether nowhere" (319). Eighteen years earlier James had complained about Trollope's "little slaps at credulity", insisting that "as a narrator of fictitious events" the novelist "is nowhere."[48] And nowhere is precisely where the fount's first-person fabulist now ends up. Seeking, once again, to "escape to other air," the deranged "I" totals his losses to withdraw back into the madness of his "method": "I *should* certainly never again, on the spot, quite hang together, even though it wasn't really that I hadn't three times her method. What I too fatally lacked was her tone" (319). James thus closes his romance on a final note of ambiguity. Fatally lacking tone not only means that the narrator has lost the kind of authoritative command over his production that Mrs. Briss has taken from him; it also means that he can no longer *tell* what her tone is. "Tone," James had written in an 1887 theater review, is "*the* great vehicle of communication".[49] Mrs. Briss's tone of voice, like Gwendolen's face in "The Figure in the Carpet," is an expression of her personality, a crucial sign of her human presence. Absorbed by his imagination, the bachelor cannot recognize tone because in the course of narrating he has become toneless himself. In the final analysis, the first person exists in an entirely different world from Mrs. Briss.

Used up in the process of plotting, the romance's narrator is the ultimate sacrificial victim of *The Sacred Fount*. Risking the terrible fluidity of self-revelation, James drives the first person into failure, fragmentation, and madness as a way of issuing from the other side with his own sanity intact. A serviceable nightmare, James's experiment in self-narration serves to dramatize the cost of penetrating experience by art, his realization that social relations can achieve a knowable form only by a kind of fiction. But as he casts his doubts about writing into writing, he also comes to cast them aside. By compelling his confessed agent to tell Newmarch's secrets, James prepares the way for his three great late novels. In *The Ambassadors, The Wings of the Dove,* and *The Golden Bowl* the sacrifices and bewilderment that take place within the fiction are kept distinct from the author's own torments and confusion without. Bounded by a third-person context, released from the burden of creating the terms that order their experience, James's characters are free to live and interact with one another, to feel the kind of intimacy, pain, and rapture that the bachelor narrating *The Sacred Fount* struggles to articulate without ever knowing. Like the mysterious host who invisibly presides over Newmarch's guests, James uses his poor hero to discover new sources of creative power *outside* his text. Giving up the first person to his unappeased desire, the author relocates his own sacred fount.

Afterword

> I am certain that what makes American success
> is American failure.
>
> GERTRUDE STEIN

Speculating in a late essay entitled "Is There a Life After Death?"
(1910), Henry James wondered what the "conception of immortality *as* personal"—"the only thing that gives it meaning or relevance"—might mean to him:

> I practically know what I am talking about when I say "I," hy-
> pothetically, for my full experience of another term of being, just
> as I know it when I say "I" for my experience of this one; but I
> shouldn't in the least do so were I not *able* to say "I"—had I to
> reckon, that is, with a failure of the signs by which I know myself.
> In presence of the great question I cling to these signs more than
> ever.... [1]

What constitutes these signs of selfhood, and how and why they
fail their first persons in the midst of discourse, has been the central
concern of this study, from the destructive returns of Poe's doubles,
to the disintegration of Coverdale's Blithedale enterprise, to the
final baffling of James's bachelor/critics, ending in *The Sacred Fount*'s
relegation of its "I" to "nowhere," a sort of death. In each case the
first person, seemingly free of all restraint, seeks to impose himself
on the world he narrates; in each case the imperial plotter falls
prey to what James called the "treacheries" of execution, entangled

by relations not of his own making. As a result, romance quickly lapses into disenchantment, disfiguring the narrative and betraying the first person. Yet to subvert the self, to give up and denaturalize the "I" as little more that an empty grammatical function, can also serve to affirm the subject's staying power, for it is the very fall from authority of the "I" which calls attention to the personal pronoun's potential to confer life. Possibility is actualized by its failure. What remains to be seen, then, is how these three writers progressively use the first person's vulnerability to their own advantage, even as they continue to risk losing the same kind of freedom and control they deny, with an increasing degree of deliberation, their fictional surrogates. I therefore want to conclude by hazarding some brief generalizations about how these particular first-person romances develop during the nineteenth century.

Moving from Poe to James, I have noted three related tendencies: a growing thematization of failure; a more and more radical undoing of the fictional "I"; and a deepening suspicion about the first-person form itself. Insofar as the first person is simultaneously tale-teller and protagonist, his personal fate and his literary form remain inextricably linked. Poe's most controlled productions, for instance, expressly take the narrator's loss of control as their main theme. In a relatively late story like "The Black Cat," to cite just one example, the comedy derives from the extravagant discrepancy between the incoherence of the storyteller's life and the apparent tightness of his artful constructions. "Here, at least, my labors have not been in vain," he brags after meticulously walling up the wife he has killed in a fit of rage. That "at least" is devastating, but the undermining aside would seem to belong to Poe as much as to his first person, who must be shielded from his own insights so that he may get on with his elaborate plotting. Exploiting the possibilities for farce in his storyteller's chilling ineptitude thus allows Poe to manage the terrors of execution without simply reduplicating them the way an earlier Gothic writer such as Charles Brockden Brown and his hapless first persons often do. Yet Poe's own desperate hope for the perfect plot, his romantic clinging to the notion of a unitary identity beyond worldly contamination, draws him into the confusion and self-betrayals of his doomed fictional creations. Denying the other as other until very late in his career, Poe falls victim to the same futile search for prelapsarian originality that plagues his lonely first persons.

The Blithedale Romance turns away from this alienating Adamic quest for perfection by treating utopianism as a communal affair out of which emerges a more modern, more dynamic notion of personal identity as contingent on social interaction. No longer assumed to be an unchanging essence, the "self" is now practically constituted through role playing within the group. In contrast to Poe's amateur criminals and detectives, Hawthorne's first-person narrator has a particular vocation—minor poet—which determines his part in Blithedale's theater of relations and helps to account for his prying interest in others as more than simply a quirk of his personality. Individualism is not an unattainable ideal, as in the case of Poe, but a problem in itself, since it is the friction among individual egos (Hollingsworth's, Zenobia's, Coverdale's) which causes the Veiled Lady and her secret family to dissolve and the Blithedale enterprise to fall to pieces. But Hawthorne clearly participates in the very thing he aims to criticize, for his self-protective retreat behind Coverdale ultimately works to return us to an analysis of individuals in isolation who can only pretend to recreate New England society in miniature. Refusing to abandon his cherished notion of the inviolability of the individual, Hawthorne in the end confesses, along with Coverdale, his reluctance to believe in collective action. The fatal disenchanting of romance entails the failure of community in addition to the disillusionment of the first person. Hawthorne thus sees how the storyteller's narrative alienation might be made to stand for antebellum Americans' sense of cultural alienation as well.

Though James also plants each of his first persons in a mysterious web of social relations, his focus is much narrower than Hawthorne's (in The Blithedale Romance) and the vocation of each fictional "I" much more specialized. If Coverdale helps to create an alternative society by acting as "half a poet [and] half a critic," the Jamesian bachelor/plotter is all critic, relentlessly interpreting signs of late nineteenth-century social rituals (the game of worshiping someone else's procreative originality, whether it be dead poet, living novelist, or metaphoric fount) rather than directly participating, however superficially, in forming these institutions. Seeking self-affirmation in the context of these firmly entrenched rituals, the first person is limited to a strictly professional relationship with his subjects; drained of its apparent autonomy, the "I" becomes something of a caricature of itself, (a "publishing scoundrel" or anonymous reviewer), until we finally end up with little more than a speculating eye/voice dispossessed of all corporeal substance. Identity is virtually obliterated.

The Sacred Fount marks an end of the line for this special brand of first-person failure, leaving the romance's governing assumptions about the freedom and power of the imagination strewn in disarray. Whereas Poe betrays both his first persons' scheming as well as his own sense of self, Hawthorne uses Miles Coverdale to regain a sense of intimacy between author and fictional narrator, but at the expense of the minor poet's personal estrangement from his imaginary enterprise. James, in turn, converts the plotter's failure to authenticate himself into the very principle of first-person plotting. Certainly twentieth-century American writers would continue to invent dramatized narrators (Fitzgerald, Faulkner, and Nabokov, to name just three), but for different ends and with different consequences. Poised on the verge of modernism, *The Sacred Fount* pushes the desperate urge to erect an ideal palace of thought to its limit, until the search for a perfectly symmetrical plot to contain identity threatens to overwhelm both James and his nameless agent. Trapped in such an endless labyrinthine nightmare, there is nowhere for the first person to go except, perhaps, the critical prefaces to the New York Edition: the ultimate professionalizing of the analytic "I."

The progressive reification, from Poe to James, of the romancer's darkest abyss proves to be one modest example of what Kenneth Burke has called "the bureaucratization of the imaginative," the historical process by which imaginative possibilities (usually utopian) are institutionalized and ordered, provided with a systematic rationale.[2] Yet if this large historical process helps to explain the increasingly deliberate ironizing of first-person American romance during the nineteenth century, it would be a mistake to assume that this growing mockery drives a wedge between author and narrator. As I have insisted throughout this study, narrating fiction in the first person is an extremely intimate business. To invoke Burke again, the attitude these authors characteristically express toward their creations partakes of "true irony," that is, irony "based upon a sense of fundamental kinship with the enemy, as one *needs* him, is *indebted* to him, is not merely outside him as an observer but contains him *within....*"[3] The authorial victimizer thus must identify absolutely with his sacrificial victim, experiencing something of the sacred but also sharing his loss. Given the romancer's desire for perfection, the first person is quite literally bound to fail. But as James's essay on immortality suggests, how and when and if one chooses to say "I," how and when and if one *can* articulate the first person, does make a difference.

Notes

Introduction

1. Throughout this study I have used as my text for Poe's tales *Collected Works of Edgar Allan Poe*, ed. Thomas Mabbott, 3 vols. (Cambridge: Harvard University Press, 1978). Page references are cited in parentheses following quotations, although I have not given page numbers in every case since many of these short passages are easy to locate within a given tale. All emphases in original.

2. The standard "story" versus "discourse" distinction stems from the classic Russian Formalist distinction between "fabula" and "sjûzet" invoked by Boris Tomashevsky in "Thématique," rpt. in *Russian Formalist Criticism*, ed. Lee T. Lemon and Marion J. Reis (Lincoln: University of Nebraska Press, 1965), p. 68. Picked up in the 1960s by various structuralists interested in establishing a grammar of narrative, the terms of this basic distinction have become notoriously slippery: what Todorov calls "discours" Barthes calls "narration," and so on. For three excellent discussions of the current status of narrative theory, see: Seymour Chatman, *Story and Discourse* (Ithaca, N.Y.: Cornell University Press, 1978); Jonathan Culler, "Story and Discourse in the Analysis of Narrative," *The Pursuit of Signs* (Ithaca, N.Y.: Cornell University Press, 1981), pp. 169–87; and Shlomith Rimmon-Kenan, *Narrative Fiction: Contemporary Poetics* (London: Methuen, 1983). Although I would agree with Culler that "story" and "discourse" are essentially incompatible, so that distinguishing between them is inevitable for the study of narrative, I am examining this double

logic specifically as it pertains to the problem of identity by locating it in a narrating subject, a first-person singular. For the most part I therefore use the terms story, plot, and narrative interchangeably, because such abstract compartmentalizing, however useful, tends to artificially isolate one narrative function from another, whereas I am more interested in seeing how such divisions dissolve during the activity of narrating. But I do maintain a basic distinction between author and narrator, that is, a distinction between a work of fiction's "outside" and "inside"—a boundary defined by that fiction's narrative form but one that can be crossed by the first-person "I."

3. Michel Foucault, "What Is an Author?" rpt. in *Textual Strategies: Perspectives in Post-Structuralist Criticism*, ed. Josué Harari, (Ithaca, N.Y.: Cornell University Press, 1979), p. 159.

4. Wayne Booth, *The Rhetoric of Fiction* (Chicago: University of Chicago Press, 1961), p. 20.

5. See Dorrit Cohn, *Transparent Minds* (Princeton, N.J.: Princeton University Press, 1978), and Franz Stanzel, *A Theory of Narrative* (New York: Cambridge University Press, 1984). Although Stanzel refers to these formal properties as "conventions," he does so in a way which does not take into account the changing conditions of literary production, in ways of reading, in the institution of literary criticism, and so on. As a result, his notion of literary form remains essentially Platonic.

6. Recent efforts to develop more dynamic models of narrative that seek to avoid the pitfalls of structuralist dualism include: Barbara H. Smith, "Narrative Versions, Narrative Theories," *Critical Inquiry* 7 (1980), 213–36; Paul Ricoeur, *Time and Narrative* (Chicago: University of Chicago Press, 1984); Peter Brooks, *Reading for the Plot* (New York: Knopf, 1984); and Ross Chambers, *Story and Seduction* (Minneapolis: University of Minnesota Press, 1984). None of these valuable studies, however, focuses specifically on the relation between author and narrator.

7. Fredric R. Jameson, "The Symbolic Inference," *Critical Inquiry* 5 (1978), 520.

8. I do not mean to minimize the substantial differences between writers as diverse as Barthes, Derrida, Foucault, Bataille, and Artaud, among many others, but structuralists, poststructuralists, and avante-garde modernists do seem to share at least one common goal, namely, what Susan Sontag has called "the disestablishment of the author." See her introduction to her edition of *Antonin Artaud: Selected Writings* (New York: Farrar, Straus, Giroux, 1976), p. xvii. The key essay representing this continental perspective remains Foucault's "What Is an Author?" In this masterful ideological analysis of the author, Foucault briefly admits that the operations of first person may allow for "certain modifications" that would complicate his attempt to distinguish neatly between discourses "provided with the author-function" and those "lacking it" (152). See also Roland Barthes,

"The Death of the Author," in *Image, Music, Text*, ed. Stephen Heath (New York: Hill and Wang, 1977), pp. 142–48. For a suggestive reply, see William H. Gass, "The Death of the Author," in his *Habitations of the Word* (New York: Simon and Schuster, 1985), pp. 265–88.

9. Jonathan Culler remarks on this critical "strategy for humanizing writing" in his *Structuralist Poetics* (Ithaca, N.Y.: Cornell University Press, 1975), pp. 200–201.

10. Emerson's phrase is cited by Lawrence Buell, *Literary Transcendentalism* (Ithaca, N.Y.: Cornell University Press, 1973), p. 267. Buell's quotation of Emerson is part of an extended discussion of the importance of the first-person "I" for transcendentalism in general.

11. Interestingly enough, American rhetoricians like Wayne Booth and French semioticians like Gérard Genette both tend to discount the distinction between first and third grammatic person as a misleading and inaccurate foundation to study narrative. Booth argues that the first-person/third-person distinction obscures more crucial discriminations to be made regarding the fiction's center of consciousness or "point of view," a critical concept that Genette in turn challenges, along with the value of grammatical person, because Booth's terminology blurs two distinct issues: who speaks (voice) and who sees (focus). See Booth, *The Rhetoric of Fiction*, pp. 150–51, and Gérard Genette, *Narrative Discourse* (Ithaca, N.Y.: Cornell University Press, 1980), pp. 186–89.

12. Stanzel, *A Theory of Narrative*, p. 93.

13. Emile Benveniste, *Problems in General Linguistics* (Coral Gables, Fla.: University of Miami Press, 1971), pp. 218, 220, 226. Benveniste's crucial observations apply to nonfictional discourse as well as fictional. But I will be restricting myself to the differences between first- and third-person fiction; including nonfictional discourse would introduce a different set of issues beyond the scope of this study, such as the relative truth claims of autobiography compared to fictionalized self-representation, ordinary versus literary language, and so on. For an interesting recent study of autobiography that takes up these issues along lines similar to my discussion of first-person fiction, see Paul Jay, *Being in the Text* (Ithaca, N.Y.: Cornell University Press, 1984). Like many other theorists of autobiography, Jay seeks to minimize the differences between fictional and non-fictional discourse.

14. Benveniste, *Problems in General Linguistics*, p. 222. For a fine discussion of Benveniste's contribution to semiotics, see Katja Silverman, *The Subject of Semiotics* (New York: Oxford University Press, 1983), pp. 43–53.

15. Explicating Lacan's notion of "the mirror stage," Terry Eagleton puts it this way: "We arrive at a sense of an 'I' by finding that 'I' reflected back to ourselves by some object or person in the world. This object is at once part of ourselves—we *identify* with it—yet not ourselves, something alien." See Eagleton's *Literary Theory* (Minneapolis: University of Minnesota

Press, 1983), pp. 164–65. We have already seen how Poe's story recounting Psyche's predicament literalizes this split in the subject.

16. Northrop Frye, *Anatomy of Criticism* (Princeton, N.J.: Princeton University Press, 1957), p. 193.

17. Booth, *The Rhetoric of Fiction*, p. 273.

18. It may be objected that I am drawing the distinction between first- and third-person fiction too sharply, that the differences are not as great as I imply, that an author's decision to use one or the other form may not be of primary importance, and that similar entanglements between plot and identity arise in many novels regardless of grammatical person. A story like James's third-person "The Beast in the Jungle," for instance, whose language so catches us up in the protagonist's way of thinking, suggests that it matters little whether John Marcher actually tells his own story or not. But the fact that James inserts an "I" (his own, not Marcher's) at a crucial moment near the end of the tale—just as Marcher is at the brink of his devastating revelation—points to the author's urgent need to emphasize the *difference* between himself and his character at the moment of their greatest intimacy. In this respect John Barth's observation is pertinent: "The more closely an author identifies with the narrator, literally or metaphorically, the less advisable it is, as a rule, to use the first-person narrative viewpoint." See his *Lost in the Funhouse* (New York: Bantam, 1968), p. 74. I am aware, however, that my approach may be taken as narrowly formalistic. Roland Barthes's speculations on converting "personal" into "impersonal" modes of address or, perhaps more telling, Franz Kafka's evidently painless decision midway through writing *The Castle* to transform his protagonist K from an "I" into a "he" certainly call into question the rigidity of formal distinctions based strictly on grammatical person. See Roland Barthes, "To Write: An Intransitive Verb," in *The Structuralist Controversy*, ed. Richard Macksey and Eugene Donato (Baltimore, Md.: The Johns Hopkins University Press, 1970), pp. 138–41; see also Cohn, *Transparent Minds*, pp. 169–71.

19. Benveniste, *Problems in General Linguistics*, p. 226. Benveniste's own emphasis.

20. It is interesting to note, for example, that Melville and Twain both displace the burden of authorship onto *third-person* characters, Ahab and Tom Sawyer, aggressive plotters who serve to express their respective authors' anxieties about the egocentric imperatives of their craft. Finding the making of fictions to be more liberating than restrictive, Ishmael and Huck can thus each get on with his business without worrying too much about the relation between story and self. To release their storytellers from the pressure of storytelling, Melville and Twain in effect transform them into passive third persons by either removing at will the interposing "I" altogether (hence Ahab's extended soliloquizing) or turning the first-

person narrator into another character (Huck's figurative "rebirth" as Tom Sawyer near the end of the novel).

Chapter 1

1. Aside from a few early satires and parodies ("Metzengerstein," "A Tale of Jerusalem," and "King Pest"), the one notable exception is "The Masque of the Red Death." Even in Poe's colloquies, dialogue quickly tends to dissolve into monologue. Citations for Poe's tales are from *Collected Works of Edgar Allan Poe*, ed. Thomas Mabbott, 3 vols. (Cambridge: Harvard University Press, 1978). Page numbers are cited parenthetically following quotations.

2. Proper names, place names, dates, family trades: the specificity with which Poe opens *The Narrative of Arthur Gordon Pym* may serve as a counterexample to my generalizations. But even here, in this imitation of a voyage journal, we note that such mimesis is undercut by a preface specifically calling attention to the hand of "Mr. Poe" at work in these opening pages. These framing allusions to Pym/Poe's credentials and credibility become even more self-enclosing once the town of "Edgarton" is introduced as the narrative's starting point.

3. Henry James, *The Art of The Novel*, ed. R. P. Blackmur (New York: Scribner's, 1934), p. 33. The previous quotation occurs on page 32.

4. Henry James, *Hawthorne* (New York: Harper and Brothers, 1880), pp. 42–43.

5. Beginning with laments by Cooper, Hawthorne, and James, the writing on American romance is extensive. Twentieth-century critical studies following James's lead include Lionel Trilling, "Reality in America," *The Liberal Imagination* (New York: Doubleday, 1953), pp. 15–32, and Richard Chase, *The American Novel and Its Tradition* (New York: Doubleday, 1957). More recent studies include Joel Porte, *The Romance in America: Studies in Cooper, Poe, Hawthorne, Melville, and James* (Middletown, Conn.: Wesleyan University Press, 1969); Eric Sundquist, *Home as Found: Authority and Genealogy in Nineteenth-Century American Literature* (Baltimore, Md.: The Johns Hopkins University Press, 1979); Michael Bell, *The Development of American Romance: The Sacrifice of Relation* (Chicago: University of Chicago Press, 1980); and Evan Carton, *The Rhetoric of American Romance* (Baltimore, Md.: The Johns Hopkins University Press, 1985). For a brief but excellent discussion that argues for a historicizing of the concept of romance, see Amy Kaplan, "'Absent Things in American Life,'" *The Yale Review* 74 (1984), 126–35. My own use of the term largely follows the line of criticism inaugurated by James, but it certainly does not preclude a more historically informed kind of analysis.

6. William Carlos Williams, "Edgar Allan Poe," *In the American Grain* (New York: New Directions, 1956), pp. 228–29. T. S. Eliot offers a similar observation while discussing Poe's influence on French writers: " 'The Philosophy of Composition' suggested to Valéry a method and an occupation—that of observing himself write." T. S. Eliot, "From Poe to Valéry," rpt. in *The Recognition of Edgar Allan Poe,* ed. Eric Carlson (Ann Arbor: University of Michigan Press, 1966), p. 218.

7. Griswold's slanderous rewriting of Poe and Baudelaire's more sympathetic though equally distorted mythologizing of the American writer from secondhand sources together make a fascinating case study of the way in which literary reputations are posthumously formed and deformed. The facts against Griswold, who was Poe's literary executor, are thoroughly documented in Arthur Hobson Quinn's *Edgar Allan Poe: A Critical Biography* (New York: Appleton-Century-Crofts, 1941). In *The French Face of Edgar Allan Poe* (Carbondale: Southern Illinois University Press, 1957) Patrick Quinn examines Baudelaire's romantic transformation of Poe into a drunken, haunted, homeless *poète maudit* figure, a persistent legend that ironically owes something to the deliberate hatchet job perpetrated by Griswold, whom Baudelaire himself passionately denounced in 1856 as a "pedagogue-vampire." See also Claude Richard's *Edgar Allan Poe: journaliste et critique* (Paris: C. Klincksieck, 1978), app. VII.

8. Richard Wilbur, "The House of Poe" (The Library of Congress Anniversary Lecture, May 4, 1959), rpt. in *The Recognition of Edgar Allan Poe,* pp. 255–77. See also Wilbur's "Introduction" to the section on Poe in *Major Writers in America,* ed. Perry Miller (New York: Harcourt, Brace and World, 1962), I, pp. 369–82. For other major critics in this tradition see Allen Tate, "The Angelic Imagination: Poe as God" and "Our Cousin, Mr. Poe," *The Forlorn Demon* (Chicago: Regnery, 1953), pp. 56–95; D. H. Lawrence, *Studies in Classic American Literature* (1923; rpt. New York: Penguin, 1977). It is interesting to note that all three writer-critics discuss Poe's work in primarily theological terms.

9. See especially James W. Gargano, " 'The Black Cat': Perverseness Reconsidered," *Texas Studies in Literature and Language* 2 (1960), 172–78; idem, "Poe's 'Ligeia': Dream and Destruction," *College English* 23 (1962), 337–42; and idem, "The Question of Poe's Narrators," *College English* 25 (1963), 177–81. G. R. Thompson's book *Poe's Fiction* (Madison: University of Wisconsin Press, 1973) represents the most extensive attempt to unify Poe's stories under the concept of Romantic irony. Derived from German Romanticism, Thompson's notion of irony is more complex, more open to unresolved ambiguity than the concept of irony customarily employed by most Anglo-American New Critics. Other key articles in this critical tradition of close readings include Roy P. Basler, "The Interpretation of 'Ligeia,' " *College English* 5 (1944), 363–72, and J. Gerald Kennedy, "The

Limits of Reason: Poe's Deluded Detectives," *American Literature* 47 (1975), 173–83.

10. Floyd Stovall offers this reading in "The Conscious Art of Edgar Allan Poe," *College English* 24 (1963), 417–21.

11. For several recent, theoretically sophisticated studies of Poe that avoid the limitations of these two critical camps, see the following: John Irwin, *American Hieroglyphics* (New Haven, Conn.: Yale University Press, 1980), pp. 43–235; John Carlos Rowe, *Through the Custom-House* (Baltimore, Md.: The Johns Hopkins University Press, 1982), pp. 91–110; Evan Carton, *The Rhetoric of American Romance* (Baltimore, Md.: The Johns Hopkins University Press, 1985), pp. 15–148, passim; Joan Dayan, *Fables of Mind* (New York: Oxford University Press, 1987); and J. Gerald Kennedy, *Poe, Death, and the Life of Writing* (New Haven, Conn.: Yale University Press, 1987). Unlike these important studies, however, my account does not make claims for Poe's profundity as a thinker on such philosophical issues as the linguistic origins of self or the relation between death and writing. I prefer instead to concentrate on the dynamic interplay between narrator and double as it develops in the process of first-person plotting. Given my interest in Poe's reliance on a strict sequence of events to sustain identity, I have steered clear of Poe's only completed novel, *The Narrative of Arthur Gordon Pym*, since its length precludes a close examination of the unfolding drama of tale-telling.

12. Bell, *The Development of American Romance*, p. 107.

13. Donald E. Pease, *Visionary Compacts* (Madison: The University of Wisconsin Press, 1987), pp. 158–202. Unfortunately Pease's excellent study came out after I had already worked out my similar argument about Poe's authorial anxieties.

14. Wilbur, *Major Writers in America*, p. 380; Thompson, *Poe's Fiction*, p. 170.

15. I suspect that Poe's brief character sketches were modeled after the seventeenth-century French work *Characters* by Jean de La Bruyère, whose crucial epigraph prefaces Poe's story. For a discussion of Theophrastian characters, see the introduction to *Characters of the Seventeenth Century*, ed. Nichol Smith (Oxford: Oxford University Press, 1918), and Benjamin Boyce, *The Theophrastian Character* (Cambridge, Mass.: Harvard University Press, 1947). Poe's innovation was to shorten the sketch to a bare minimum and then plant the character in an urban crowd.

16. See Poe's early review of Dickens's *Watkins Tottle* in *The Complete Works of Edgar Allan Poe*, ed. James Harrison, 16 vols. (1902; rpt. New York: AMS Press, 1965), VIII, 45–48. Subsequent references to Poe's critical prose are parenthetically cited by volume and page number from this edition.

17. Paul de Man, "Literary History and Literary Modernity," *Blindness*

and Insight (New York: Oxford University Press, 1971), p. 159. For a discussion of the significance of the story's urban setting, see Walter Benjamin, "On Some Motifs in Baudelaire," *Illuminations* (New York: Schocken, 1968), pp. 170–76. In keeping with his somewhat curious view of Poe as a traditional storyteller, Benjamin reads the tale as a conventional representation of the crowd that predates Baudelaire's more modern cityscapes. Georg Simmel offers a stunning analysis of the relationship between anonymity and subjectivity in modern urban life in "The Metropolis and Mental Life," *The Sociology of Georg Simmel* ed. Kurt. H. Wolff (New York: The Free Press, 1950), pp. 409–24. For an interesting, if not entirely convincing, recent reading of the story that attempts to historicize Poe's treatment of London, see Robert Byer's "Mysteries of the City: A Reading of Poe's 'The Man of the Crowd' " in *Ideology in Classic American Literature*, ed. Myra Jehlen and Sacvan Bercovitch (New York: Cambridge University Press, 1986), pp. 221–46.

18. The best synopsis of the Romantic quest convention remains M. H. Abrams's *Natural Supernaturalism* (New York: Norton, 1971), pp. 255–56.

19. See especially Marie Bonaparte, *The Life and Works of Edgar Allan Poe* (London: Imago, 1949), and Daniel Hoffman, "Voyages," *Poe Poe Poe Poe Poe Poe Poe* (New York: Doubleday, 1972), pp. 135–77.

20. Irwin, *American Hieroglyphics*, Chaps. 4, 5, and 7.

21. Kenneth Burke, *A Grammar of Motives* (Berkeley: University of California Press, 1969), p. 430. For a similar account of narrative's distinct capacity to function chronologically and logically at once, see Roland Barthes, "Structural Analysis of Narratives," in *Image, Music, Text*, ed. Stephen Heath (New York: Hill and Wang, 1977), pp. 94, 98.

22. Although it might make sense to treat *Eureka* as yet another of Poe's first-person plots, I am more interested in using it as a critical commentary that sheds light on Poe's more overtly fictional narratives.

23. James, *The Art of the Novel*, p. 5.

24. Ibid., p. 42.

25. Ibid., p. 319.

26. Kenneth Burke, "The Principle of Composition," *Poetry* 99 (1961), 46–53.

27. Boris Tomashevsky, "Thématique," rpt. in *Russian Formalist Criticism*, ed. Lee T. Lemon and Marion J. Reis (Lincoln: University of Nebraska Press, 1965), p. 68.

28. Hoffman, *Poe Poe Poe Poe Poe Poe Poe*, p. 235.

29. Charles Brockden Brown, *Wieland or The Transformation* (Port Washington, N.Y.: Kennikat Press, 1963 [rpt. of 1887 McKay edn.]), pp. 140, 188, and 166.

30. Yvor Winters offers the most extreme articulation of this attack when he writes that the "underlying defect in all of Poe's work [is] the

absence of theme." See his "Edgar Allan Poe: A Crisis in the History of American Obscurantism," *In Defense of Reason* (New York: Swallow Press, 1947), p. 256. Winters's moral indignation against such "absence" is refreshingly blunt, if somewhat misguided, but there are other recent, more refined versions. See, for example, Taylor Stoehr, " 'Unspeakable Horror' in Poe," *South Atlantic Quarterly* 78 (1979), 317–32.

31. For a convincing demonstration that the old man functions as the narrator's double, see E. Arthur Robinson, "Poe's 'The Tell-Tale Heart,' " *Nineteenth-Century Fiction* 19 (1965), 369–78.

32. Robert Caserio, *Story, Plot, and the Novel* (Princeton: Princeton University Press, 1979), p. 87.

33. Martin Price, "Irrelevant Detail and Emergence of Form," in *Aspects of Narrative*, ed. J. Hillis Miller (New York: Columbia University Press, 1971), p. 82.

34. For such symbol hunting, see, in particular, Darrel Abel, "A Key to the House of Usher," *University of Toronto Quarterly* 18 (1949), 176–85.

35. William James offers a striking correlative to Poe's contriving by fear: "The more a conceived object excites us, the more reality it has." See his *Principles of Psychology* (Chicago: Encyclopaedia Britannica, 1952), p. 652.

36. James Cox, "Edgar Poe: Style as Pose," rpt. in *Twentieth Century Interpretations of "The Fall of the House of Usher,"* ed. Thomas Woodson (Englewood Cliffs, N.J.: Prentice-Hall, 1969), p. 115.

37. Poe's "Autography" series proved so popular that he produced a second version in 1841. While the first version presents a series of signed letters written by famous authors in reply to one bogus "Joseph Miller," Poe formalizes his procedures in the 1841 version by appending a short biographical sketch after each author's signature that he analyzes.

38. See Frank Mott, *A History of American Magazines* (Cambridge, Mass.: Harvard University Press, 1957), I, 502–3.

39. Michael Allen, *Poe and the British Magazine Tradition* (New York: Oxford University Press, 1969), pp. 141, 162.

40. Hoffman, *Poe Poe Poe Poe Poe Poe Poe*, p. 197, and William Whipple, "Poe's Political Satire," *Texas Studies in English* 35 (1956), 81–95, respectively.

41. Michael Rogin, "The Romance of the Self in Jacksonian America," *Partisan Review* 44 (1977), 88. Rogin's entire analysis is pertinent to Poe's story.

42. *The Letters of Edgar Allan Poe*, ed. John Ostrom (New York: Gordian, 1966), vol. 1, p. 202. Hereinafter cited as *Letters*.

43. *Letters*, p. 258.

44. Benjamin, "On Some Motifs in Baudelaire," pp. 158–59.

45. Allen, *Poe and the British Magazine Tradition*, p. 84.

46. *Letters*, p. 257.

47. Wayne Booth, *The Rhetoric of Fiction* (Chicago: University of Chicago Press, 1961), p. 201.

48. Robert Adams, *Nil* (New York: Oxford University Press, 1966), p. 43.

49. See Floyd Stovall, "Poe's Debt to Coleridge," *Texas Studies in English* 10 (1935), 70–127; and, more recently, Robert D. Jacobs, *Poe: Journalist and Critic* (Baton Rouge: Louisiana State University Press, 1969).

50. For a history of the dailies, particularly the *New York Sun*, see Frank Mott, *American Journalism* (New York: Macmillan, 1962), pp. 220–227.

51. Quoted in Mabbott, *Collected Works of Edgar Allan Poe*, 1067.

52. Roland Barthes, "Analyse textuelle d'un conte d'Edgar Poe," in *Semiotique narrative et textuelle*, ed. Claude Chabrol et al. (Paris: Librarie Larousse, 1973), p. 49.

53. It is interesting to note that Poe was quite surprised at the sensation caused by the hoax, which he did not think would be believed, as an 1849 letter suggests: "In my 'Valdemar Case' (which *was* credited by many) I had not the slightest idea that any person should credit it as any thing more than a 'Magazine-paper' " (*Letters*, p. 433).

54. *Letters*, p. 427.

55. *Letters*, p. 433. Emphasis in original.

56. Burton R. Pollin, *Discoveries in Poe* (Notre Dame, Ind.: Notre Dame University Press, 1970), pp. 166–87. I am also indebted to a suggestive reading of the story by Jerome J. McGann, "Shall These Bones Live?" *Text: Transactions of the Society for Textual Scholarship* 1 (1981), 21–40.

Chapter 2

1. Nathaniel Hawthorne, "Preface to *Twice-Told Tales*," in his *Tales and Sketches*, ed. Roy Harvey Pearce (New York: The Library of America, 1982), p. 1152. Subsequent page references to this one-volume printing of *The Centenary Edition* (see no. 4) are cited parenthetically.

2. My emphasis throughout this book on the first-person narrator who must act as the story's hero as well as its historian precludes me from discussing in more detail Hawthorne's most interesting first-person tales and sketches in which the fictional "I" functions as a kind of dramatic showman/guide ("Alice Doane's Appeal," "Little Annie's Ramble," "Wakefield," and "Main-Street") or an imaginatively charged auditor (the frame sections of "Legends of the Province-House"). For a thoughtful discussion of these and other Hawthorne tales that attends closely to Hawthorne's development as a short story writer, see Nina Baym, *The Shape of Hawthorne's Career* (Ithaca, N.Y.: Cornell University Press, 1976), pp. 15–122.

Focusing on Hawthorne's strong desire to attract an audience, Baym's reading, like my own, tends to stress the relatively conventional, social aspect of the tales Hawthorne published in the 1830s. For another, shorter survey of the stories that argues for Hawthorne's early self-doubts and uncertainty, see J. Donald Crowley, *Hawthorne: The Critical Tradition* (London: Routledge & Kegan Paul, 1970), pp. 1–10.

3. Even though the evidence suggests that Hawthorne wrote "The Custom-House," as well as his subsequent prefaces, after each respective romance was already virtually completed, I am taking the convention of a "pre-face" literally in this discussion by assuming that Hawthorne's explanatory remarks are meant to introduce the fiction that follows. I am therefore mainly interested in "The Custom-House" for the light it sheds on the romance proper, and not as a subtle first-person fiction in its own right. For a provocative discussion that takes up the complex relation between the preface and the romance, see Jonathan Arac, "The Politics of *The Scarlet Letter*," in *Ideology in Classic American Literature*, ed. Myra Jehlen and Sacvan Bercovitch (New York: Cambridge University Press, 1986), pp. 247–66.

4. *The Centenary Edition of the Works of Nathaniel Hawthorne*, ed. William Charvat, Roy Harvey Pearce, and Claude M. Simpson (Columbus: Ohio State University Press, 1965), (*The Scarlet Letter*), I, 33. Subsequent references to this volume and other volumes in *The Centenary Edition* are cited parenthetically by volume and page number; only page numbers are given in repeated references to the same volume.

5. Both phrases occur in Irving Howe's *Politics and the Novel* (London: New Left Books, 1957), p. 174.

6. This phrase is from Richard Brodhead, *Hawthorne, Melville, and the Novel* (Chicago: University of Chicago Press, 1976), pp. 110.

7. Elaine Scarry, *The Body in Pain* (New York: Oxford University Press, 1985), p. 166.

8. Michel Butor, "L'Usage des pronoms personnels dans le roman," *Répertoire II* (Paris: Les Editions de Minuit, 1964), pp. 62–63.

9. Henry James, *Hawthorne* (New York: Harper and Brothers, 1880), p. 130.

10. Major articles in the ongoing debate about Coverdale's reliability include: Frederick Crews, "A New Reading of *The Blithedale Romance*," *American Literature* 29 (1957), 147–70; William Hedges, "Hawthorne's *Blithedale*: The Function of the Narrator," *Nineteenth-Century Fiction* 14 (1960), 303–16; Kelley Griffith, "Form in *The Blithedale Romance*," *American Literature* 40 (1968), 15–26; and Louis Auchincloss, "*The Blithedale Romance*: A Study of Form and Point of View," *Nathaniel Hawthorne Journal* (1972), 53–58. Virtually every interpretation of the book accepts the New Critical assumption that Coverdale is an untrustworthy narrator, with one notable

exception: the fine recent discussion by Evan Carton, *The Rhetoric of American Romance* (Baltimore, Md.: The Johns Hopkins University Press, 1985), pp. 228–52.

11. The most lucid and authoritative presentation of the concept of narrative unreliability remains Wayne Booth's *The Rhetoric of Fiction* (Chicago: University of Chicago Press, 1961). Treating unreliability as a relative notion dependent on conventions of reading, Booth's discussion is generally more judicious and useful than the practical criticism of many of his followers.

12. John McElroy and Edward McDonald, "The Coverdale Romance," *Studies in the Novel* 14 (1982), 1–16.

13. Dorrit Cohn, *Transparent Minds* (Princeton, N.J.: Princeton University Press, 1978), p. 144.

14. "Contemporary Literature of America," *Westminster Review* 58 (October 1852), 592–98. Rpt. in *The Blithedale Romance*, ed. Seymour Gross and Rosalie Murphy (New York: Norton, 1978), p. 281. The reviewer is thought to be George Eliot.

15. James, *Hawthorne*, p. 131.

16. Leo Bersani, *A Future for Astyanax* (Boston: Little, Brown, 1976), pp. 77–79.

17. Hawthorne, *Our Old Home* (Columbus: Ohio State University Press, 1965), V, 4.

18. R. W. B. Lewis, *The American Adam* (Chicago: University of Chicago Press, 1955), p. 118.

19. Brodhead, *Hawthorne, Melville, and the Novel*, p. 110.

20. Taylor Stoehr, *Hawthorne's Mad Scientists* (Hamden, Conn.: Archon, 1978), p. 182.

Chapter 3

1. Henry James, *Hawthorne* (New York: Harper and Brothers, 1880), p. 84. Subsequent references to this edition are cited parenthetically by page number.

2. This critical tradition begins with F. O. Matthiessen (*American Renaissance* [New York: Oxford University Press, 1941], pp. 292–304, 351–68), is advanced by Marius Bewley (*The Complex Fate* [London: Chatto and Windus, 1952; rpt. 1967], pp. 1–149), and Richard Poirier, *A World Elsewhere* (New York: Oxford University Press, 1966), pp. 93–143), and culminates in the recent fine study by Richard Brodhead (*The School of Hawthorne* [New York: Oxford University Press, 1986], pp. 114–200).

3. James's mixed attitude toward Poe is discussed in Burton Pollin's "Poe and Henry James: A Changing Relationship," *Yearbook of English Studies* 3 (1973), 232–42.

4. Henry James, *The Art of the Novel*, ed. R. P. Blackmur (New York: Scribner's, 1934), p. 3. Subsequent references to this edition will be cited parenthetically by page number.

5. Steven Gilman, *The Confusion of Realms* (New York: Random House, 1963), p. 78.

6. Lionel Trilling, *Sincerity and Authenticity* (Cambridge, Mass.: Harvard University Press, 1972), p. 131.

7. Henry James, *The Awkward Age* (New York: Scribner's, 1908), p. 310 (vol. IX of the New York Edition).

8. Henry James, "Anthony Trollope," in *Partial Portraits* (London: Macmillan, 1888), pp. 97–133. In his preface to *Roderick Hudson* James remarks that the only detachment available to the responsible author is "the detachment of aversion" (AN, 11).

9. For a good discussion of the relation between consciousness and containment in James, see Ruth Bernard Yeazell, *Language and Knowledge in the Late Novels of Henry James* (Chicago, Ill.: University of Chicago Press, 1976), pp. 1–15.

10. In a notebook entry that works out the plot of his story "The Friend of the Friends," James decides to create a "3rd person" whose observation of the two main characters is designed to keep the tale "intensively objective." See *The Notebooks of Henry James*, ed. F. O. Matthiessen and Kenneth Murdock (New York: George Braziller, 1955), p. 231. In *The Space of Literature* (Lincoln: University of Nebraska Press, 1982), p. 26, Maurice Blanchot paraphrases Kafka as saying that he knew he had entered into literature as soon as he could substitute "he" for "I." For an interesting discussion of Kafka's pronominal shifts from first to third person, see Dorrit Cohn, *Transparent Minds* (Princeton, N.J.: Princeton University Press, 1978), pp. 169–71.

11. In this connection James's complaint about "the narrator mixing himself up with the narrative in 'Heart of Darkness' " is particularly revealing. Ian Watt discusses the relation between Conrad and James in terms of their differing attitudes about first-person narration in "Marlow, Henry James, and 'Heart of Darkness,' " *Nineteenth-Century Fiction* 33 (1978), 159–74. James's objection is cited on page 165. For a fascinating set of later remarks that James made about another first-person novel by Conrad, see his essay "The New Novel" in his collection of essays entitled *Notes on Novelists* (New York: Scribner's, 1914). James notes that the use of a first-person narrator in Conrad's *Chance* leads to the novel's "general and diffused lapse of authenticity," which leaves the reader to admire "the genius" behind the fiction, "simply Mr. Conrad himself" (pp. 349–50).

12. This analogy between art and life is closely examined by Laurence Holland (*The Expense of Vision* [Princeton, N.J.: Princeton University Press, 1964], pp. 155–82), and by Leo Bersani ("The Jamesian Lie," in *A Future for Astyanax* [Boston: Little, Brown, 1976], pp. 128–55. My discussion of

the critical prefaces is heavily indebted to Holland's work. For an excellent recent discussion of the prefaces as well as James's other first-person writings, see William Goetz, *Henry James and the Darkest Abyss of Romance* (Baton Rouge: Louisiana State University Press, 1986). Published after this book was essentially completed, Goetz's study independently confirms much of the theoretical aspects of my own argument about James and the first person, although I tend to place greater emphasis on the nightmarish consequences of James's assumption of an "I" than he does.

13. James's belief that first-person narration is acceptable only for short works of fiction raises an interesting point of comparison with Poe's preference for works that could be read in a single sitting. When he was deciding between first and third person for the narration of *The Sense of the Past*, James recognized that the length of the novel would prohibit the effect of "intense simplification" that first-person narration could afford. See *The Notebooks of Henry James*, p. 301.

14. This first-person anonymity is a more controlled version of the obtuseness which Poe assumes to protect himself from his first-person speakers.

15. Roland Barthes, following Emile Benveniste, analyzes the consequences of this motivation—how the "I" reflects the instance of discourse— "in a strictly a-psychological way." See "To Write: Intransitive Verb?" in *The Structuralist Controversy*, ed. Richard Macksey and Eugenio Donato (Baltimore, Md.: The Johns Hopkins University Press, 1970), pp. 138–39.

16. It is a risky business to generalize about any author with a literary output as massive as James's, but I would argue that all of the fifty or so works of fiction he wrote in the first person fall into three or four basic categories. First, there are the kinds of tales which I am discussing, stories whose narrators are identified as analytic men of letters. Other examples include two important tales published in the mid 1890s, "The Death of the Lion" and "The Next Time." A second group of first-person narratives are overtly Gothic, stories like "The Turn of the Screw" and "The Friend of the Friends." As R. P. Blackmur first suggested in "The Country of the Blue" (1943), James's ghost stories bear a clear resemblance to his fables for critics, insofar as imagination and individuality are inversely related in both kinds of tales. But in the Gothic tales James is more interested in using the first-person form to achieve an intensity of effect than in treating the narrator solely as a mediator between life and art. A third group is comprised of miscellaneous experiments in point of view. This group includes an early series of Browning-like attempts at dramatic monologue utilizing the diary or epistolary form ("A Landscape-Painter," "A Light Man," and "The Point of View"), another set of early stories whose first-person narrators provide an ironic but sympathetic perspective on the central character ("A Passionate Pilgrim" and "The Madonna of the Future"), and a cluster of tales about portrait painting written in the 1890s

("The Real Thing," "The Special Type," "The Tone of Time," and "The Beldonald Holbein"). Concerned more with the difficulty of seeing than with narrating, these late stories are told by painters rather than writers. I have also deliberately chosen not to consider first-person prose such as *A Small Boy and Others* and *The American Scene* in this discussion, because an author's commitment to "fact," whether it be autobiographical or by way of a travel sketch, raises a different set of theoretical issues than the formal problems arising from explicitly fictional narratives.

17. Henry James, "The Author of Beltraffio," in *The Author of Beltraffio* (New York: Scribner's, 1909), p. 6 (vol. XVI of the New York Edition). Subsequent references to this edition are cited in parentheses by page number.

18. Henry James, *The Aspern Papers* (New York: Scribner's, 1908), p. 9. (New York Edition, Vol. XII). Subsequent references to this edition are cited in parentheses by page number.

19. It is interesting to note that in earlier versions of the tale James used the word "editor" instead of the New York Edition's substitution of the word "commentator," which more explicitly connects his profession with his role as narrator. Perhaps this connection would have been clearer to James himself in 1908 after having written his other first-person fictions.

20. *The Art of the Novel*, p. 161. The entire critical preface, with its anxious talk of exploitation and peering into gardens, closely imitates the first person's own speech in the tale.

21. It is curious to see how often critics feel compelled to assign blame for the tale's tragic outcome. The classic indictment against the narrator is offered by Wayne Booth in *The Rhetoric of Fiction* (Chicago: University of Chicago Press, 1961), pp. 254–65. Though Booth perceives the way James's own "voice" enters into the narrator's "unreliable" account, he simply blames James for this confusion: "How can I, then, excuse him [James] when I find his narrator to be one kind of man in one paragraph and another kind of man in the next?" (363). How indeed? The crucial distinction between "man" and "commentator" helps to answer Booth's question. In recent years the tale's narrator has been defended, most often by finding fault with the two women. Daniel Schneider attacks Juliana ("The Unreliable Narrator: James's 'The Aspern Papers' and the Reading of Fiction," *Studies in Short Fiction* 13 [1976], 43–49), while Miss Tina is treated as conniving by John Crowley ("The Wiles of a 'Witless' Woman: Tina in *The Aspern Papers*," *ESQ* 22 [1976], 162) and by Joseph Waldmeir ("Miss Tina Did It: A Fresh Look at *The Aspern Papers*," *Centennial Review*, 26 [1982], 256–67. A more suggestive reading of the tale as an inverted romance which accounts for the problem of the narration is offered by James Mellard ("Modal Counterpoint in James's *The Aspern Papers*," *Papers on Language and Literature*, 4 [1968], 299–307).

22. Cf. *The Art of the Novel*, p. 160: "One must pay one's self largely

with words, I think, one must induce almost any 'Italian subject' *to make believe* it gives up its secret, in order to keep at all on working..." (James's own emphasis).

23. The suggestion that the letters are only presumed to exist by the two women in order to force the narrator into marriage was first made by Jacob Korg, "What Aspern Papers? A Hypothesis," *College English* 23 (1962), 378–81.

24. For an interesting discussion of the meaning of money in James's late works, see Donald Mull, *Henry James' "Sublime Economy"* (Middletown, Conn.: Wesleyan University Press, 1973).

25. Susanne Kappeler, *Writing and Reading in Henry James* (London: Macmillan, 1980), p. 58.

26. In his preface to *The Golden Bowl* James calls the first person of *The Aspern Papers* "intelligent but quite unindividualised" (AN, 329), an assessment borne out by the tale itself. If I continue to attribute emotional qualities to the first person, it only attests to the persistence with which his language creates these emotive shades rather than reflects any inner essence or personality.

27. Contrasting third- with first-person narration, David Goldknopf notes that the narrating "I" "ruptures the screen [between reader and text] from the fictional side. Someone inside the novel is talking to someone *outside* the novel" (emphasis in original). See his *The Life of the Novel* (Chicago: University of Chicago Press, 1972), pp. 32–33. Even in the narcissistic doublings of Poe's first persons, we might remember, there remains an unknown "other" beyond the solipsistic confines of the narrative.

28. Henry James, "The Figure in the Carpet," in *The Lesson of the Master* (New York: Scribner's, 1909), p. 23 (vol. XV of the New York Edition). Subsequent references to this edition are cited in parentheses by page number.

29. Three quintessential New Critical readings of the story were published in the early 1960s: Seymour Lainoff, "Henry James's 'The Figure in the Carpet': What Is Critical Responsiveness?" *Boston University Studies in English* 5 (1961), 122–28; Lyall H. Powers, "A Reperusal of James's 'The Figure in the Carpet,'" *American Literature* 33 (1961), 224–28; and Leo B. Levy, "A Reading of 'The Figure in the Carpet,'" *American Literature* 33 (1962), 457–65. Levy explicitly identifies the story as a parable illustrating the Intentional Fallacy (p. 459). The most thorough structuralist analysis is Shlomith Rimmon's *The Concept of Ambiguity: The Example of James* (Chicago, Ill.: University of Chicago Press, 1977), pp. 95–115. More recent accounts informed by French criticism include J. Hillis Miller's "The Figure in the Carpet," *Poetics Today*, 1, no. 3. (1980), 107–18, and Peter Lock's "'The Figure in the Carpet': The Text as Riddle and Force," *Nineteenth-Century Fiction* 36 (1981), 157–75. Just as Miller's discussion of the nar-

rative's labyrinthine threading gets interesting, he breaks off by concluding
that the comic tale simply does not permit itself to be read. Lock offers a
more careful look at the tale's ambiguities, noting in particular how the
effects of the figure on each participant come to reproduce the figure
itself.

30. James, *The Notebooks of Henry James*, pp. 220–21. A notebook entry
dated June 4, 1895, on a similar critical fable ("The Next Time") likewise
suggests the author's investment in his anonymous first-person agents: "I
become the narrator, either impersonally or, in my unnamed, unspecified
personality" (201).

31. G. A. Finch, "A Retreading of James's Carpet," *Twentieth-Century
Literature* 14 (1968), 99. Finch is virtually unique among readers of the
story in refusing to condemn the narrator. Even a critic as theoretically
sophisticated as Wolfgang Iser needs to ignore the first person's value as
narrator in order to fault him as a *reader*. See Iser's *The Act of Reading*
(Baltimore, Md.: The Johns Hopkins University Press, 1978), pp. 3–10.
He follows the main critical tradition by identifying Corvick as the "good"
reader and the narrator as the "bad" one without considering how the first
person's flaws derive directly from his function as narrator.

32. In an 1891 article entitled "Criticism" (reprinted in *Essays in London and Elsewhere* [New York: Harper, 1893], pp. 259–66), James offers
his most extended and acute analysis of "the conditions of contemporary
journalism" (259). Identifying periodical reviewing as "a new and flourishing
industry" (260–61), James brilliantly anticipates Walter Benjamin's work
on journalism by comparing the "commodity" of periodical literature—"a
huge, open mouth which has to be fed"—to a train which can only run if
all of its spaces are filled, no matter how many "dummies," or blocks of
meaningless print, it takes. For a more charitable view, published just a
few months earlier, see Oscar Wilde's "The Critic as Artist," in *Essays by
Oscar Wilde*, ed. Hesketh Pearson (London: Methuen, 1950), pp. 100–188.
Wilde raises many of the same troublesome issues posed by James's essay
but conceals any anxieties in a dismissive blanket of wit. The year 1891
also saw the publication of Gissing's *New Grub Street*, which satirized the
new breed of professional journalists and book reviewers. For an interesting examination of the growth of popular critics in late nineteenth-
century England, see John Gross, *The Rise and Fall of the Man of Letters*
(London: Macmillan, 1969), pp. 190–232. Gross points out that from 1881
to 1891 the number of individuals listing themselves in census reports as
"authors, editors, journalists" nearly doubled.

33. This charge of inauthenticity has been made by many critics,
especially Levy and Lainoff, who also quotes Quentin Anderson, *The American Henry James* (New Brunswick, N.J.: Rutgers University Press, 1957).

34. Rachel Solomon, "A Marriage of Opposites: Henry James's 'The

Figure in the Carpet' and the Problem of Ambiguity," *ELH* 47 (1980), 801. Solomon's approach is closest to mine, although, like other critics, she feels compelled to call the narrator "unreliable."

35. In the first volume of his biography of James, Leon Edel makes the broad generalization that throughout the writer's career "to be led to the marriage bed was to be dead" (*Henry James: The Untried Years* [New York: Lippincott, 1953], p. 55). While this may hold true for his early works, I am suggesting that James had to overcome his fear of marriage, see it in terms of his own first-person celibacy, in order to arrive at his late phase.

36. I am indebted to Geoffrey Hartman's brief though highly suggestive comments about marriage as a form of consciousness for James in *Beyond Formalism* (New Haven, Conn.: Yale University Press, 1970), pp. 54–55.

37. Henry James, *The Sacred Fount* (New York: Grove Press, 1953), p. 205. All subsequent references are cited parenthetically by page number.

38. Paul Ricoeur, *Freud and Philosophy* (New Haven, Conn.: Yale University Press, 1970), p. 32. The identification of the narrator of *The Sacred Fount* as a "proto-Freudian analyst" was first made by Maxwell Geismar in *Henry James and the Jacobites* (Boston: Houghton Mifflin, 1963), p. 208. The Lacanian implications of this comparison have recently been discussed by Susanne Kappeler in *Writing and Reading in Henry James*, pp. 153–58.

39. R. P. Blackmur, "In the Country of the Blue," *Kenyon Review* 5 (1943), 597.

40. The facts about the novel's initial intention and execution can be found in Leon Edel's *The Treacherous Years* (New York: Lippincott, 1969), pp. 338–39. The best discussion of the novel's length in terms of its first-person form remains Claire Raeth's "Henry James's Rejection of *The Sacred Fount*," *ELH* 16 (1949), 308–24.

41. For an intriguing discussion of James's self-duplicating "talk," see Leo Bersani's *A Future for Astyanax*, pp. 140–41.

42. Reading the critics on *The Sacred Fount* is even more disheartening and exasperating than reading the novel itself. The tendency to decide, once and for all, if the narrator is crazy has led—as in the case of "The Turn of the Screw"—to all kinds of equally obsessive readings that try to get at the "facts." See, for instance, Jean Frantz Blackall's book-length study *Jamesian Ambiguity and "The Sacred Fount"* (Ithaca, N.Y.: Cornell University Press, 1965). Assuming that commonsense evidence can easily be brought to bear on the story, Blackall painstakingly probes the gaping holes in the narrator's elaborate theory. At the other extreme there is a tendency to dismiss both narrator and James as crazy in a brief sentence or two; see, for instance, Rebecca West's account in *Henry James* (New York: H. Holt, 1916), pp. 107–8. One way out of this naively mimetic morass is

to turn the narrator into a figure representing the novelist at work. Wilson Follett initially raised the issue of self-parody in "Henry James's Portrait of Henry James," *New York Times Book Review*, August 23, 1936, pp. 2, 16. This issue has been elaborated by R. P. Blackmur ("The Sacred Fount," *Kenyon Review* 4 [1942], 328–52) and rejuvenated by Naomi Lebowitz (*The Imagination of Loving* [Detroit, Mich.: Wayne State University Press, 1965], pp. 119–29) and Phillip Weinstein (*Henry James and the Requirements of the Imagination* [Cambridge, Mass.: Harvard University Press, 1971], pp. 97–120), among others. However illuminating, this approach threatens to reduce the novel to a self-reflexive exercise by slighting the social value of the narrator's search—how his problems are shared by the other Newmarch guests. Some readings that avoid this pitfall include Robert Andreach's "Henry James's *The Sacred Fount*: The Existential Predicament," *Nineteenth-Century Fiction* 17 (1962), 197–216, and Joseph Wiesenfarth's *Henry James and the Dramatic Analogy* (New York: Fordham University Press, 1963). Andreach views the narrator's habit of confusing objective and subjective reality as an existential predicament common to all of us, while Wiesenfarth argues that we should rest easy with the novel's ambiguity by treating it as a study of the way signs can be read. Two of the best studies are Holland's and Kappeler's; the latter includes an excellent analysis of the criticism on the novel up to the late 1970s.

43. Lebowitz, *The Imagination of Loving*, p. 120.

44. Laurence Holland has made the same point: "[A]s creator of the forms which shape their passion he is cut off from the passion which they know." *The Expense of Vision*, p. 210.

45. The connection between May Server and Priscilla has also been made in a more general discussion comparing *The Sacred Fount* and *The Blithedale Romance*; see Elizabeth Keyser's "Veils and Masks: *The Blithedale Romance* and *The Sacred Fount*," *Henry James Review*, 2 (1981), 101–11. For a similarly general account of James's debt to Poe in *The Sacred Fount*, see Judith L. Sutherland's *The Problematic Fictions of Poe, Hawthorne and James* (Columbia: University of Missouri Press, 1984), pp. 45–50.

46. In *Through the Custom-House* (Baltimore, Md.: The Johns Hopkins University Press, 1982), p. 181, John Carlos Rowe also notes the narrator's "growing sense that he has no being outside the confines of a text, whether it be the arranged world of Newmarch or the record of his own story."

47. The first person's disintegration bears a striking resemblance to the "deconstruction of self" that Leo Bersani has discussed in *A Future for Astyanax*. But while Bersani celebrates the modernist fragmentation of personality as a way to desublimate desire, for James it is clearly a source of great anxiety, for he still clings to a bourgeois notion of organic form, what Bersani might call the fetishism of the Whole.

48. James, "Anthony Trollope", pp. 116–17.

49. James, "Coquelin," in *The Scenic Art*, ed. Allan Wade (New York: Hill and Wang, 1957), p. 209.

Afterword

1. James, "Is There a Life After Death?" rpt. in F. O. Matthiessen, *The James Family* (New York: Knopf, 1947), p. 607.

2. Kenneth Burke, *Attitudes Toward History* (Boston: Beacon Press, 1937; rpt. 1961), p. 225.

3. Kenneth Burke, "Appendix D," *A Grammar of Motives* (Berkeley: University of California Press, 1969), p. 514.

Index

Abel, Darrel, 185 *n*.3
Abrams, M. H., 184 *n*.18
Adams, Robert, 60
Allen, Michael, 53
Anderson, Quentin, 193 *n*.33
Andreach, Robert, 195 *n*.42
Arac, Jonathan, 187 *n*.3
Artaud, Antonin, 178 *n*.8
Auchincloss, Louis, 187 *n*.10

Barth, John, 180 *n*.18
Barthes, Roland, 65, 178 *n*.8, 180 *n*.18, 184 *n*.21, 190 *n*.15
Basler, Roy P., 182 *n*.9
Bataille, Georges, 178 *n*.8
Bauderlaire, Charles, 24, 31
Baym, Nina, 186 *n*.2
Bell, Michael, 25, 181 *n*.5
Benjamin, Walter, 57, 184 *n*.17, 193 *n*.32
Benveniste, Emile, 13-14, 17
Bersani, Leo, 114, 189 *n*.12, 194 *n*.41
Bewley, Marius, 188 *n*.2
Blackall, Jean Franz, 194 *n*.42
Blackmur, R. P., 160, 190 *n*.16, 195 *n*.42

Blanchot, Maurice, 189 *n*.10
Bonaparte, Marie, 184 *n*.19
Booth, Wayne C., 7-8, 9, 15, 60, 179 *n*.11, 188 *n*.11, 191 *n*.21
Boyce, Benjamin, 183 *n*.15
Brodhead, Richard, 115, 187 *n*.6, 188 *n*.2
Brooks, Peter, 178 *n*.2
Brown, Charles Brockden, 23, 43, 173
Browning, Robert, 190 *n*.16
Buell, Lawrence, 179 *n*.10
Burke, Kenneth, 34-35, 39, 175
Butor, Michel, 88-89, 93, 144
Byer, Robert, 184 *n*.17

Carton, Evan, 181 *n*.5, 183 *n*.11, 188 *n*.10
Caserio, Robert, 46
Chambers, Ross, 178 *n*.2
Chase, Richard, 181 *n*.5
Chatman, Seymour, 177 *n*.2
Cohn, Dorrit, 8, 94, 180 *n*.18, 189 *n*.10
Coleridge, Samuel Taylor, 31, 37, 61-62
Confession, 13, 38, 43, 45, 78, 83, 95, 107–8

Conrad, Joseph, 189 *n.*11
Cooper, James Fenimore, 181 *n.*5
Cox, James, 50
Crews, Frederick, 181 *n.*10
Crowley, J. Donald, 187 *n.*2
Crowley, John, 191 *n.*2
Culler, Jonathan, 177 *n.*2, 178 *n.*9

Dayan, Joan, 183 *n.*11
Defoe, Daniel, 21-22
de Man, Paul, 31
Derrida, Jacques, 178 *n.*8
Dickens, Charles, 29
Dickinson, Emily, 18
Doubling, and first-person narration,
    5-6, 8, 20-21, 30-31, 77-78, 95,
    134, 145, 157, 165
Duyckinck, Evert, 68

Eagleton, Terry, 179 *n.*15
Edel, Leon, 194 *n.*35, 194 *n.*40
Eliot, George, 16, 188 *n.*14
Eliot, T. S., 182 *n.*6
Emerson, Ralph Waldo, 5, 10, 98

Failure, 11, 24-27, 40, 87, 117, 140,
    165, 173-75
Faulkner, William, 175
Fielding, Henry, 123
Finch, G. A., 147
First-person fiction, maintaining dif-
    ference in, 12, 26; as motivated,
    11-12, 130; as romance, 126-28;
    as slippage from third person,
    88-89
Fitzgerald, F. Scott, 175
Flaubert, Gustave, 123
Follett, Wilson, 195 *n.*42
Foucault, Michel, 7, 178 *n.*8
Frye, Northrop, 14

Gargano, James W., 182 *n.*9
Gass, William, 179 *n.*8
Geismar, Maxwell, 194 *n.*38

Genette, Gérard, 7, 179 *n.*11
Gilman, Steven, 124
Gissing, George, 193 *n.*32
Goetz, William, 190 *n.*12
Goldknopf, David, 192 *n.*27
Gothic fictional conventions, 3, 30, 50,
    58-60, 87, 132, 159, 167
Greimas, A. J., 7
Griffith, Kelley, 187 *n.*10
Griswold, Rufus, 24
Gross, John, 193 *n.*32

Hartman, Geoffrey, 194 *n.*36
Hawthorne, Nathaniel, compared with
    Poe, 71-79, 120; on egotism,
    104-5, 110, 112-13, 174; on
    romance, 80-88, 90-92, 97-98;
    self-criticism in, 79-81; and voy-
    eurism, 93, 103-4
"Alice Doane's Appeal," 73-74, 186
    *n.*2
"Artist of the Beautiful, The," 74
Blithedale Romance, The, 8, 13, 15, 17,
    80, 87-117
"Chippings with a Chisel," 72
"Custom-House, The," 74
"Drowne's Wooden Image," 74
"Earth's Holocaust," 74
"Foot-prints on the Sea-Shore," 73
"Fragments from the Journal of a
    Solitary Man," 73
"Hall of Fantasy, The," 74
"Haunted Mind, The," 73
House of the Seven Gables, The, 83-86,
    90, 91, 111, 115, 120
"Legends of the Province-House,"
    186 *n.*2
"Little Annie's Ramble," 186 *n.*2
"Main-Street," 186 *n.*2
Marble Faun, The, 101, 111
"Monsieur du Miroir," 76-79
"My Visit to Niagara," 72
"Night-Sketches," 73
"Old Apple-Dealer, The," 75-76
"P's Correspondence," 73
Preface to *Mosses on an Old Manse*,
    79-80

Preface to *Our Old Home*, 188 *n*.17
Preface to *Twice-Told Tales*, 73, 79
"Prophetic Pictures, The," 74
Scarlet Letter, The, 74, 81-86, 88, 110
"Sights from a Steeple," 87
"Snow-Flakes," 72
"Sunday at Home," 72
"Virtuoso's Collection, A," 74
"Wakefield," 186 *n*.2
Hedges, William, 187 *n*.10
Hoffman, Daniel, 42, 184 *n*.19, 185 *n*.40
Holland, Laurence, 189 *n*.12, 195 *n*.44
Howe, Irving, 87
Howells, William Dean, 92

Information, as substitute for experience, 45, 57-58, 156
Irving, Washington, 23
Irwin, John, 34, 183 *n*.11
Iser, Wolfgang, 193 *n*.31

Jacobs, Robert D., 186 *n*.49
James, Henry, compared with Hawthorne, 92, 118-19, 165; compared with Poe, 36-38, 119-21, 145, 159-60, 190 *n*.13, 190 *n*.14; on critics, 193 *n*.32; on immortality, 172; inauthenticity in, 124, 135, 155; marriage in, 140, 153-58, 160; showing versus telling, 7; on tone, 196 *n*. 49; on Trollope, 189 *n*.8, 196 *n*.48
Ambassadors, The, 171
American Scene, The, 191 *n*.16
Aspern Papers, The, 8, 119, 130-31, 134-44, 149, 157-58, 164, 165
"Author of Beltraffio, The," 131-34, 136, 138, 144, 157
Awkward Age, The, 161
"Beast in the Jungle, The," 133, 180 *n*.18
"Beldonald Holbein, The," 191 *n*.16
"Death of the Lion, The," 190 *n*.16
"Figure in the Carpet, The," 8, 119, 130-31, 144-58, 162, 164, 170

"Friend of the Friends, The," 189 *n*.10
Golden Bowl, The, 139, 171
Hawthorne, 118, 120
"Landscape-Painter, A" 190 *n*.16
"Lesson of the Master, The," 133, 158
"Light Man, A," 190 *n*.16
"Madonna of the Future, The," 190 *n*.16
"Next Time, The," 190 *n*.16, 193 *n*.30
"Passionate Pilgrim, A," 190 *n*.16
"Point of View, The," 190 *n*.16
Prefaces, 22, 36, 124-30, 192 *n*.26
"Private Life, The," 158
"Real Thing, The," 191 *n*.16
Roderick Hudson, 161
Sacred Fount, The, 8, 11, 19, 119, 130-31, 155, 159-71
Small Boy and Others, A, 191 *n*.16
"Special Type, The," 191 *n*.16
Spoils of Poynton, The, 138, 139, 141
"Tone of Time, The," 191 *n*.16
"Turn of the Screw, The," 190 *n*.16
Wings of the Dove, The, 139, 141, 171
James, William, 185 *n*.35
Jameson, Fredric, 9
Jay, Paul, 179 *n*.13

Kafka, Franz, 189 *n*.10
Kaplan, Amy, 181 *n*.5
Kappeler, Susanne, 192 *n*.25, 194 *n*.38
Kennedy, J. Gerald, 182 *n*.9, 183 *n*.11
Keyser, Elizabeth, 195 *n*.45
Korg, Jacob, 192 *n*.23

La Bruyère, Jean de, 183 *n*.15
Lacan, Jacques, 179 *n*.15, 194 *n*.38
Lainoff, Seymour, 192 *n*.29
Lawrence, D. H., 182 *n*.8
Lebowitz, Naomi, 164, 195 *n*.42
Levy, Leo B., 192 *n*.29
Lewis, R. W. B., 114
Lock, Peter, 192 *n*.29

Longfellow, Henry Wadsworth, 62
Lubbock, Percy, 7

McDonald, Edward, 188 n.12
McElroy, John, 188 n.12
McGann, Jerome J., 186 n.56
Matthiessen, F. O., 188 n.2
Mellard, James, 191 n.21
Melville, Herman, 10, 18, 51, 180 n.20
Miller, J. Hillis, 192 n.29
Modernity, 26, 31, 104, 175
Mott, Frank, 185 n.38, 186 n.50
Mull, Donald, 192 n.24

Nabokov, Vladimir, 175

Pease, Donald, 25-26
Persona, New Critical assumptions
    about, 15, 86-87, 161-62. See also
    Reliability
Pierce, Franklin, 114
Plot, as inducing paranoia, 46-47; rela-
    tion to personal identity, 17-18,
    27, 37-38, 61-62, 131; as sacri-
    fice, 95-96, 124-25, 154, 170; as
    substitute for community, 87,
    96-98, 106-11, 115, 128, 174
Poe, Edgar Allan, audience, sense of,
    51-53; essays and marginalia,
    36, 52, 55, 61, 62, 69; and Jack-
    sonian democracy, 55-56; and
    journalistic style, 63, 67; obtuse-
    ness in, 26; on perfect plot, 17,
    37-38, 61-62; and plagiarism,
    23, 52, 62; reviews of Haw-
    thorne, 6, 36, 120; and voice,
    43-44, 54, 58, 65
"Al Aaraaf," 36, 60
"Balloon-Hoax, The" 63, 64
"Berenice," 22, 32, 47, 49, 53, 60
"Black Cat, The," 39-45, 47, 58, 150,
    173
"Descent into the Maelström, A," 34
"Eleonora," 49
Eureka, 34-38, 46, 68

"Facts in the Case of M. Valdemar,
    The," 44, 53, 64-67, 70
"Fall of the House of Usher, The,"
    3, 25-26, 32, 44, 47-51, 53, 54,
    66, 74, 132, 159
"Gold-Bug, The," 47
"How to Write a Blackwood Article,"
    3-8, 13, 20, 23, 32-33, 44, 54
"Island of the Fay, The," 42
"King Pest," 181 n.1
"Ligeia," 3, 22, 24, 32, 38, 44, 49, 53
"Loss of Breath," 54, 57
"Man of the Crowd, The," 19, 27-
    35, 38, 41, 45, 57, 61, 63, 95, 99
"Man That Was Used Up, The," 53-
    57, 70
"Masque of the Red Death, The,"
    181 n.1
"Mesmeric Revelation," 64
"Metzengerstein," 181 n.1
"Morella," 44, 49, 58
"MS. Found in a Bottle," 21-22, 34,
    60
"Murders in the Rue Morgue, The,"
    27, 39, 44-45, 58
Narrative of Arthur Gordon Pym, The,
    34, 181 n.2, 183 n.11
"Philosophy of Composition, The,"
    6, 18, 36, 38-39, 65
"Power of Words, The," 34
"Premature Burial, The," 53, 58-60,
    64
"Purloined Letter, The," 27
"Raven, The," 38-39
"Shadow—A Parable," 35
"Tale of Jerusalem, A," 181 n.1
"Tell-Tale Heart, The," 45-47, 62
"Unparalleled Adventure of One
    Hans Pfaall, The," 63
"Von Kempelen and His Discovery,"
    53, 67-70
"William Wilson," 3, 25, 44, 53, 54,
    76-79
Poirier, Richard, 188 n.2
Pollin, Burton R., 186 n.56, 188 n.3
Porte, Joel, 181 n.5
Powers, Lyall H., 192 n.29
Price, Martin, 46